Low-salt meals don't have to be bland and boring—and reducing the sodium in your diet can be easier than you think. Here are five tips to help get you started:

1. *Choose the right cooking equipment.*
Investing in a quality nonstick skillet will significantly reduce the fat you will need to use while cooking.

2. *Use only fresh ingredients.*
Frozen foods and canned goods are packed and stored in sodium. Fresh foods are healthier, tastier, and almost always lower in salt.

3. *Stock up on herbs and spices.*
.One of cooking's best-kept secrets, they add a variety of wonderful flavors to food. Don't be afraid to experiment!

4. *Call ahead when eating out.*
Most restaurants will be happy to prepare low-salt dishes in advance.

5. *Exercise, exercise, exercise!*
Not only does it improve circulation, cardiovascular strength, and overall health—it allows your body to sweat out excess salt.

ELMA W. BAGG
SUSAN BAGG TODD
& ROBERT ELY BAGG

Cooking Without a Grain of Salt

BANTAM BOOKS

New York · Toronto · London

Sydney · Auckland

COOKING WITHOUT A GRAIN OF SALT
A Bantam Book

PUBLISHING HISTORY
Doubleday hardcover edition published May 1964
Bantam paperback edition published February 1972
Bantam revised paperback edition/December 1998

ISBN 0-553-57951-7

Bantam Books are published by Bantam Books, a division of Bantam
Doubleday Dell Publishing Group, Inc. Its trademark, consisting of the
words "Bantam Books" and the portrayal of a rooster, is Registered in
U.S. Patent and Trademark Office and in other countries. Marca
Registrada. Bantam Books, 1540 Broadway, New York, New York 10036.

PRINTED IN THE UNITED STATES OF AMERICA

OPM 10 9 8 7 6 5

·Contents·

Cooking Without a Grain of Salt

·Introduction·

Elma Bagg wrote *Cooking Without a Grain of Salt* in the early sixties, organizing it from a series of notes and ideas that she hoped would benefit others who were told to follow a low-salt diet. Her cookbook arrived at a time when the effects of salt on health were just beginning to be better understood. She popularized an attitude toward low-sodium cooking that was much in evidence in her home—that it could be fun, that you could cope with its demands and live a perfectly normal life.

Thirty years later, the original *Cooking Without a Grain of Salt* was still in print, a classic guide to low-sodium cooking with down-to-earth advice to help make that diet work in a world where people almost automatically salt their food.

Elma's book met a need for practical help in preparing tasty low-sodium meals; today that need is even greater and more universal than when the book first appeared. But much else has been discovered in the last quarter century about the essentials of maintaining a healthy diet, particularly for those who must protect their hearts and their arteries from their appetites. We have accordingly updated and revised *Cooking Without a Grain of Salt* to take advantage of present nutritional wisdom.

Each recipe is followed by a complete nutritional

analysis so that specific dietary requirements can be met. We have expanded the choice of recipes with reduced cholesterol and fat levels. We have also added new dishes from vegetarian, regional, ethnic, and international cuisines, which, with a good sense that predates modern medical knowledge, were already low in sodium and high in flavor.

This book grew from Elma's personal challenge: to serve her husband meals in which the sodium content had to be closely monitored. Ted Bagg's need for that diet arose in dramatic fashion, though probably not much differently than it has in many households. Ted—who, in fact, earned his living selling insurance—had decided to increase the coverage on his own life when he was in his late fifties. After hearing the results of his physical exam, he casually told Elma (over his shoulder, as he was walking out the door on his way to work) that the insurance company doctors judged him to be uninsurable. He shrugged it off, saying "Too bad," not seeing that much could be done about it. "Hey, I feel fine," was his assessment of the situation. Elma was not reassured. After learning that it was his alarmingly high blood pressure reading that made him uninsurable, she went into high gear—asking questions that led to a good doctor, a new diet, her discoveries in the kitchen, and this book.

Ted enjoyed good food, disliked blandness, and did not hide his preferences. So Elma's problem was real and immediate. She clearly thought that her efforts to engage Ted's appetite at mealtime would determine his chances of survival. We children remember how the liberal sprinkling of dill weed on his poached egg made the automatic pass of the saltshaker no longer missed—even by us, when we tried the eggs with the unfamiliar shaggy topping.

As Ted's health improved, his blood pressure decreased, and he learned not only to relish, but to be grateful for, what Elma cooked. And Ted proved the insurance company doctors wrong: he lived to be 89.

Elma made her learning experiences part of her story; she realized that other dieters and their families could benefit from her kitchen struggles, her always playful improvisations and adjustments in restaurants and friends' houses, her slowly acquired expertise and discipline.

One day Elma was sitting in the kitchen with her daughter, not long after Susan's first child was born. Elma said: "You know, Susan, I think my book will go on and on. And someday I'd like you to revise it." Quietly, she brought together the book's enduring power and her own mortality.

When Susan was 19 Elma gave her a copy of the *Gourmet Cookbook, Volume I.* But Susan wasn't just learning to cook in the classical tradition, she was learning to cook under Elma's tutelage . . . without salt. Mother and daughter would mull over haute cuisine recipes and figure out how to adapt them for a salt-free diet. In retrospect we see Elma's spirit here. It was her desire to keep that spirit alive, and she thought it best to do it while she and her daughter were learners together.

Elma's kitchen was a work of art, or rather, many works of art—a kind of witty domestic museum. A stranger would have had difficulty finding the appliances. There was too much else to look at: a waist-high fireplace, put in after Elma and Ted came home from France; a cobbler's bench full of whimsical antiques sat in front of the fireplace; two rocking chairs calmed the usual frenetic activity in the kitchen. Candles were everywhere. Potatoes and onions had their own baskets. The refrigerator was behind a shutter, and the stove, the narrowest you could buy, was tucked in a corner. Beside the stove was a small wooden square on which her most faithful salt-fighting allies stood at the ready: a pepper grinder, a flask of olive oil, a garlic bulb. There was no dishwasher.

A dynamic is played out around eating in countless households. From our perspective, it seemed that both our parents worked hard to achieve change in their habits. The partnership they developed as parents and friends was solidified as they entered together into the salt-free adventure.

Susan Bagg Todd
Robert Ely Bagg
January 1, 1998

THE ROLE OF SODIUM: NUTRITIONAL BACKGROUND

Sodium is a mineral basic and necessary to animal and plant life, and salt (sodium chloride) has been used as a seasoning since ancient times. But medical consensus tells us that excess sodium can cause us all eventual harm. The kidneys are the organs that control the level of salt in our bodies. If there is too much salt, healthy kidneys excrete it into our urine. When kidneys are faulty, or if too much salt enters the system, the excess salt stays in the bloodstream, absorbing water to keep it dissolved. That excess liquid in the confined space of our circulatory system causes swelling that puts dangerous hydraulic pressure on the walls of blood vessels and leaves us at risk for strokes and heart attacks. If arteries are clogged with fat, that risk is compounded.

But we can lessen the risk of such damage by maintaining adequate potassium in our diet. A healthy body needs more potassium than sodium in order to ensure the efficient workings of its cells. These minerals work cooperatively to activate the intake of nutrients and the excretion of wastes on the cellular level in a process governed by the sodium-potassium pump, a kind of engine that drives cell activity. To maintain the essential high-potassium ratio, known as the "K factor," people must eat fresh fruits and vegetables. The National Academy of Science recommends between 1,600 and 2,000 milligrams of potassium a day. Foods particularly high in potassium include dried apricots, bananas, potatoes (especially sweet potatoes), dried beans and peas, meat, peanut butter, and orange juice.[1]

As you use this book you will notice that every nu-

---

[1] *For additional information, read* The K Factor *by Richard D. Moore and George D. Webb (Macmillan, 1986).*

tritional analysis contains figures for both sodium and potassium and that the potassium amounts will nearly always be considerably higher than the sodium ones, as in the following:

BLACK BEANS WITH CILANTRO

Calories	221	Protein	12 g.
Fat	4 g.	Carbohydrate	35 g.
Saturated Fat	1 g.	**Sodium**	**8 mg.**
Cholesterol	3 mg.	**Potassium**	**855 mg.**

Maintaining this ratio, in which potassium amounts are far greater than sodium, is critical to cellular health.

Primitive societies lived close to their plant and animal food, did not salt food as a matter of course as we do, and ate much of it uncooked. Potassium was plentiful in this natural diet. Sodium wasn't. Thus humans were genetically programmed millennia ago to excrete potassium and retain sodium. There is even a particular place at the edge of the tongue that detects saltiness in foods. As civilizations developed and some groups moved away from their food source, salt became the indispensable preserving ingredient so that food could both travel and keep. So honored was the role of salt that it entered the language both as a measure of value and an index of excellence. Hence we are paid a *sala*ry; good folk are the salt of the earth.[2]

[2]   *It is interesting to note just how effective a preserving agent salt became in ancient Egypt. Mummification depended on salt! When the Nile receded from its yearly floods, it left behind pockets of a substance the Egyptians called* natron, *a sodium-based chemical essential to the technology of preserving mummies.*

As people discovered that salt could preserve foods for long periods, they also discovered that they liked the taste it gave to food. As salt came into common use, the proportion of sodium to potassium in human diets reversed, with sodium gaining dominance. The effect of sodium dominance on whole societies has been dramatic and destructive. Hypertension, once unknown in cultures that traditionally followed low-sodium diets, now affects tens of millions as those societies adapt to the high-sodium diet of "commerce" or "civilization." As much as 95 percent of the sodium we eat is put in our foods by someone else, most typically in the processed foods that are, unfortunately, a staple of the American diet. It is by informing ourselves of the sodium content of the foods we buy that we most usefully exercise our salt vigilance.

Medical demographers estimate that around 15 percent of the general population is particularly sensitive to the adverse effects of salt. That works out to be roughly 40 million people. At least 50 percent of those with hypertension risk harm by maintaining a high-sodium diet. Several other conditions are also commonly treated by salt-free diets. These include congestive heart failure, diabetes, migraines, premenstrual tension, and Ménière's disease. Women after menopause are encouraged to reduce salt because studies show that sodium contributes to the loss of calcium, which is needed to prevent osteoporosis. Current research has determined that certain forms of cancer are related to high-sodium levels. Many cancer therapies, in fact, involve eliminating salt intake. Certain kinds of stress have been shown both to be sodium-caused and to increase desire for salt; lowering salt intake lowers stress levels.

Thirty years ago there was a sharp distinction between those for whom it was medically necessary to limit salt intake and those who had no need to do so. Today we know better: most of us would be healthier if we used less salt.

We conclude this nutritional note with a statement of two convictions. The first is that sodium has invaded our culture in a highly dangerous way, because it is all too often silently present and frequently unsuspected. Sometimes we can't taste it even when it is there in startlingly high concentrations—in milkshakes, for instance, which contain nearly 300 milligrams of sodium. The use of sodium in preparing fast foods, most baked goods, and most canned and frozen foods, is common and under-recognized. The current federal truth-in-packaging guidelines make it increasingly easier for consumers to learn the exact ingredients of what they buy and eat. On the other hand, as the nutritionist Dodie Anderson has said, "You won't have to bother reading labels because the foods I want you to eat don't have labels."

Our second conviction is that an addiction to salt, because it is an acquired taste or acquired craving, can be unlearned. (Babies are born with no interest in salty foods and breast milk is very low in sodium.) Because the taste for salt is a habit, developed both by cultures and by individuals, it can be changed and replaced by a taste for flavors and textures and smells much better for our health. In just a matter of weeks you'll lose the desire for salt and become newly sensitive to the array of seasonings that await you.

Work with Your Doctor

The simplest way to monitor your sodium susceptibility is to ask your doctor to test your sodium blood level.[3] A reading of between 137 and 144 indicates you should maintain a moderate salt intake of about 2,000

[3] Get the Salt Out by Ann Louise Gittleman, M.S., C.N.S. Crown Publishers (New York, 1996), p. 24.

milligrams a day. If your reading is over 144, it indicates an unhealthy salt retention in your tissues, and your doctor will probably urge you to identify and cut sharply the sources of salt in your diet. A sodium blood level under 137 means you may need to slightly increase your sodium intake.

In our parents' case, the doctor placed Ted on a low-sodium diet and he followed it, with Elma's help. Thirty years ago, before more sophisticated medications, doctors treated hypertension with diet. It is still the preferred method, but, probably because of the less arduous alternatives, many doctors find that it is too difficult to get people to comply. There are countless approaches to the curing of illness in the medical profession. Some doctors rely primarily on medication; others look first at dietary changes, along with weight loss and exercise. Many suggest a combination, believing that a low-sodium diet contributes to the effectiveness of medication. Make sure you and your doctor are of a mind. Because you have this book in your hands you are embracing a nutritional approach, but you also will need the advice and encouragement of your doctor as you set out.

The original recipes in *Cooking Without a Grain of Salt* were created so that they might be used for a sodium-restricted diet of 500 milligrams per day (in 24 hours). Most people need not follow such a limited low-sodium diet. But if you must, there is a range of recipes from which you may select your menu. To ensure well-balanced meals, careful planning will be needed for 500 milligrams. But if your sodium restriction is under 500 milligrams, *very* careful planning must be employed. You and your doctor should be certain you are receiving adequate nutrition, especially for the recommended amount of calcium, perhaps in the form of a supplement. (An 8-ounce cup of milk contains between 120 and 125 milligrams of sodium. One glass would then limit you to 375 milligrams of sodium for the rest of the day.)

If your diet permits more than 500 milligrams per day, the recipes in this book are adaptable. Many doctors restrict all added salt, rather than prescribing a specific milligram limit. Your doctor may allow light salting in the cooking or in the preparation of food. If the food was prepared without salt, a limited amount may be permitted at the table. But keep in mind that there are 570 milligrams of sodium in $1/4$ teaspoon of salt, about 2,300 in a teaspoon. It will take discipline and ingenuity to stay safely within your limit.

If there are foods on the permitted lists or ingredients in these recipes that your doctor forbids, follow those orders and do not use those foods. On the other hand, as you gain understanding of the principles of salt-free cooking, you will take responsibility for how it applies to you and allow yourself occasional foods on the off-limits list as you learn to balance and combine ingredients during a single day.

Your doctor will explain your individual dietary needs. But the only way any doctor can truly assist and benefit your health is for you to fully participate in the process. Take to heart the instructions your doctor lays out for you. Make sure the instructions make sense. Ask questions. Read and learn on your own. Work and live within the dietary guidelines and understand that in following them with determination you are creating your own health.

Our susceptibility to sodium's harmful effects tends to increase with age. If we learn to limit our intake early in life, we reduce our risk of sodium-induced diseases later on.

THE BIG PICTURE:
HOW SODIUM FITS INTO BASIC NUTRITION

The human body needs close to 50 nutrients to maintain good health. All of these nutrients are not found in every food. Vitamin pills are not a substitute for adequate nutrition. Although each food is important in some way, we need to eat more of some and less of others in order to prevent or postpone certain diseases.

The United States Department of Agriculture developed the Food Guide Pyramid to illustrate how your daily food intake should be proportioned.

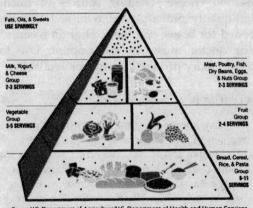

Food Guide Pyramid
A Guide to Daily Food Choices

Fats, Oils, & Sweets
USE SPARINGLY

Milk, Yogurt, & Cheese Group
2-3 SERVINGS

Meat, Poultry, Fish, Dry Beans, Eggs, & Nuts Group
2-3 SERVINGS

Vegetable Group
3-5 SERVINGS

Fruit Group
2-4 SERVINGS

Bread, Cereal, Rice, & Pasta Group
6-11 SERVINGS

Source: U.S. Department of Agriculture/U.S. Department of Health and Human Services

1. Fats, oils, sweets—use sparingly (no more than 30 percent of daily caloric intake). Focus on consuming mostly monounsaturated and poly-

unsaturated fats such as olive oil, canola oil, safflower oil, sunflower oil, soybean oil, and sesame seed oil.

2. Proteins: 2–3 servings. Meat, poultry, fish, beans, eggs, and nuts are protein sources that also provide B vitamins, iron, magnesium, and zinc. 1 serving = 3 ounces cooked seafood, poultry, meat, $^1/_2$ cup cooked fried beans, 1 egg, or 1 ounce nuts.

Note: One large egg and 3 ounces of beef would quickly take you over the 300-milligram cholesterol recommendation, so remember to distribute your cholesterol intake over time and compensate where necessary by cutting back on some days.

3. Dairy products: 2–3 servings. A serving size: 1 cup of low-fat milk or yogurt, $1^1/_2$ ounces unsalted cheese. Leading sources of calcium, high-quality protein, riboflavin, and Vitamin A needed for bones and teeth. High in sodium, so your doctor must set the amount. Use low-sodium dairy products whenever available.

CALCIUM IS A UNISEX MINERAL

We have known for some time of the increased risk to women of calcium loss to bone structure as their sodium-intake levels rise. We now know that many men are also at risk for the same dangerous loss of bone calcium if their bodies cannot assimilate the sodium in their diets. All of us will better preserve the essential calcium needed for healthy bones and optimum health if our diet contains less sodium.

4. Fruits: 2–4 servings. Excellent sources of Vitamins A and C as well as dietary fiber. Serving

size: 1 medium apple, orange, or banana. $^1/_2$ cup diced fruit or berries, and $^3/_4$ cup of juice.

5. Vegetables: 3–5 servings. Excellent sources of vitamins, minerals, and fiber. Also low in fat. Serving consists of 1 cup raw leafy greens, $^1/_2$ cup of others. For dry beans and peas count $^1/_2$ cup cooked as a serving of vegetables.

6. Breads, cereals, rice, and pasta: 6–11 servings. Abundant sources of complex carbohydrates, iron, B vitamins, fiber, minerals, and energy. Suggested serving: 1 slice of low-sodium bread, $^1/_2$ low-sodium muffin, 1 ounce dry, ready-to-eat low-sodium cereal, $^1/_2$ cup cooked low-sodium cereal, rice, or pasta.

Remember: Dietary fiber, the indigestible part of plant foods, helps the body regulate fat and cholesterol levels.

WATER: 6–8 GLASSES A DAY

Adequate water will help your body flush excess sodium. Remember this essential part of your daily diet.

Check with your local board of health to learn the sodium count in your town's water supply. Or take a sample of your own water supply to your local extension service to have it analyzed. Many of us rely on bottled water, and there are now low-sodium brands on the market. Check the labels. The standard for sodium in tap water is 20 milligrams per 8 ounces. If your roads are salted in the winter, this amount may vary. Do not drink water that has been softened. It contains high levels of sodium. And don't bathe in it, either. Salt-softened water will absorb easily into your body through your skin.

More is learned about the importance of diet every day, though many of the old truths still apply. Read to educate yourself about food values and nutrition and new ideas for great flavors, and use your common sense. Discuss your questions with your doctor. A safe principle for low-sodium nutritious eating is:

Think about balance, variety, freshness, moderation, and proportion when choosing your foods. Read your labels, and remember that following a low-sodium diet does not simply mean you are eliminating salt, but that you are including in your diet the proper levels of all the nutrients necessary for health.

COPING WITHOUT SODIUM IN THE WIDER WORLD

The beginning is the most important part of the work.
—*Plato*

Keep a Notebook

Learn to count milligrams of sodium. Use a pocket notebook so you can record the numbers and also jot down the combinations of herbs and seasonings that taste good to you. Make sure you date your entries and note everything you eat, along with the milligram counts and calorie counts, if you are also trying to lose weight. This exercise will help you become more accustomed to the diet and will provide a useful history of your progress. Keep a pocket folder, as well, for clippings of great ideas.

The Hospital Patient

If you are hospitalized and need to enhance an institutional diet, suggest that a member of your family or a friend help by filling a shoe box with twelve seasoning shakers (formerly saltshakers) containing curry powder, cayenne, dill, dry mustard, garlic powder, onion powder, nutmeg, oregano, thyme, cinnamon, allspice, and paprika. Include a small bottle of cider or flavored vinegar, low-sodium catsup, unsalted horseradish, and hot sauce, as well. Tuck in some fresh lemons and limes. There are only 3 milligrams of sodium in 1 tablespoon of low-sodium catsup and 9 milligrams of sodium in $^1/_4$ teaspoon of Tabasco sauce. The rest of the herbs and seasonings on this list you don't have to count.

Eating Out

Restaurants of every kind will try to fulfill your requests, and the more expensive ones will tend to cook to order from a wider variety of fresh ingredients. Call ahead. It is much appreciated if you give advance warning, especially since people so often don't, putting added burdens on an already hard-pressed kitchen staff.

Most natural-food-store delis have a take-out department already stocked with the ingredients needed for a good sandwich or simple lunch. Pita and bean sprouts and low-sodium cheese and unsalted turkey are available most places, and they generally have low-sodium condiments on hand, as well. Salad bars are everywhere. (Just remember to use oil and vinegar and stick with the raw, fresh ingredients. Avoid the relishes and already mixed salads.)

Fast-food establishments have a reputation for being treacherous territory for anyone on a low-sodium diet. If you find yourself at one, the best option is always a garden or chicken salad with a light vinaigrette (used sparingly), especially in the pizza places. (You might carry with you a stash of bottled, low-sodium dressing, or containers of oil and vinegar.) Most burger emporiums will make anything you want to order, such as an unsalted hamburger or unsalted french fries (if you can afford the fat). In Tex-Mex spots avoid all corn products because they contain preservatives high in sodium. Eat the salad, but leave the taco shell it comes in. Flour tortilla burritos can be made to order with beans and rice, and lettuce and tomato. These may be higher in sodium than you'd like, but still better than the standard fare. Always ask for help. You may be surprised at how accommodating a fast-food establishment can be.

HOW TO ORDER LOW-SODIUM FROM A MENU

First ask if your choice may be cooked to order. If something isn't on the menu, ask if the chef could fill a request.

Appetizers: sliced melon and berries with lime, raw oysters with lemon, crudités, green salad dressed with oil and vinegar or lemon juice (see if there's young arugula or fresh dill available), fruit soup (most other soups will be loaded with sodium).

Entrées: Ask specifically that your entrée be grilled, broiled, baked, steamed, or roasted without salt. Avoid anything sautéed, creamed, or au gratin. Choose a 3-ounce (cooked weight) serving of: center cut roast beef, breast of chicken, fresh fish, lamb chop, pork chop, steak, or turkey without gravy. Remember: a 3-ounce serving is about the same size as a deck of cards.

Vegetables, grains, pasta: Ask that the vegetables be steamed and served with a small amount of unsalted

(continued)

butter and lemon juice. (The best restaurants generally cook only with unsalted butter.) Vegetables grilled or roasted without salt are also good choices. Otherwise the vegetables might be very salty. Baked potato (use nonfat yogurt as a topping), baked sweet potato, ear of corn, plain steamed rice, or pasta with olive oil.

Dessert: Choose sorbet, frozen yogurt, or fresh fruit of the season with a little honey. (Honey is said to promote a good night's sleep!)

Drinks: Coffee, decaf, herbal, black, and green teas.

Snacks

Besides fruit, air-popped popcorn with a little garlic powder and olive oil drizzled on top is a good snack. Take your own to the movies. Also, you can make your own trail mix, combining unsalted nuts, seeds, chopped dried fruit, and a few yogurt chips.

BOON COMPANIONS:

Ideas for Your Insulated Bag or Portable Cooler

Low-sodium crackers
Low-sodium cheese
Unsalted butter (with parsley)
Carrot sticks
Low-sodium hot sauce
Frozen grapes
Slices of unsalted French bread
Spiced, unsalted nuts
Nonfat yogurt

Microwaves: Double-Edged Sword

Most workplaces have microwave ovens. Put together a careful arrangement of last night's dinner on a microwavable plate, cover with plastic wrap, and carry it in an insulated bag or cooler: you'll have a lunch to anticipate all morning. But don't let this tool lure you into buying high-sodium microwave dinners.

The First Dinner Invitation

If you are on a very strict low-sodium diet, do not be afraid to explain to your hosts that your sodium intake must be monitored. Reassure them that they need prepare nothing special, and offer to contribute a dish that was made without salt for you or to share. Once you've disclosed your medical needs, it won't seem odd to bring your insulated bag or a contribution to the gathering. Of course, your hosts may wish to plan their meal around your special needs, and if so, they are friends to be cherished. You may even be surprised at how many people there are who quietly cook and eat without salt.

> **FOREIGN TRAVEL**
>
> If you're traveling abroad, you may want a somewhat larger cooler or insulated bag. You'll be able to buy fresh fruit (lemons for flavoring) and vegetables, dip bread in olive oil, and will probably come home with many ideas for food combinations you'd never thought of before. Airlines and cruise companies are most cooperative if notified 24 hours ahead of time about your diet. An added benefit is that you'll most likely be served first. When you reach your destination and you don't want salt added to your food, be sure to say:

(continued)

Arabic	*ma Fii mil Hah*
Chinese	*wu yen*
French	*sans sel*
German	*ohne Saltz*
Greek	*horis alati*
Italian	*senza sale*
Japanese	*shio nuki*
Lithuanian	*be druskos*
Portuguese	*falto de sel*
Russian	*bez soli*
Spanish	*sin sal*
Swedish	*utan salt*
Yiddish	*una zaltz*

Salt Outside Mealtimes: When to Worry and When Not to Worry

One highly effective way to reduce salt levels is through all forms of aerobic exercise. The salt comes out in our sweat.

Dental care: Rinse carefully after gargling with salt water. Toothpaste, toothpowder, and mouthwashes are safe as long as you rinse after brushing. A toothbrushing can provide as much as 40 milligrams sodium. Sodium fluoride is the great cavity fighter. You can, however, make your own salt-free toothpaste. Ask your pharmacist for chemically pure precipitated calcium carbonate. This is basically found in capsule form as a calcium supplement. Ask the pharmacist to grind it. Then mix it with a little glycerin as you use it.

Sodium in Over-the-Counter Drugs

Many over-the-counter drugs are safe for restricted diets, but some are not. Most pain relievers have less than 5 milligrams of sodium, but it is important to check the label, as it is to check the labels of all drugs you buy, including vitamins, for their exact sodium content. Antacids can be high in sodium: Alka-Seltzer has 995 milligrams of sodium per two-tablet dose; Bromo-Seltzer has 761. Many brands, however, also sell low-sodium versions. A tea brewed with freshly grated ginger and sage steeped in hot water will soothe upset stomachs.

Certain foods can tend to bring on headaches: cured meats (e.g., ham, bacon, hot dogs), dishes made with monosodium glutamate (MSG), aged cheese, chocolate, and nuts. A low-salt diet might mean, literally, fewer headaches! A small (25 milligrams) daily dose of the herb feverfew acts as a headache preventative.

Prune juice, which has only 2 milligrams of sodium in a half cup, is preferable to drugstore laxatives.

One more thing. Don't lick postage stamps. Use the self-adhesive ones.

CHANGING HABITS

Great is the person who does a thing for the first time.
— *Alexander Smith*

Eliminating salt from one's diet nearly always means radical change. It means using unfamiliar ingredients, experimenting with new combinations, and walking a different route through the supermarket. It may seem, at first, to have all the fear and excitement of a voyage into the unknown.

When we begin any new venture, we prepare. We lay plans and gather materials. We don't begin until we are ready. Beginning to cook without salt is no different. But by driving away salt as a seasoning shortcut, we can appreciate fully the true elements of flavor and food preparation. No longer dependent on salt, we can begin to respond to ingredients afresh. We imagine combinations that might work, study sodium counts, and plot how our likes and dislikes figure into the picture.

One reader wrote many years ago with a useful idea that we'd like to pass along. He said his wife, when told she had to eliminate salt from her diet, took *Cooking Without a Grain of Salt* and went to the supermarket and spent $30 on ingredients. She didn't know what she was going to cook that night, but she knew she needed at her fingertips a whole new selection of seasonings to reinvent her recipes.

We are passing on that suggestion to you (though $30 certainly went a lot further 30 years ago!). But first we'll give you some lists to prepare you for change and to help you reinvent your own way of cooking.

The 10-Foot Pole

Copy the list on the following pages to keep in your wallet or in your notebook at all times. It is more valuable than money to someone on a salt-free diet.

When food is transported between states, federal law requires that the label on all packaged and canned foods show whether food contains salt in any form.

DON'T BUY FOOD WITH THE FOLLOWING INGREDIENTS:

As you read over this list, notice that many of these additives are used to preserve food, another reason why "fresh is best."

Salt (sodium chloride) NaCl	To season, to preserve, to can, and to process food
Baking soda (sodium bicarbonate)	To leaven bread and cakes
Brine (salt and water)	To check bacteria growth To clean and blanch vegetables and fruits
Monosodium glutamate (MSG)	To flavor food
Baking powder	To leaven breads and cake
Di-sodium phosphate	Found in some quick-cooking cereals and processed cheeses
Sodium alginate	To smooth texture of chocolate milk and ice cream
Sodium benzoate	To preserve condiments
Sodium hydroxide	To soften and loosen skin of certain fruits and vegetables, such as olives
Sodium propionate	To inhibit growth of mold in pasteurized cheese and in some breads and cakes

(continued)

Sodium sulfite	To bleach fruits, to obtain artificial color as in maraschino cherries, glazed fruit *Note: Sulfites are added to wine barrels to prevent mold, but these are in the form of sulfur dioxide or raw sulfur. No sodium is added.*
Sodium nitrate	To preserve bacon, hot dogs and ham, lunch meats, and smoked fish. It inhibits the growth of botulism-causing bacteria and keeps red meat red.
Na	Chemist's symbol for sodium

The following are the Food and Drug Administration's definitions of the claims made on labels regarding the sodium content of food:

- Sodium-free: less than 5 milligrams per serving
- Very low-sodium: 35 milligrams or less per serving
- Low-sodium: 140 milligrams or less per serving.
- Reduced or less sodium: at least 25 percent less per serving than regular or reference food
- Light in sodium: 50 percent less sodium than regular or reference food. (Any food that still does not meet the definition for "low-

sodium" is required to include the phrase
"not a low-sodium food" on the label.)

> If anyone in your family is a normal salt user, it is
> preferable to use salt in a natural, unrefined form, such
> as sea salt, which retains about 60 healthy minerals
> and does not contain the aluminum-based compound
> added to improve its pourability. These additives have
> been identified as potential sources of several diseases,
> including Alzheimer's.

Off-Limits Seasonings, Flavors, and Blends

Bouillon cubes (except low-sodium)
Candies (commercial and homemade with salt)
Catsup (except low-sodium)
Celery flakes
Celery salt
Chili sauce (except low-sodium)
Garlic salt
Gelatin, flavored
Horseradish with salt
Mayonnaise (except low-sodium)
Meat extracts
Meat sauces (salted)
Meat tenderizers (except low-sodium)
Miso
Monosodium glutamate (MSG)
Mustard (except low-sodium)
Olives
Onion Salt
Pickles (except low-sodium)

Pudding mixes (except low-sodium)
Relishes (except low-sodium)
Rennet tablets
Salt (except what your doctor may allow you)
Salted nuts
Salt substitutes (except what your doctor allows)
Soy sauce (except low-sodium)
Sugar substitute (sodium cyclamate)
Worcestershire sauce (except low-sodium)

Off-Limits Drinks

Cocoa, instant mixes
Chocolate milk
Malted milk
Milk shakes
Salted buttermilk
Tomato or vegetable juice (except low-sodium)
Nutritional or diet supplements (except low-sodium)

Off-Limits Vegetables

All canned vegetables (except low-sodium)
All canned or packaged vegetable soups (except low-sodium)
Sauerkraut

Note: You can eliminate a good percentage of the salt in canned vegetables by rinsing the food before heating. Some brands of frozen peas and lima beans, as well as frozen vegetable combinations or those with sauces, are high in sodium. Check the labels.

Off-Limits Meats

Bacon
Bologna
Brains
Chipped beef
Corned beef
Frankfurters
Ham (except fresh)
All canned meat soups and stews (except low-sodium)
Kidneys
Kosher meats*
Salt pork
Sausage
Smoked tongue
Liverwurst
Luncheon meats
Salami
Canned meat (except low-sodium)
Pickled meat
Salted meat
Smoked meat
Spiced meat

Kosher meat is salted. If you are on a low-sodium diet, Jewish law excuses you from the consumption of kosher meat.

Off-Limits Breads/Grains

Commercial or homemade with salt:
Bagels
Bread

Crackers

Rolls

Cakes and cake mixes (except low-sodium)

Cookies

Waffles

Pancakes

Self-rising cornmeal and flour

Quick-cooking or instant cereals made with salt (except Cream of Wheat, Ralston, Maltex, Wheatena, Quaker Oats, Quaker Oat Bran, farina, kasha, and bulgur wheat)

Dry cereals (except puffed rice, puffed wheat, puffed kasha, shredded wheat, granola, and muesli, or low-sodium varieties)

Salted popcorn, potato chips, tortilla chips, and pretzels

Seasoned rice or other grain dishes

Off-Limits Dairy and Farm Foods

All salted cheeses

Commercial and homemade salted ice cream and sherbet

Salted butter

Salted buttermilk

Off-Limits Fish

Frozen fish fillets

All canned fish (except low-sodium)

All salted fish

All shellfish (except oysters, if doctor permits, or occasional servings of shrimp or scallops)

All smoked fish
Anchovies
Caviar
Clams
Cod, dried
Cod, salted
Crabs
Herring
Lobster
Sardines

Cooking Wine

Salt is added to cooking wine to make it undrinkable. In this way it can be sold by stores without liquor licenses. In any case, cooking wine should never be used for cooking, whether or not you are required to restrict your salt intake.

No Worries

Your foods shall be your remedies, and your remedies shall be your foods.

—*Hippocrates*

The following are lists of all the foods to choose from if you're on a low-sodium diet, along with portions, sodium count in milligrams, and calories per serving. Sodium is found naturally in most foods, and, in general, in quite low amounts. If a food is somewhat higher in sodium (or fat) and should be used carefully, we've marked it with an asterisk [*]. Remember that the processing of food provides as much as 95 percent of the sodium in American diets.

In the cooking of meat, poultry, or fish, the shrinkage is approximately 25 per cent. For instance, 4 ounces of raw meat, poultry, or fish becomes 3 ounces cooked. The sodium content, however, doesn't shrink and is valued in the raw weight. All sodium contents of meats are figured after the removal of excess fat. Remember, a 3 ounce portion is about the size of a deck of cards.

cooked weight	milligrams sodium	calories
3 oz. beef	80	250
3 oz. chicken (white)	89	186
3 oz. duck breast	80	200
3 oz. pork	64	280
3 oz. rabbit	53	140
3 oz. buffalo	48	111
1 quail (3.8 oz.)	58	210
3 oz. venison	46	134
3 oz. chicken (dark)	124	196
3 oz. duck leg	108	228
3 oz. lamb	100	220
3 oz. liver (calf)	125	180
3 oz. sweetbreads	100	188
3 oz. tongue	90	220
3 oz. turkey (dark)	104	245
3 oz. veal	110	228

Unsalted gravy (if your doctor allows gravy), made from the liquid left in the pan, may be used with the portion of meat, fish, or chicken allowed in your diet.

FRESH FISH CHOICES

cooked weight	milligrams sodium	calories
3 oz. bass	75	150
3 oz. bluefish	75	144
3 oz. cod	88	80
3 oz. flounder	64	75
3 oz. haddock	68	88
3 oz. halibut	60	144
3 oz. mackerel	60	204
3 oz. trout	60	116
9 medium oysters	90	280
3 oz. salmon	90	225
3 oz. sole	100	115
3 oz. swordfish	90	140
3 oz. tuna	90	225
4 large shrimp*	49	22
3 oz. scallops*	137	75

FRESH VEGETABLE CHOICES

Frozen vegetables are permissible if processed without salt. Check the label.

	milligrams sodium	calories
6 stalks asparagus	2	22
1/2 cup beans (green and wax)	1	23
1/2 cup beans (lima)	1	100
1/2 cup broccoli	10	22
9 brussels sprouts	11	60
1 cup cabbage (shredded)	12.8	20
1 large carrot*	48	20
1/2 cup cauliflower	18	15
1 ear sweet corn	3	85
1 cucumber	7.2	20
1/2 eggplant	8.2	48
4 escarole leaves	3	3
4 endive leaves	3.6	7
1/4 head lettuce (solid)	12	13
8 large mushrooms	10	25
10 pods okra	1	30
1 medium onion	6	25
2 tablespoons parsley	2	2

$^1/_2$ cup peas	1	56
1 green pepper	1	16
1 potato (white)	4	97
1 potato (sweet)	12	183
$^1/_2$ cup mustard greens	7	7
1 medium artichoke*	114	108
$^1/_2$ cup beets*	49	30
1 rib celery*	35	6
$^1/_2$ cup dandelion greens*	21	13
$^1/_2$ cup kale	15	15
$^1/_2$ cup beet greens*	173	20
1 cup pumpkin	2	66
1 radish	3	2
$^1/_2$ cup summer squash	0.6	15
$^1/_2$ cup winter squash	0.6	45
1 tomato	3	30
$^1/_2$ cup turnip greens	10	22
$^1/_2$ cup yellow turnips	5	25
$^1/_2$ cup watercress	11	2

Note: Many canned tomato products are made without salt. These include crushed tomatoes, stewed tomatoes, and tomato paste. Also, canned pimentos are low in sodium.

FRESH FRUIT CHOICES

	milligrams sodium	calories
1 apple (skinned)	2	75
1 apricot	0.4	18
1 avocado*	6	485
1 banana	1.4	99
1/2 cup blackberries	2	41
1/2 cup blueberries	1	43
1/4 cantaloupe	6	18
1/2 cup cherries	3	40
1 cup coconut (grated)*	18.4	352
1 cup cranberries	1	54
1/2 cup currants	1.3	30
1/2 grapefruit	3	75
30 grapes	3.5	70
1/2 cup lemon juice and pulp	2	32
1 mango	4	133
1 orange	2	70
1 papaya	6	43
1 peach	2	51
1 pear	2	60
1/2 cup pineapple	1	32

1 plum	0.6	29
1 kiwi	4	46
1 cup raspberries	1	84
1 cup rhubarb	2	20
10 strawberries	0.8	35
1 tangerine	0.6	35
8 oz. watermelon	0.6	75

DAIRY AND FARM CHOICES

	milligrams sodium	*calories*
1 tablespoon sweet or unsalted butter	0.7	100
8 oz. nonfat unsalted buttermilk	120	85
8 oz. evaporated milk (reconstituted)	126	166
8 oz. skim milk	127.9	87
8 oz. whole milk	122	166
8 oz. low-sodium dry milk (reconstituted)	7	79
8 oz. low-sodium fresh milk	12	166
8 oz. low-fat milk	123	102
8 oz. plain yogurt (nonfat)	110	140

8 oz. fruit yogurt	88	220
1 oz. low-sodium cheese	12	100
1 tablespoon cream	5.7	49
1 tablespoon sour cream	5.7	49
1 tablespoon whole milk	7.6	11
1 egg	68	77
1 egg yolk	13	61
1 egg white	55	16

BREAD CHOICES

	milligrams sodium	*calories*
1 slice low-sodium bread	4	75
1 low-sodium roll	4	75
1 low-sodium melba toast	1.6	15
1 matzo	0.2	112
2 low-sodium bread sticks	15	120
7 unsalted pretzels	0	50
1 oz. corn chips, unsalted	2	160
1 oz. potato chips, unsalted	1	160
1 pita bread	10	70
1 rice cake, unsalted	0	35

COOKED CEREAL CHOICES

	milligrams sodium	*calories*
2 oz. bulgur wheat	0	200
1 oz. Cream of Wheat	0	100
1 cup corn grits	0	146
3/4 cup farina	1	87
2 oz. kasha	5	177
1/3 cup Quaker Oat Bran	1	92
1 cup old-fashioned Quaker Oats	2	145
1 cup multigrain Quaker Oats	2	145
1 cup Ralston High Fiber	5	90
1/3 cup Maltex	2	71
1/2 cup Wheatena	0.4	77

READY-TO-EAT CEREAL CHOICES

	milligrams sodium	*calories*
1/2 cup apple-cinnamon squares	5	90
1/4 cup wheat germ	2	103
1 oz. low-sodium bran flakes	1	100
1 oz. low-sodium cornflakes	5	110

1 oz. Frosted Mini-Wheats	0	100
1 cup puffed rice	1	54
1 cup puffed wheat	1	50
1 cup puffed kasha	2	74
2 biscuits shredded wheat	1	132
1 oz. whole-grain shredded wheat	0	90
1/4 cup granola	3	138

BAKING INGREDIENT CHOICES

	milligrams sodium	*calories*
1/3 cup tapioca	0.5	174
1 tablespoon unflavored gelatin	3.6	34
1 tablespoon cornstarch	0.5	29
1 cup flour	2.7	400
1 tablespoon flour	0.1	25
1 teaspoon cream of tartar	8	tr
1 tablespoon yeast (compressed)	0.6	20
1 teaspoon egg replacer	0	10
1/4 cup soya powder	2	100

VINEGAR CHOICES

	milligrams sodium	calories
1 tablespoon vinegar (cider and distilled)	tr	2
1 tablespoon red wine vinegar	4	2
1 tablespoon white wine vinegar	5	2
1 tablespoon balsamic vinegar	5	3
1 tablespoon champagne vinegar	4	2
1 tablespoon rice vinegar	4	2

OIL AND FAT CHOICES

	milligrams sodium	calories
1 tablespoon un-salted butter	1	100
1 tablespoon low-sodium margarine	1.5	100

Note: Avoid margarine whenever possible. The hydrogenation process used to produce margarine creates substances that the body cannot absorb properly. It is better to use, instead, small amounts of unsalted butter, which, in addition, has a superior taste. You can flavor butter with such low-sodium ingredients as citrus juices, peaches, strawberries, or unsalted ground nuts mixed with brown sugar.

1/2 cup vegetable shortening	0.8	880
1 tablespoon low-sodium mayonnaise	6.0	92

$^1/_2$ cup corn oil	0.3	1,000
$^1/_2$ cup olive oil	0.3	1,000
1 tablespoon olive oil	tr	125
$^1/_2$ cup safflower oil	0.3	1,000
$^1/_2$ cup soybean oil	0.3	1,000
$^1/_2$ cup peanut oil	tr	955
1 tablespoon canola oil	0	120
1 tablespoon rice bran oil	tr	125
1 tablespoon walnut oil	tr	125
1 tablespoon hazelnut oil	tr	125
1 tablespoon sesame oil	tr	125
1 sec. of cooking spray	0	2

Note: The best oils for cooking are olive oil, canola oil, and peanut oil because they remain stable at higher temperatures.

DRINKS CHOICES (SEE DAIRY CHOICES)

	milligrams sodium	*calories*
8 oz. low-fat soy drink	120	120
2 oz. lite coconut milk	6	53
1 teaspoon cocoa	2	7
1 teaspoon coffee (instant)	1.7	0
1 teaspoon coffee (regular)	1.5	0

1 teaspoon Postum (instant)	0.4	2
1 teaspoon Sanka	0.1	0
1 teaspoon tea (regular)	0.1	0
1 teaspoon decaf coffee (instant)	0	4
1 teaspoon coffee with chicory (instant)	5	6
1 teaspoon herb tea	tr	0
1 teaspoon green tea	tr	0

FRUIT JUICES

	milligrams sodium	calories
1/2 cup apple cider	1	62
1/2 cup apple juice	6	62
1/2 cup apricot juice	4	51
1/2 cup cranberry juice	3	90
1/2 cup grapefruit juice	2	65
1/2 cup grape juice	2	32
1/2 cup orange juice	2.5	54
1/2 cup pineapple juice	0.6	60
1/2 cup prune juice	2	85
1/2 cup tangerine juice	2	47
1/2 cup fresh tomato juice	6	25
1/2 cup canned low-sodium tomato juice	6	28

SODAS

	milligrams sodium	calories
6¹/₂ oz. Coca-Cola	1.8	80
8 oz. ginger ale	18.4	75
7 oz. 7UP	13.9	66
12 oz. diet cola	21	2
8 oz. White Rock club soda	1.7	80

MINERAL AND SELTZER WATERS BY BRAND

	milligrams sodium	calories
1 liter Evian	5	0
1 liter San Pellegrino	41	0
6 oz. Adirondack	5	0
Poland Spring	0	0
Perrier	0	0
Appolinaris	0	0

DRINKS CHOICES
(WITH DOCTOR'S PERMISSION)

	milligrams sodium	calories
12 oz. beer	19	146
12 oz. light beer	10	100
1 oz. brandy	1.3	80
1 oz. gin	0.2	70

1 oz. rum	0.5	90
1 oz. whiskey	0.9	86
3^1/$_2$ oz. red table wine	6	74
3^1/$_2$ oz. white wine ·	5	70
2 oz. sweet dessert wine	5	90
1 tablespoon sherry	2.3	22

NUT CHOICES

	milligrams sodium	*calories*
20 almonds	5	170
4 Brazils	4	125
8 cashews	4	171
6 chestnuts	1	49
20 hazelnuts	1	200
30 peanuts	3.2	171
6 pecans (whole)	2.4	185
6 walnuts	2	156
2 oz. water chestnuts	10	14

BEAN AND GRAIN AND PASTA CHOICES

	milligrams sodium	*calories*
^{1}/$_2$ cup cooked white rice	2	131
^{1}/$_2$ cup cooked popcorn	0.4	60
2 oz. spaghetti	0	210
2 oz. brown rice	1	200

^{1}/$_2$ cup arborio rice	5	100
^{1}/$_2$ cup wild rice	3	83
2 oz. lasagna	4	210
2 oz. spinach spaghetti	20 ·	212
2 oz. whole wheat spaghetti	5	198
2 oz. black beans	10	190
1 cup cooked black-eyed peas	6	198
2 oz. chickpeas	11	200
1 cup cooked kidney beans	4	225
^{1}/$_2$ cup cooked barley	2	97
^{1}/$_2$ cup split peas	25	354
^{1}/$_2$ cup lentils	4	347
^{1}/$_2$ cup soybeans	4	348
^{1}/$_2$ cup navy beans	1	321
^{1}/$_2$ cup pea beans	1	321

SWEET CHOICES

	milligrams sodium	*calories*
1 tablespoon honey	1.5	62
1 tablespoon jam or jelly (without preservatives)	1	55

1 cup white sugar	0.8	770
1 tablespoon white sugar	tr	48
1 tablespoon powdered sugar	0.1	31
1 tablespoon brown sugar	3.4	51
1 tablespoon maple syrup (pure)	2.8	57
1 square unsweetened chocolate	3	142
1 marshmallow	3.1	20
2 tablespoons dark molasses	20	110
date sugar, 1 teaspoon sucanat	7	12

CANNED FRUIT CHOICES

Most canned fruit may be used. Check the label. Here are a few suggestions:

	milligrams sodium	calories
1/2 cup applesauce	5	90
1/2 cup cherries	1	61
1/2 cup cranberry sauce	1.2	274
1/2 cup grapefruit	3	100
2 halves peaches	3	79

3 slices pineapple	3	100
3 plums	3	100

DRIED FRUIT CHOICES

Sometimes sodium sulfite has been added to dried fruit. Check the label.

	milligrams sodium	calories
5 apricots	5	82
2 dates	tr	43
3 peaches	5	133
8 prunes	3	144
1 tablespoon raisins	3	35
2 large figs	16	114
10 pears	5	230
1 sun-dried tomato*	8	6
2 dried banana slices	0	140

Sodium levels vary according to brands and packing.

Herbs, Spices, Seasonings, Flavors, and Blends

He causeth the grass to grow for the cattle, and herbs for the service of his people . . .

—Psalm 104:14

Herbs are a special service to us all, and they are sold everywhere. Even small cities offer an array of fragrant herbs all year round. In the dead of winter you can often find vibrant and inexpensive pots of a variety of familiar and hard-to-find herbs. Farmer's markets sell quantities of herbs in the summer. If you have even a small plot of land or just a sunny window, grow your own. Rosemary can test the greenness of your thumb, but mint, parsley, chives, lemon balm, basil, dill, cilantro, fennel, arugula (rocket), and oregano are among the flavorful plants that flourish with little tending. And considering the price of dried herbs, it's definitely worth your while. Even if you buy a supermarket potted herb on impulse and it lasts only a few weeks, it's worth the small expense for the heartwarming flavor it will add to your meals. Remember that 1 tablespoon of a fresh herb may be substituted for 1 teaspoon of dried.

This list is the longest of all, and so it receives its own section. The sodium content of the following ingredients is low, and because they are used in small amounts, you may use them as you wish.

Herbs and Spices

Allspice

Anise seed

Apple-pie spice

Basil

Bay leaf

Cajun no-salt seasoning

Caraway seed

Cardamom

Celery seed (ground or whole)

Chili con carne seasoning powder (check label)

Chives

Cinnamon
Cloves (ground or whole)
Coriander (ground or whole)
Cumin
Curry
Dill weed
Fennel
Five-spice powder
Garlic powder
Ginger (ground)
Juniper berries
Lemongrass
Lemon peel
Mace (ground or whole)
Marjoram
Mint
Mushrooms, powdered
Mustard, dry
Nutmeg
Onion powder
Orange peel
Oregano
Paprika
Pepper, black, red, and white (Tellicherry is
    particularly good)
Poppy seed
Poultry seasoning
Pumpkin-pie spice
Rosemary
Saffron

Sage
Summer savory
Sesame seeds
Tarragon
Thyme
Turmeric

Use the above list when you are shopping and add to it the following flavors, blends, and fresh ingredients. Also include staples such as low-sodium tomato products and condiments.

Flavors

Almond extract
Cocoa
Instant coffee
Lemon juice
Lemon extract
Orange extract
Peppermint extract
Saccharin (if doctor says so)
Salt substitutes (if doctor says so)
Vanilla extract
Vinegar, white, cider, or wine
Wine (with doctor's permission)
Walnut extract

Blends

All low-sodium:

Bouillon cubes
Catsup

Chili sauce
Mustard
Pickles
Tomato sauce
Worcestershire sauce

Fresh, Raw Ingredient Flavors

Onions, Vidalia, yellow, or red
Garlic
Scallions
Shallots
Hot green chili pepper
Green pepper
Red pepper
Ginger
Lemons
Limes

Enlightenment by Contrast

These lists of comparisons bring home the vast differences in sodium content between certain foods.

	milligrams sodium
1 tablespoon low-sodium catsup	0.7
1 tablespoon catsup	221
1 oz. lean beef	20
1 oz. dried beef	1,219
1 low-sodium beef bouillon cube	31

1 bouillon cube	960
1/2 cup cabbage	12.8
1/2 cup sauerkraut	536
1 oz. low-sodium Cheddar	15
1 oz. Cheddar cheese	198
1 cucumber	14.4
1 dill pickle	1,900
1 oz. fresh codfish	22
1 oz. salted codfish	2,296
1 oz. low-sodium ham	14
1 oz. cured ham	312
8 unsalted peanuts	0.5
8 salted peanuts	35
1 tablespoon low-sodium peanut butter	7
1 tablespoon peanut butter	19
10 unsalted potato chips	1
10 salted potato chips	70
Poached egg on low-sodium toast	72
Roy Rogers breakfast sandwich with sausage	1,281
Fresh ocean perch (1 lb.)	111
Frozen fish fillet	415

Raw rice ($^1/_2$ cup)	9
Wild and long-grain rice mix	442
1 stick chewing gum	tr
1 tablespoon caviar	352
$^1/_2$ cup fresh cauliflower	5
Frozen cauliflower with cheese sauce	450
5 oz. dry fettuccine	0
Frozen fettuccine Alfredo	1,195
Corn on the cob	0
$^1/_2$ cup canned corn	302

Regroup

These lists should prepare you for the next step. Look at your pantry. Read the labels and take stock. Separate out the items you know have high levels of salt. If you don't want to have them around, give them away. Assemble all the other foods you'll be able to keep and use. Organize your spice shelf and throw out the contents of old bottles of herbs that may have lost their flavor. (Save the bottles to fill with herbs bought in bulk. It's far cheaper.) Empty your refrigerator and check every item. Really look at what you have on hand. Repeat the process frequently. Then, using the previous lists, create your own grand shopping list and go shopping. Imagine a balance. On the one side is salt, on the other is a panorama of flavors awaiting discovery, even if you have cooked for years.

Supermarkets, Whole-Food Stores, and Food Co-ops

In any supermarket, the most valuable principle to keep in mind is: Shop the periphery. The outside aisles contain the fresh foods.

Most supermarkets have a section that will offer some low-sodium items not available elsewhere in the store. But most basic low-sodium items are mixed in with the salted ones. You'll grow to recognize the distinctive and welcome packaging. Excellent brand names for low-sodium foods include:

Boar's Head
Featherweight
Hain's
Westbrae
Herb Ox low-sodium broths
Cento tomato products without salt

Some ingredients, however, you'll only find in a health-food or specialty store. But remember that not everything they sell is low-sodium—Brewer's yeast can come mixed with salt! And many low-fat items are unusually high in sodium. Check the labels. A health-food-store lasagna, low in fat, might contain nearly 700 milligrams of sodium. Health-food stores, however, can order almost anything, and they have access to low-sodium specialty brands that can help you get started at once on your diet, until you have time to cook using your own staples. People who work in a health-food store are trained to answer your questions and make you feel comfortable navigating the aisles of unfamiliar ingredients. Their herb and spice collections are usually vast. Some health-food stores will offer free nutritional consultations and suggest cooking teachers who can guide you with your diet. They may also be able to recommend doctors who are skilled at helping people lower their salt intake, and they can order food in bulk, generally giving you their discount. You also might find yourself in very helpful conversations with fellow customers.

A food co-op can also be an excellent way to order economically in bulk, though you may not find the variety that a whole-foods store can offer. Also, search out ethnic markets in your area. These will educate you in new ingredients nearly as powerfully as a trip to another country.

SPECIAL LOW-SODIUM ITEMS AND THEIR SODIUM CONTENTS

	milligrams sodium	*calories*
Low-sodium beef broth, 1 packet	5	10
Low-sodium chicken broth, 1 packet	5	10
Sodium-free bread, 1 slice	<5	7
Catsup, no salt added, 1 tablespoon	0	20
Swiss cheese, no salt, 1 oz.	10	100
Chickpeas, water pack, 1/2 cup	5	105
Cottage cheese, dry curd, 1 cup	19	123

	milligrams sodium	calories
Mayonnaise, low-sodium, 1 tablespoon	45	50
Milk, low-sodium, 1 cup	6	149
Mustard, no salt added, 1 tablespoon	6	10
Peanut butter, no salt, 1 tablespoon	<5	100
Dill pickle, low-sodium, 1	12	12
Canned salmon, diet, $1/2$ cup	45	188
Soy milk, 1 cup	30	79
Soy sauce, Kikkoman lite, $1/2$ teaspoon	100	5
Stewed tomatoes, no salt, 4 oz.	20	35
Canned tomatoes, whole, no salt added	15	20
Tomato paste, no salt, 2 oz.	25	45
Tomato juice, no salt, 6 oz.	25	35
Tuna, chunk light Tongol, 2 oz.	55	50
Worcestershire, Lea & Perrins, 1 teaspoon	55	5

STARTING TO COOK WITHOUT SALT

1. GO SLOWLY.

Habits of eating are developed over many years. Change will take time. You, your body, and your mind need to become accustomed to a new way of eating. Concentrate on one area at a time—main courses or lunches—and then move on to another area—salads or vegetables.

2. TREAT FOOD SHOPPING AS A VITAL, ACTIVE EXPLORATION.

Seek freshness and variety. Buy at least one new item every week. So often we tend to fill our shopping basket with the same ingredients, following a fixed, safe path through the supermarket. Something different can make us nervous, but active exploration is one of the joys of cooking. Foods from around the globe are now in our supermarkets. Take one home. Remember to concentrate on the outside aisles, where most of the unprocessed food is stocked.

3. APPEAL TO THE SENSES.

A grain of salt is nearly invisible, has no smell, and very little texture. Think of putting ingredients on an imaginary palette, then draw on their variety to involve every sense. Think about aroma, color, texture, crunch, and taste.

4. PUT FOOD INTO A WIDER CONTEXT.

Candlelight, flowers, music, fine linens, firelight, and conversation enhance the eating experience.

5. KEEP YOUR INGREDIENTS TIDY.

Napoleon said, "Order is progress." If you always know what you have on hand, you can be much more daring and versatile. Organization gives you security.

6. EXPERIMENT AND PLAY WITH FOOD.

Teachers who use hands-on materials to teach their students generally give them the opportunity to explore first, free of instruction. The same applies to cooking. What if you've never used chili peppers? Buy one. Put on some rubber gloves or put your hands inside a plastic bag (hot peppers can sting your hands and eyes), slice it in half, take out the seeds, cut it up. Maybe cook it. Use it in a recipe another day.

7. COOK WITH A FRIEND.

Find someone whose healthful cooking you admire. Arrange to cook together. You will be amazed at how much you learn just by watching someone else use ingredients that are unfamiliar to you.

8. DECORATE WITH FOOD.

Capture the eye with a garnish. If food looks pretty, you've attracted your eater. Think not only of what to use but how to present it. Here are some ideas:

- grate apples, lemons, oranges, limes, carrots, and zucchini
- cut citrus triangles or half circles, sprinkle with mint or parsley
- snip 5-inch lengths of herbs, such as thyme, rosemary, chives, oregano, cilantro, tarragon, lavender, dill, and fennel—wrap in bundles
- use leaves either under or over a dish, such as edibles: mint, basil, arugula, spinach,

celery, and kale; or inedibles: maple, gingko, raspberry, blueberry, oak

- grind nuts
- arrange flowers, with or without stem, such as buttercup, nasturtium, marigold, violet, or bachelor's button *on* the table-cloth or around the food
- slice disks of radish, cucumber, kiwi, ba-nanas, or grapes
- make patterns of combinations
- use whole raspberries, blueberries, cherry tomatoes, strawberries, sunflower seeds, corn kernels in groups of three

9. EXPERIMENT AND FAIL—THEN KEEP LEARNING.

Failure generally teaches us to be good at something.

USEFUL EQUIPMENT FOR ENHANCING FLAVOR IN LOW-SALT COOKING

Nothing great was ever accomplished without enthusiasm.

—*Emerson*

Much can be done with very little. Energy, commitment, and enthusiasm take us a long way. Beyond the usual pots and pans, here are the essentials for preparing tasty food without salt.

Nonstick skillet: A good, sturdy nonstick skillet means that you can cut way down on the amount of fat you use in preparing food. Make sure you get a high-quality one with a guarantee. Cheap ones lose their nonstick surface and flake into your food. Use wooden spoons to stir.

Garlic press: A strong, well-made garlic press is essential for the preparation of many great dishes, low sodium or not. It's worth spending a little more on a good one.

Citrus squeezer: Lemon, lime, and orange juice flavor a wide variety of ingredients. Having a squeezer close at hand is very helpful.

Grater: The classic metal grater is important for adding grated citrus peel or ginger or onion to a number of dishes. It's very easy to clean.

Bread maker: Bread makers or bread attachments can be a boon to those who prefer to make their own low-sodium bread at home. The expense can be well worth it.

Mortar and pestle: If you would like to devise your own herb and spice blends, this will inspire you to do so, though it's certainly not necessary.

Scale, measuring cups, and measuring spoons: Make sure that these items are accessible and easy to read. If you've cooked for many years by guesswork, you will need to rely more on weighing and measuring until you are comfortable with the nutritional values and proportions of the ingredients you'll be using to begin cooking a low-sodium diet.

Bread & Breakfast

Few of us can afford the time to bake all our own bread, and low-sodium bread can be bought in almost any good bakery or market. Still, nothing cheers up a house like the smell of hot loaves in the oven, and baking bread at home does provide an opportunity to include all kinds of nutritious grains, fruits, and nuts. Similarly, most breakfasts these days seem to be eaten on the run. But in just a few more minutes than it takes to toast a bagel, hot cereals cooked without salt can be ready for the table. Try topping them with warm fruit or honey and a sprinkle of nutmeg.

We've included some breakfast treats to remind us what this first meal of the day is supposed to be about—enjoy preparing them on a leisurely weekend morning. If you have a houseful of guests to feed, take a hint from innkeepers and make breakfast buffet-style. Lay out bowls of fruit salad or fresh whole fruit, containers of yogurt, varieties of low-sodium cold cereal, baskets of sliced bread, and pitchers of juice, tea, and coffee.

WHITE BREAD

2 tablespoons sugar
3 tablespoons vegetable shortening (unsalted)
1 cup lukewarm water
1/2 cake compressed yeast
3 cups plus 1 tablespoon flour
1 tablespoon unsalted butter

Put the sugar and the vegetable shortening in a large bowl. Add the water. Sprinkle the yeast over the lukewarm mixture. Mix. Add half of the flour and stir with wooden spoon. Add rest of flour and stir well. Knead the dough with floured hands until smooth and place in greased bowl. Spread melted butter over dough, cover with towel, and let rise in warm place until dough doubles in size. Knead again. Shape into loaf. Place in greased loaf pan. Spread the remaining butter on top and cover. Let rise until double in bulk. Bake at 400 degrees for about 30 to 35 minutes. Dough will rise twice as fast without salt. Makes 1 loaf.

Entire loaf:

Calories.......... 1,875	Protein........... 38 g.
Fat .... 54 g.	Carbohydrate .... 306 g.
Saturated Fat...... 18 g.	Sodium......... 17 mg.
Cholesterol...... 33 mg.	Potassium ..... 449 mg.

Slice:

Calories 117	Protein............ 2 g.
Fat .... 3 g.	Carbohydrate ..... 19 g.
Saturated Fat....... 1 g.	Sodium .... 1 mg.
Cholesterol....... 2 mg.	Potassium ...... 28 mg.

FRENCH BREAD

Preparing this homemade bread is so easy when you use a food processor.

1 teaspoon yeast
1 cup lukewarm water
3 cups flour

Dissolve the yeast in the water. Place 2 cups of flour in the work bowl of the food processor and add half of the yeast mixture to the flour. Pulse the food processor 4 or 5 times. Add the remaining yeast mixture and pulse another 4 or 5 times. Add the last cup of flour to the work bowl and blend for no more than 1 minute. If dough is sticky, slowly add more flour until it is well bound and springy to the touch. Put rounded dough on a greased baking sheet, cover with a clean dish cloth, and let rise for 2 hours or until doubled in bulk. Preheat oven to 400 degrees. Form and place loaf on greased baking sheet, then let rest for 20 minutes. Bake for exactly 30 minutes.

Slice:

Calories 79	Protein. . . . . 2 g.
Fat. . . . . tr	Carbohydrate . . . . . 17 g.
Saturated Fat . . . . tr	Sodium . . . . 1 mg.
Cholesterol. . . . . . . 0 mg.	Potassium . . . . . . 26 mg.

150 PERCENT WHOLE WHEAT BREAD

1 cup lukewarm water
2 packages active dry yeast
1 teaspoon honey
5 to 6 cups whole wheat flour
1 cup raw bulgur or cracked wheat
1 cup boiling water
¼ cup unsalted butter
¼ cup molasses
½ cup golden seedless raisins

Pour the water in a small bowl. Dissolve the yeast in the water, add honey, and let stand for 5 minutes. Beat in half the flour, cover, and let rise for 30 to 60 minutes. In a large bowl combine remaining ingredients, except for the remaining flour, and let stand 30 minutes uncovered and 30 minutes covered. Add risen sponge to bulgur wheat mixture and stir in remaining flour until dough is smooth. Knead, adding flour as necessary, to make an elastic dough. Cover and let rise until double in bulk, about 1 to 1½ hours. Divide dough in 2, form into loaves, and place in greased loaf pans. Let rise for another hour, covered, until double in bulk. Bake in preheated 375-degree oven for 30 to 40 minutes. Makes 2 loaves.

Slice:

Calories	113	Protein	4 g.
Fat	2 g.	Carbohydrate	22 g.
Saturated Fat	1 g.	Sodium	3 mg.
Cholesterol	4 mg.	Potassium	151 mg.

RANDALL'S ORDINARY CORIANDER AND GINGER LOAF

This traditional New England recipe was adapted from *Great Cooking with Country Inn Chefs* by Gail Greco, Rutledge Hill Press, 1992.

1/4 cup warm water
1 package active dry yeast
1/4 cup sugar
1 cup warm low-fat milk
1/4 teaspoon coriander
1/2 teaspoon cinnamon
1/2 teaspoon ginger
1/4 teaspoon cloves
1/4 teaspoon mace
1/4 cup canola oil
1/4 cup chopped, peeled orange
1 lightly beaten egg
3 1/2 cups or more unbleached flour

In a measuring cup dissolve the yeast in warm water. Add sugar and let bubble. Set aside. In a large mixing bowl combine the remaining ingredients. Add the yeast mixture and stir to form a dough. Turn dough onto a floured board and knead, adding more flour until the dough is smooth, not sticky. Place the dough in a warm, greased bowl. Cover the bowl with a towel and let the dough rise until doubled in bulk. Preheat the oven to 375 degrees. Punch the dough down. Shape it into a loaf and place it in a greased 9-by-5-inch loaf pan. Bake the bread for 45 to 50 minutes, or until golden brown.

Remove the bread from the pan and let it cool on a wire rack. Makes 1 loaf.

Slice:

Calories	164	Protein	5 g.
Fat	4 g.	Carbohydrate	26 g.
Saturated Fat	1 g.	Sodium	12 mg.
Cholesterol	14 mg.	Potassium	73 mg.

BREAD MACHINE APPLE AND CURRY BREAD

This is great for sandwiches.

1 package dry yeast
2 cups bread flour
2 tablespoons wheat flour
2 tablespoons rolled oats
2 tablespoons nonfat dry milk
1$1/2$ teaspoons curry powder
$1/4$ cup green apple, chopped with skin
$1/4$ cup walnuts, chopped
1 tablespoon honey
$2/3$ cup water

Mix ingredients and proceed as suggested by bread machine manufacturer's instructions. Makes 1 1-pound loaf.

Slice:

Calories	91	Protein	3 g.
Fat	2 g.	Carbohydrate	16 g.
Saturated Fat	tr	Sodium	4 mg.
Cholesterol	tr	Potassium	56 mg.

OTTO'S BANANA BREAD

1¾ cups white flour
½ cup sugar
½ teaspoon cinnamon
½ teaspoon nutmeg
2½ teaspoons low-sodium baking powder
¼ cup unsalted butter or margarine
2 very ripe bananas
1 egg slightly beaten
½ cup chopped walnuts

Preheat oven to 350 degrees. Grease and flour a 9-by-5-inch loaf pan. In a large bowl, use a fork to mix flour, sugar, cinnamon, nutmeg, and baking powder. With pastry blender or 2 knives cut in butter until mix resembles coarse crumbs. Stir in bananas and egg until just blended. Mix in walnuts. Spread batter evenly in pan. Bake for 45 to 55 minutes or until a toothpick inserted in the center comes out clean. Cool. Makes 8 to 10 slices.

Slice:

Calories	211	Protein	4 g.
Fat	8 g.	Carbohydrate	33 g.
Saturated Fat	3 g.	Sodium	8 mg.
Cholesterol	34 mg.	Potassium	259 mg.

ORANGE BREAD

Nobody can believe this recipe (inspired by *San Francisco à la Carte*) calls for a whole orange!

2 eggs
1/2 cup canola oil
4 cups all-purpose flour, sifted
1 cup sugar
2 tablespoons low-sodium baking powder
1 teaspoon cinnamon
1 large, organic orange, unpeeled
1 cup buttermilk
1/2 cup skim milk
butter and flour for pans

Beat eggs until thick and lemon-colored. Gradually add oil. Beat for 1 minute. Sift dry ingredients and add to egg mixture. Cut the orange into pieces and chop in blender or food processor. Add to batter. Add milk slowly, continuing to beat for 2 minutes. Divide the batter between two 8-by-5-inch loaf pans that have been lightly buttered and floured. Let stand for 20 minutes. Bake for 20 minutes in a 400-degree oven. Turn oven temperature to 300 and continue baking for 20 minutes or until a knife inserted in the middle comes out clean. Let rest for 10 minutes before removing from the pan. Makes 2 loaves.

Slice:

Calories 236	Protein. . . . . 5 g.
Fat . . . . 8 g.	Carbohydrate . . . . . 38 g.
Saturated Fat. . . . . . . 1 g.	Sodium. . . . . 29 mg.
Cholesterol. . . . . 27 mg.	Potassium . . . . . 272 mg.

SPOON BREAD

1 cup cornmeal
1 cup water
1 tablespoon unsalted butter
1½ cups low-fat milk, scalded
1 egg, well beaten

Combine cornmeal and water in a medium-size saucepan. Cook over low heat, stirring occasionally, for 15 minutes. Remove from heat. Melt butter in scalded milk, add to corn mixture, and mix until smooth. Slowly stir beaten egg into hot mixture. Pour into oiled 1-quart casserole. Bake at 350 degrees for 35 minutes. Serve with pure maple syrup. Serves 10.

Serving:

Calories 155	Protein . . . . 3 g.
Fat . . . . 10 g.	Carbohydrate . . . . . 13 g.
Saturated Fat . . . . 6 g.	Sodium . . . . 27 mg.
Cholesterol . . . . . . 48 mg.	Potassium . . . . . . 88 mg.

DOUBLE CORN BISCUITS

1¾ cups flour
½ cup cornmeal
1 tablespoon honey
1 tablespoon low-sodium baking powder
4 tablespoons unsalted butter
1 cup fresh or thawed frozen corn kernels
¾ cup nonfat plain yogurt

In a medium bowl combine flour, cornmeal, honey, baking powder, and butter. Mix thoroughly. Add corn kernels and yogurt. Knead on a floured surface 10 to 12 times. Pat into an 8-inch greased square pan and cut into 2-inch squares. Bake in a 450-degree preheated oven for 10 to 12 minutes or until lightly brown. Makes 16 biscuits. Serve warm with honey or jam.

Serving:

Calories 113	Protein . . . . 3 g.
Fat . . . . 3 g.	Carbohydrate . . . . . 19 g.
Saturated Fat . . . . 2 g.	Sodium . . . . 11 mg.
Cholesterol . . . . 8 mg.	Potassium . . . . . 164 mg.

DATE AND APPLE BREAKFAST BARS

1½ cups oatmeal
1 cup apples, finely chopped
1 tablespoon grated orange rind
2 tablespoons canola oil
¾ cups water
¾ cup dates, chopped
¼ cup walnuts, chopped
1 teaspoon vanilla

Blend half of oatmeal to make flour. Combine flour thoroughly with remaining ingredients. Spread mixture evenly on greased 8-by-eight-inch baking pan. Bake at 375 degrees for 20 to 25 minutes.

Per bar:

Calories 85	Protein . . . . 2 g.
Fat . . . . 3 g.	Carbohydrate . . . . . 13 g.

Saturated Fat . . . . tr   Sodium . . . . 1 mg.
Cholesterol. . . . . . . 0 mg.   Potassium . . . . . . 99 mg.

ANN PATCHETT'S HEALTHY PANCAKES

You can keep the dry ingredients mixed and ready to go—just multiply the first 5 ingredients by 6 and keep sealed in a container. Then dole out a cup of mix and add an egg, oil, and yogurt for instant pancakes.

1/3 cup whole wheat flour
2 teaspoons low-sodium baking powder
1/3 cup rolled oats
1/3 cup Miller's bran
2 tablespoons wheat germ
1 egg
1 tablespoon vegetable oil
1 cup nonfat vanilla yogurt
1/2 teaspoon unsalted butter

Combine dry ingredients. Beat egg with oil and yogurt and stir in with butter and dry mixture. Tastes great with honey. Makes 8 pancakes.

Per pancake:

Calories 90   Protein. . . . . 4 g.
Fat . . . . 3 g.   Carbohydrate . . . . . 13 g.
Saturated Fat. . . . . . . 1 g.   Sodium. . . . . 26 mg.
Cholesterol. . . . . . 27 mg.   Potassium . . . . . 265 mg.

GINGERBREAD PANCAKES

This recipe was inspired by one of Brinna Sands's recipes in *The King Arthur Flour 200th Anniversary Cookbook*. The seltzer helps the pancakes rise high.

1½ cups white flour
2½ teaspoons low-sodium baking powder
2 teaspoons ground ginger
1 teaspoon cinnamon
½ teaspoon allspice
¼ teaspoon ground cloves
1 egg, separated
½ cup skim milk
3 tablespoons molasses
3 tablespoons vegetable oil
½ to 1 cup low-sodium seltzer water

Combine dry ingredients in a bowl. Beat egg yolk in milk and then add molasses and oil. Mix with dry ingredients. Beat egg white until stiff. Fold egg white and seltzer into batter. Makes about 12 pancakes.

Calories	108	Protein	2 g.
Fat	4 g.	Carbohydrate	16 g.
Saturated Fat	1 g.	Sodium	12 mg.
Cholesterol	18 mg.	Potassium	188 mg.

Variation: Substitute beer for ¹/₂ of the seltzer.

BANANA PANCAKES

These pancakes laced with bananas are just lovely. The recipe is adapted from Eleanor Early's *New England Cookbook.*

- 1½ cups flour
- 2½ teaspoons low-sodium baking powder
- 2 tablespoons sugar
- ¼ teaspoon nutmeg
- 1 egg, separated
- 1¼ to 1½ cups low-fat milk
- 3 tablespoons corn oil
- 1 cup finely diced banana
- 1 teaspoon vanilla
- ½ cup walnuts, roasted in 350-degree oven for 5 to 10 minutes (optional)

Sift together dry ingredients. Combine egg yolk, milk, and oil and add to flour mixture. Stir until ingredients are barely mixed. Beat egg white until stiff. Fold bananas, vanilla, egg white, and optional walnuts into batter. Makes about 12 pancakes.

Variations: For blueberry pancakes, substitute ¾ cup of blueberries, tossed with 1 teaspoon of sugar, for bananas. A cup of apples sprinkled with cinnamon is another delicious alternative.

Per pancake:

Calories	122	Protein	3 g.
Fat	4 g.	Carbohydrate	18 g.
Saturated Fat	1 g.	Sodium	20 mg.
Cholesterol	19 mg.	Potassium	212 mg.

CRÊPES

½ cup sifted all-purpose flour
1 egg
1 egg yolk
5 tablespoons milk (about)
1 teaspoon unsalted butter
3 tablespoons currant or red raspberry jelly
Powdered sugar

Combine flour, egg, egg yolk, and milk. Beat with rotary beater until smooth. Cover and chill ½ hour in refrigerator—or make night before. Heat heavy small iron skillet, wipe out with paper that has been dipped in unsalted butter. Pour in enough batter to barely cover bottom of skillet. Brown pancakes on both sides. Remove from skillet, spread with unsalted butter, and serve. If you like, spread with jelly, roll up jelly-roll-fashion, and sprinkle with a little powdered sugar. Place under broiler to glaze. Serve with pure maple sugar or honey. Makes 12 crêpes.

Per crêpe:

Calories 66	Protein . . . . 1 g.
Fat . . . . 3 g.	Carbohydrate . . . . . . 8 g.
Saturated Fat . . . . 2 g.	Sodium . . . . 10 mg.
Cholesterol . . . . . . 41 mg.	Potassium . . . . . . 25 mg.

JOHNNYCAKES

Try baked bananas and Waldorf salad with these for Sunday supper.

1 cup white cornmeal
1 teaspoon sugar
1/8 teaspoon mace
1 1/4 cups boiling water
1/4 cup milk

In a warm bowl mix cornmeal with sugar and mace. Pour boiling water over dry ingredients and mix well. When thoroughly mixed, add milk. Drop by tablespoons on hot heavy skillet. Turn and cook on the other side as you do pancakes. Serve with unsalted butter and jelly or honey. Makes 12 cakes.

Per cake:

Calories	46	Protein	1 g.
Fat	tr	Carbohydrate	10 g.
Saturated Fat	tr	Sodium	4 mg.
Cholesterol	tr	Potassium	27 mg.

BANANA SMOOTHIES

2 bananas
1 1/4 cup skim milk
1 teaspoon pure vanilla extract

Peel the bananas, cover with plastic wrap, and put in freezer overnight. Mix together frozen bananas, milk, and vanilla in blender at high speed until mixture is smooth. Add a sprinkling of nutmeg if you like. Serves 2.

Variations: Combine bananas with other fruits, such as strawberries or raspberries.

Per serving:

Calories	271	Protein	8 g.
Fat	1 g.	Carbohydrate	62 g.
Saturated Fat	1 g.	Sodium	81 mg.
Cholesterol	3 mg.	Potassium	1,156 mg.

POACHED EGG

2 teaspoons cider vinegar

1 egg

1 slice low-sodium bread, toasted

1 teaspoon unsalted butter

Pepper to taste

If you like, a sprinkle of curry, sage, dill, or mustard

Fill saucepan $^2/_3$ full of water. Bring water to a boil. Add vinegar. Stir water fast until a whirlpool has formed; break egg in middle. Immediately reduce heat and simmer $1^1/_2$ to 2 minutes. Remove with slotted spoon. Place on toasted bread. Top with unsalted butter and seasonings. Serves 1.

Per serving:

Calories	190	Protein	9 g.
Fat	9 g.	Carbohydrate	17 g.

Saturated Fat. . . . . . . 4 g.	Sodium. . . . . 65 mg.
Cholesterol. . . . . 224 mg.	Potassium . . . . . . 89 mg.

Note: If for tomorrow's breakfast you would like a scrambled egg, try flavoring the egg with savory and basil or dill.

EGGS BENEDICT

1 egg
2 teaspoons low-sodium mayonnaise
½ teaspoon lemon juice
Pinch of sage, curry powder, turmeric, or mustard
1 slice tomato

Poach egg any saltless way you wish. Place poached egg in individual flat dish. Place on top 2 teaspoons of warmed low-sodium mayonnaise that has been mixed with ½ teaspoon lemon juice. Add a dash of sage, curry, turmeric, or mustard if you like. Serve on a tomato slice. Serves 1.

Calories 145	Protein. . . . . 6 g.
Fat . . . . 13 g.	Carbohydrate . . . . . . 1 g.
Saturated Fat. . . . . . . 2 g.	Sodium. . . . . 100 mg.
Cholesterol. . . . . 216 mg.	Potassium . . . . . . 68 mg.

SPANISH OMELET

2 cups canned dietetic tomatoes
3 tablespoons unsalted butter
Pepper to taste
Few grains cayenne
¼ teaspoon thyme
1 tablespoon fresh chopped parsley
1 bay leaf
2 cloves garlic, minced
½ cup minced onions
1 cup chopped green pepper
1 tablespoon flour
½ cup white wine
6 medium mushrooms, chopped
4 eggs
1 tablespoon olive oil

Combine tomatoes and 1 tablespoon of butter in saucepan. Simmer 10 minutes, stirring occasionally. Add pepper and cayenne. Cook 10 minutes more. Add thyme, parsley, bay leaf, and garlic. Cook 15 minutes until sauce thickens.

In a small skillet, melt 1 tablespoon of butter. Add onions and green pepper; sauté until slightly soft. Remove pan from heat and stir in flour. Return to low heat and cook a few minutes more. Add wine, stirring constantly until slightly thickened. Add mushrooms and cook until heated through.

Beat eggs in bowl until well blended. Add green pepper mixture. Heat remaining tablespoon of butter and olive oil in skillet. Pour in egg mixture. Shake skillet until eggs begin to set, lifting edges of omelet with a spatula to let uncooked mixture flow to bottom. Cover skillet until egg mixture is fully set. Place a few spoons of tomato sauce inside omelet and fold. Garnish with remaining sauce and parsley. Serves 4.

Per serving:

Calories 260	Protein. . . . . 9 g.
Fat . . . . 18 g.	Carbohydrate . . . . . 14 g.
Saturated Fat. . . . . . . 7 g.	Sodium. . . . . 84 mg.
Cholesterol. . . . . 236 mg.	Potassium . . . . . 563 mg.

Note: Since this analysis was done, ¹⁄₂ cup peas were omitted from the recipe and 5 tablespoons green pepper was changed to 1 cup.

FRENCH TOAST

1 egg, beaten
¹⁄₈ cup milk
¹⁄₄ cup sugar
1 teaspoon pure vanilla extract
3 slices low-sodium bread
Nutmeg

Mix egg, milk, sugar, and vanilla. Remove crust and soak bread in the egg mixture for 5 minutes. Brown on greased griddle. Sprinkle with nutmeg. Serve with honey, jelly, or pure maple syrup.

Note: French toast also can be cooked in the oven. Dip each slice in the egg mixture. Place slices on oiled baking dish. Bake in 450-degree oven for 7 minutes on one side, then turn and brown 5 minutes longer. Try a sprinkle of cardamom or grated orange peel.

Per slice:

Calories 128	Protein . . . . 5 g.
Fat . . . . 2 g.	Carbohydrate . . . . . 22 g.
Saturated Fat . . . . 1 g.	Sodium . . . . 27 mg.
Cholesterol . . . . . . 71 mg.	Potassium . . . . . . 62 mg.

CRANBERRY AND BANANA TOAST

1 slice low-sodium bread
1 teaspoon unsalted butter
1 tablespoon cranberry sauce
1/2 banana, sliced
1 teaspoon brown sugar
1/4 teaspoon cinnamon or allspice

Place bread under broiler and toast on one side, spread butter on other side, spread with cranberry sauce, cover with sliced banana, sprinkle with brown sugar and cinnamon or allspice. Broil slowly until bananas are light brown and the sauce bubbling. Try a sprinkle of anise sometimes. Serves 1.

Per slice:

Calories 212	Protein . . . . 3 g.
Fat . . . . 5 g.	Carbohydrate . . . . . 42 g.
Saturated Fat . . . . 3 g.	Sodium . . . . 9 mg.
Cholesterol . . . . . . 11 mg.	Potassium . . . . . 276 mg.

BUCKWHEAT BREAKFAST CEREAL WITH APPLES

Buckwheat (kasha) is a fruit and not a grain, so it's both wheat- and gluten-free.

2½ cups water
¼ teaspoon mace
½ cup whole kasha
1 apple, chopped
Honey to taste

In a saucepan bring water to boil and add mace and kasha. Cook uncovered, keeping at a low boil, for 12 to 15 minutes. Stir frequently. Fold in apple and serve with honey. Serves 4.

Per serving:

Calories	92	Protein	2 g.
Fat	1 g.	Carbohydrate	21 g.
Saturated Fat	tr	Sodium	7 mg.
Cholesterol	0 mg.	Potassium	106 mg.

GRANOLA

6 cups uncooked quick or old-fashioned rolled oats
1/2 cup brown sugar
3/4 cup wheat germ
1/2 cup shredded coconut
1/3 cup sesame seed or sunflower seed kernels
1 cup chopped unsalted walnuts, pecans,
    peanuts, or unchopped raisins
1/2 cup salad oil
1/3 cup honey
1 1/2 teaspoons vanilla extract
1/2 teaspoon cinnamon or nutmeg

Heat oats in shallow baking pan in 350-degree oven for about 10 minutes. Combine toasted oats, brown sugar, wheat germ, coconut, seeds, cinnamon or nutmeg, and nuts. Add oil, honey, and vanilla. Mix to coat dry ingredients. Divide mixture in half. Return 1 portion to shallow baking pan and heat at 350 degrees for 20 to 25 minutes, stirring every 5 minutes or so to brown evenly. Cool then stir until crumbly. Heat the other half the same way. Store in airtight container; keeps refrigerated for about 1 month. Makes about 10 cups or 40 servings.

Per serving:

Calories	129	Protein	3 g.
Fat	7 g.	Carbohydrate	16 g.
Saturated Fat	1 g.	Sodium	5 mg.
Cholesterol	0 mg.	Potassium	95 mg.

Appetizers

Most things coming your way on a silver platter are bad news, and that's very true of those little things wrapped in bacon or flaky crust at the cocktail party. Happily, party givers these days tend to serve crudités and low-sodium crackers or tortilla chips with fresh salsa and bean dips among traditional hors d'oeuvres. Here are some tasty items that won't compromise your salt-free diet.

DIP FOR FRUIT AND VEGETABLES

Mix 2 tablespoons of low-sodium mayonnaise with $1/8$ teaspoon of curry. Arrange vegetables and fruits (see below) in a festive way. Pick leaves from your trees for a background; they are especially colorful in the fall. In the winter, use evergreens. If you're not lucky enough to have trees in your yard, use parsley. Wash your parsley, drain, and keep in a covered jar or plastic bag in refrigerator. Parsley should not look "tired."

FRUITS AND VEGETABLES FOR DIPPING

Apple slices (keep the skin on)

Pineapple chunks

Cauliflower florets

Radishes

Broccoli florets

Jicama slices

Scallions

Carrots (watch sodium content if you are close to your day's allowance)

Cherry tomatoes

Green beans

Red and green peppers, sliced

Brinna Sands's Rainbow of Peppers

3 peppers, red, yellow, and orange

Core, seed, and slice peppers lengthwise. Stand them all together, like a bunch of flowers, in a small, but proportionately high bowl. That's it. You have a colorful, simple, and healthy appetizer.

Roasted Chestnuts

Here's a simple idea for an appetizer. Cut an X on the flat side of each chestnut, then wrap them in foil and roast in the oven (or in the fire) for about an hour or until tender.

Yogurt Cheese

Most cheeses are very high in sodium. This is an easy and tasty substitute. Flavor it with fresh herbs and serve with vegetables or crackers as an appetizer or mix it with garlic to fill pasta.

2 cups low-fat yogurt

Place a colander inside a bowl and line the colander with a double thickness of cheesecloth. Pour in yogurt. Let it drain for 15 to 20 minutes. Drain bowl and cover colander with foil or plastic wrap. Refrigerate for 24 hours. Squeeze out any remaining liquid from yogurt and transfer to a container with a lid. Yields $^2/_3$ cup.

Suggested Flavors to Add:

Garlic
Olive oil
Dill
Chopped jalapeño pepper
Freshly ground pepper
Chives
Scallions
Mint

Great idea: During the summer months fill day lily blossoms with yogurt cheese, sprinkled with chives and serve with raw vegetables or unsalted crackers.

Also: The strained yogurt liquid makes a delicious marinade for poultry or lamb. Add lemon juice, garlic, ginger, turmeric, cumin, and pepper and marinate for several hours. This method is used in India before roasting in a clay oven called a *tandoor,* but may be used before roasting or grilling in conventional ways, as well.

Total recipe:

Calories	254	Protein	26 g.
Fat	1 g.	Carbohydrate	35 g.
Saturated Fat	1 g.	Sodium	348 mg.
Cholesterol	8 mg.	Potassium	1,158 mg.

Black Bean and Mango Dip

1 red onion, chopped

1 red pepper, chopped

1 orange pepper, chopped

1 jalapeño pepper, minced

3 pressed garlic cloves

Juice of 2 limes

1 bunch of cilantro, chopped

2 15-oz. cans unsalted black beans or one 16-oz.
    package black beans cooked without salt

1 mango, chopped

Combine all ingredients. If you would like, you may combine onion, peppers, garlic, lime juice, and cilantro in a food processor for a finer texture and then mix with beans and mango.

Refrigerate for at least an hour to give flavors a chance to blend. Serve with unsalted tortilla chips. This makes about 6 cups and lasts for several days. It is a marvelous appetizer but may be served as an additional salad with grilled meats or used to fill a pita for an easy lunch.

Per cup:

Calories 251	Protein . . . . 15 g.
Fat . . . . 1 g.	Carbohydrate . . . . . 48 g.
Saturated Fat . . . . tr	Sodium . . . . 12 mg.
Cholesterol . . . . . . 0 mg.	Potassium . . . . . 912 mg.

Susana's Eggplant and Garlic Dip

This dip is great with fresh vegetables.

1 head of garlic
1 large eggplant (about 1½ pounds)
¼ cup chopped fresh cilantro (or parsley, if desired)
1 tablespoon fresh lemon juice
1 tablespoon extra-virgin olive oil

Preheat oven to 450 degrees. Wrap the garlic in a double thickness of foil and place it in a dish with the eggplant. Bake for about 30 minutes. Let cool for about 15 minutes. Peel the eggplant. Separate the garlic head into cloves. Cut off the end of each clove and squeeze the soft garlic into a food processor. Add the eggplant and chopped cilantro (or parsley). Process until smooth. Add lemon juice and olive oil. Mix well. Refrigerate until ready to serve.

Total recipe:

Calories 350	Protein . . . . 8 g.
Fat . . . . 15 g.	Carbohydrate . . . . . 54 g.
Saturated Fat . . . . 2 g.	Sodium . . . . 26 mg.
Cholesterol . . . . . . 0 mg.	Potassium . . . . 1,598 mg.

Curried Avocado Dip

1 mashed avocado
¼ teaspoon curry powder
2 teaspoons vinegar

Cut avocado into halves lengthwise and remove seed and skin. Mash the avocado with a fork and blend in curry and vinegar. Serve with unsalted melba toast or unsalted tortilla chips.

Total recipe:

Calories	342	Protein	5 g.
Fat	27 g.	Carbohydrate	28 g.
Saturated Fat	5 g.	Sodium	16 mg.
Cholesterol	0 mg.	Potassium	1,502 mg.

GRILLED BREAD

Rather than serving crackers, slice low-sodium French bread and brush with olive oil. Place under broiler (or on grill) until lightly toasted. Serve with low sodium cheese, dips, or the antipasto platter (see below).

Olive Oil, Balsamic Vinegar, and Crusty Bread

¼ cup olive oil
2 tablespoons balsamic vinegar

Put olive oil in bowl, swirl with vinegar, and serve with low-sodium bread to dunk.

Total recipe:

Calories	507	Protein	0 g.
Fat	54 g.	Carbohydrate	7 g.
Saturated Fat	7 g.	Sodium	5 mg.
Cholesterol	0 mg.	Potassium	0 mg.

Sun-dried Tomato Dip

Serve this dip in a small bowl on a plate of vegetables for spreading. Endive leaves, zucchini rounds, and jicama slices are particularly good companions.

1½ ounces sun-dried tomatoes
1 tablespoon olive oil
2 cloves garlic, pressed
4 tablespoons nonfat yogurt
6 basil leaves
¼ cup parsley

Snip sun-dried tomatoes into small pieces. Pour boiling water over them to soften. Let rest about 10 minutes. Drain. Place tomatoes and remaining ingredients in a blender or food processor. Blend until mixture is smooth. Makes about 1 cup.

Per cup:

Calories	287	Protein	9 g.
Fat	14 g.	Carbohydrate	37 g.
Saturated Fat	2 g.	Sodium	102 mg.
Cholesterol	1 mg.	Potassium	1,060 mg.

ANTIPASTO

A choice from among the following may be arranged on a large platter to be served as hors d'oeuvres or on smaller plates for individual appetizers. Accompany either with cruets of balsamic vinegar and extra-virgin olive oil flavored with garlic and bowls of freshly clipped basil or oregano, as well as low-sodium bread.

Tomato wedges
Fennel or celery hearts
Roasted red, green, and yellow peppers
Roasted eggplant
Flaked low-sodium or Tongol tuna
Marinated mushrooms
Melon wedges
Low-sodium cheese slices
Marinated garbanzo beans
Hard-boiled egg slices
Scallions

HUMMUS

There are about as many ways to make hummus as there are people who make it. Served with low-sodium pita bread, it is a beloved appetizer.

1 cup uncooked garbanzo beans
Water to cover
2 cloves garlic, crushed
1 tablespoon olive oil
Juice of one lemon

3 to 4 tablespoons tahini
2 scallions, chopped
1/2 teaspoon cumin
Freshly ground pepper
Options: cayenne pepper, oregano, cilantro, parsley

Soak garbanzo beans for 6 hours or overnight. Drain and rinse, cover with water in a kettle, and cook for 2 hours or until tender. Drain, reserving cooking liquid. In a blender or food processor puree garbanzo beans with oil and lemon juice until smooth. Add a little cooking water if needed for smoothness. Spoon into a bowl and add tahini, scallions, and pepper. Include optional ingredients, if desired.

Total recipe:

Calories	1,160	Protein	51 g.
Fat	51 g.	Carbohydrate	137 g.
Saturated Fat	7 g.	Sodium	54 mg.
Cholesterol	0 mg.	Potassium	1,928 mg.

SALSA

Even if you're not serving Mexican food, salsa is an excellent accompaniment to many meat and bean dishes. It's also great on baked potatoes.

3 lbs. tomatoes
2 small onions
3 to 4 fresh jalapeño peppers, sliced and seeded*
Handful of fresh cilantro
Juice of 1 lemon or of 2 limes
Freshly ground pepper

Chop tomatoes, onions, and peppers. Mix together in bowl with chopped, fresh cilantro. Add juice of lemon or limes and ground pepper.

Variation: Substitute chopped mangoes for half of the tomatoes.

*Take care when chopping the jalapeño—don't rub your eyes afterward!

Total recipe:

Calories 379	Protein . . . . 15 g.
Fat . . . . 5 g.	Carbohydrate . . . . . 86 g.
Saturated Fat . . . . 1 g.	Sodium . . . . 134 mg.
Cholesterol . . . . 0 mg.	Potassium . . . . 3,570 mg.

BLACK-EYED PEAS SALSA

This versatile salsa is a boon companion to chicken, pork, and rice salads and can be used to fill wedges of low-sodium pita bread for sandwiches with bite.

2 cups black-eyed peas, cooked without salt

1 red pepper, chopped fine

2 tablespoons onion, finely chopped

1 jalapeño pepper, seeded, washed, finely
     chopped

2 tablespoons chopped parsley

2 tablespoons chopped cilantro

2 tablespoons olive oil

1 tablespoon wine vinegar

1 garlic clove, crushed

Freshly ground pepper

Mix all ingredients except pepper and refrigerate several hours before serving. Let the salsa come to room temperature and sprinkle with pepper just before serving. Makes 2 ¹/₂ cups.

Total recipe:

Calories	622	Protein	13 g.
Fat	29 g.	Carbohydrate	82 g.
Saturated Fat	4 g.	Sodium	23 mg.
Cholesterol	0 mg.	Potassium	1,806 mg.

GUACAMOLE

---

2 large ripe avocados, peeled and cut into chunks

1 small onion, chopped

Juice of 1 lemon

4 drops of hot pepper oil

1 small tomato, seeded and chopped

2 garlic cloves, minced

Optional: ¹/₂ jalapeño pepper, finely chopped
  2 tablespoons finely chopped cilantro

Combine all ingredients in a blender or food processor, including the pepper and cilantro if you wish, and puree. Or mash ingredients in a bowl with a fork. Leave the avocado pit in mixture until serving to keep it from discoloring. Makes about 2 cups.

Tablespoonful:

Calories	23	Protein	tr
Fat	2 g.	Carbohydrate	2 g.
Saturated Fat	tr	Sodium	6 mg.
Cholesterol	0 mg.	Potassium	105 mg.

GREMOLATA

In Italy this is served on top of crusty bread as an appetizer, but you can also offer it in a small bowl to accompany fish.

Finely grated peel of 1 lemon

2 to 3 tablespoons parsley (Italian or curly), finely chopped

2 garlic cloves, crushed

Combine lemon peel, parsley, and garlic in bowl and mix thoroughly. Makes about ¼ cup.

Entire recipe:

Calories 16	Protein. . . . . 1 g.
Fat . . . . tr	Carbohydrate . . . . . . 4 g.
Saturated Fat . . . . tr	Sodium . . . . 5 mg.
Cholesterol. . . . . . . 0 mg.	Potassium . . . . . . 87 mg.

SWEDISH MEATBALLS

1 tablespoon minced onions

1 tablespoon vegetable oil

1 lb. lean ground round beef

½ lb. ground pork

1 beaten egg

½ cup wheat germ or low-sodium bread crumbs or low-sodium cornflakes

1 teaspoon brown sugar

¼ teaspoon ground pepper

½ teaspoon nutmeg

½ teaspoon cloves
½ teaspoon ginger
½ teaspoon allspice
2 cups boiling low-sodium beef broth

Fry onions in the oil. Mix all ingredients except broth with onions, form into small balls, brown well in onion fat. Cover with boiling broth and simmer meatballs, covered, for 20 to 30 minutes. Remove meatballs to warm casserole.

Gravy

2 cups stock
2 tablespoons flour
4 teaspoons lemon juice

Pour all but 4 tablespoons of the stock into pan. Blend in flour. Stir the gravy until thick. Add rest of stock, slowly, stirring constantly. Add lemon juice. Pour over meatballs. Serves 6.

Per serving:

Calories 295	Protein . . . . 23 g.
Fat . . . . 18 g.	Carbohydrate . . . . . 93 g.
Saturated Fat . . . . 6 g.	Sodium . . . . 75 mg.
Cholesterol . . . . . 109 mg.	Potassium . . . . . 525 mg.

SALMON MOUSSE

1 cup canned low-sodium or fresh-cooked
    salmon
1/2 cup finely chopped cucumber
1/2 tablespoon chopped fresh dill
1/4 cup minced onion
1/4 cup low-sodium catsup
1/8 cup vinegar
1 tablespoon unflavored gelatin
1/4 cup cold water
1/2 cup low-sodium mayonnaise
Tomatoes or lemons
Parsley

Drain flaked salmon, reserve liquid. Mix with cucumber, dill, and onion. Combine reserved salmon liquid, catsup, and vinegar. Bring to boil. Soften gelatin in
water, then add to liquid and stir until dissolved. Blend
hot liquid with salmon mixture. Stir in mayonnaise. Stir
into oiled mold. Chill. Garnish with tomatoes or lemons
and parsley. Serves 4. Serve with crackers as an appetizer
or with cucumbers as a first course.

Per serving:

Calories	298	Protein	12 g.
Fat	27 g.	Carbohydrate	4 g.
Saturated Fat	3 g.	Sodium	225 mg.
Cholesterol	27 mg.	Potassium	349 mg.

COCKTAIL OYSTERS

1 pint oysters (about 2 dozen)
1 pint oyster liquor
$^1/_2$ tablespoon whole black pepper
$^1/_2$ tablespoon allspice
$^1/_2$ lemon, cut in thin slices
Vinegar and cayenne to taste

Place oysters and liquor in top of double boiler. Heat enough to curl edges, drain. Keep liquor. Dry oysters with paper towels. Boil liquor with pepper and allspice about 30 minutes. Pour over oysters and lemon. Add vinegar and cayenne. Let stand in refrigerator for 24 hours. Will keep for 2 or 3 days.

Per oyster:

Calories	29	Protein	3 g.
Fat	1 g.	Carbohydrate	2 g.
Saturated Fat	0 g.	Sodium	83 mg.
Cholesterol	21 mg.	Potassium	96 mg.

DEVILED EGGS

4 hard-boiled eggs
1 tablespoon low-sodium mayonnaise
1 teaspoon tarragon vinegar
½ teaspoon mustard
¼ teaspoon chervil
¼ teaspoon rosemary
⅛ teaspoon cumin
Parsley
Paprika

Cut eggs in two, mash yolks, add the next six ingredients. Cream well. Fill eggs. Garnish with parsley and paprika. Serves 4.

Calories 104	Protein . . . . 6 g.
Fat . . . . 8 g.	Carbohydrate . . . . . . 1 g.
Saturated Fat . . . . 2 g.	Sodium . . . . 84 mg.
Cholesterol . . . . . 214 mg.	Potassium . . . . . . 70 mg.

STUFFED MUSHROOMS

½ lb. mushrooms
¼ cup melted unsalted butter
1 minced medium onion
1 teaspoon thyme
1 tablespoon sherry

Wash mushrooms and remove stems. Brush mushrooms with butter. Place in baking pan and broil 4 inches from heat until browned. Chop stems. Add stems, thyme, and onion to remaining butter. Cook until well browned. Add sherry, mix well. Fill mushrooms with mixture. Broil 5 minutes or until mixture is lightly browned. Serves 4.

Per serving:

Calories	132	Protein	2 g.
Fat	12 g.	Carbohydrate	6 g.
Saturated Fat	7 g.	Sodium	4 mg.
Cholesterol	31 mg.	Potassium	241 mg.

CUCUMBER SANDWICHES

A hot summer teatime classic. It's the way the cucumber is sliced that makes all the difference.

Low-sodium bread
Low-sodium, low-fat mayonnaise
Cucumber
Freshly ground pepper
Dill weed, fresh or dried
Chopped dill or parsley

Remove crusts from bread. Spread mayonnaise on one side of each piece. Thinly slice a peeled cucumber lengthwise. Lay the cucumber strips on top of mayonnaise-coated bread, sprinkle with ground pepper and dill weed. Top with another slice of bread. Cut into desired shapes. If you like you can spread a little mayonnaise on the top or sides and sprinkle chopped dill or parsley on coated areas.

Per serving:

Calories	59	Protein	1 g.
Fat	2 g.	Carbohydrate	9 g.
Saturated Fat	tr	Sodium	10 mg.
Cholesterol	1 mg.	Potassium	34 mg.

FRUIT PUNCH

1 12-oz. can frozen orange juice concentrate

1 12-oz. can frozen lemonade concentrate

1 quart cranberry juice

1 quart, more or less, low-sodium club soda

1 to 2 quarts ginger ale

$1/2$ bag of ice cubes

Unless you have a very large container, mix slowly, varying amounts according to the size of the bowl and replenish according to how many people you're serving. Float a ring of ice, frozen with flowers, in the punch bowl.

Variation: Add frozen limeade and/or pineapple juice.

Per serving:

Calories 99	Protein . . . . tr
Fat . . . . tr	Carbohydrate . . . . . 25 g.
Saturated Fat . . . . tr	Sodium . . . . 7 mg.
Cholesterol. . . . . . . 0 mg.	Potassium . . . . . 120 mg.

MULLED CIDER

2 quarts apple cider

1 cup cranberry juice

2 cinnamon sticks

$1/2$ teaspoon allspice

$1/2$ teaspoon cloves

Combine ingredients in a large saucepan or Crock-Pot. Heat thoroughly and serve in mugs. Serves 8 to 10.

Per serving:

Calories 114	Protein . . . . tr
Fat . . . . tr	Carbohydrate . . . . . . 7 g.
Saturated Fat . . . . tr	Sodium . . . . 2 mg.
Cholesterol. . . . . . . 0 mg.	Potassium . . . . . . 11 mg.

Soups

No matter what the tempting name on the label, most canned soups have one predominant flavor: saltiness. Now, thanks to blenders, food processors, and the huge variety of fresh ingredients available, you can easily declare independence from the commercial soup manufacturers and enjoy delicacies of taste that just can't be found on the shelf. For really inventive soups, think leftovers. Last night's vegetables or legumes can instantly be transformed into soups with a blender, a little broth, yogurt, a dollop of cream, and fresh herbs added at the last minute.

Please note that all nutritional information at the end of each recipe refers to 1 serving size.

HOMEMADE STOCK

A Versatile Base for Chicken, Vegetable, Beef, and Fish Recipes

No matter how useful low-sodium bouillon packets are, there is no substitute for homemade stock. One way to simplify the process is to have one basic recipe for stock that can be adapted for chicken, beef, vegetable, or fish recipes. If you are used to having the key ingredients on hand, then you can assemble them quickly, let the stockpot boil, and get in the habit of freezing cupfuls in plastic containers, carefully labeled. You can also freeze greatly reduced stock in ice cube trays, then place them in plastic freezer bags for adding concentrated flavor to a variety of dishes.

2 onions, chopped
3 cloves garlic, chopped
2 leeks, white parts sliced
4 to 6 carrots, scraped and sliced
2 to 3 ribs celery, chopped
1 bunch chopped parsley stems
Peppercorns
Bay leaves
3 quarts water

For chicken: Add 2 to 4 pounds chicken bones and/or parts, thyme, tarragon. Roast bones for 40 minutes in oven at 350 degrees. Then combine with remaining ingredients and simmer for 3 hours.

For beef: Add 2 to 4 pounds beef bones, thyme, rosemary. Roast bones in oven at 350 degrees for 40 minutes.

Combine with remaining ingredients and simmer for 3 hours.

For vegetable: Add thyme and marjoram. Combine all ingredients and simmer for 1 hour.

For fish: Add 4 pounds of fish bones, 6 large sliced mushrooms, juice of one lemon. Combine all ingredients and simmer for 45 minutes.

Strain stock. (For a more intense flavor return this strained stock to the stove and simmer until reduced by half.) Let cool. Skim off any fat. If not used immediately, store covered in refrigerator for up to 10 days or freeze in plastic containers or ice cube trays.

Homemade stock (1/2 cup reduced stock):

Calories	34	Protein	1 g.
Fat	tr	Carbohydrate	8 g.
Saturated Fat	tr	Sodium	32 mg.
Cholesterol	0 mg.	Potassium	204 mg.

Chicken stock (1/2 cup reduced stock):

Calories	230	Protein	18 g.
Fat	14 g.	Carbohydrate	8 g.
Saturated Fat	4 g.	Sodium	81 mg.
Cholesterol	60 mg.	Potassium	315 mg.

Vegetable stock (1/2 cup reduced stock):

Calories	35	Protein	1 g.
Fat	tr	Carbohydrate	8 g.
Saturated Fat	tr	Sodium	32 mg.
Cholesterol	0 mg.	Potassium	206 mg.

Homemade beef stock (1/2 cup reduced stock):

Calories	203	Protein	24 g.
Fat	8 g.	Carbohydrate	8 g.

Saturated Fat. . . . . . . 3 g.	Sodium. . . . . 81 mg.
Cholesterol. . . . . . 68 mg.	Potassium . . . . . 472 mg.

Homemade fish stock (¹/₂ cup reduced stock):

Calories 176	Protein. . . . . 31 g.
Fat . . . . 2 g.	Carbohydrate . . . . . . 9 g.
Saturated Fat . . . . tr	Sodium. . . . . 177 mg.
Cholesterol. . . . . 107 mg.	Potassium . . . . . 840 mg.

HEARTY BEEF SOUP

---

1 tablespoon butter

1 tablespoon extra-virgin olive oil

2 lbs. beef shinbone

Flour

Freshly ground pepper

1 onion, chopped

1 carrot, sliced

7 garlic cloves, minced

3 cups of water

3 cups of low-sodium beef broth

1 teaspoon dried thyme

3 bay leaves

1 teaspoon dried marjoram

**1 teaspoon dried rosemary, crumbled between
    fingers**

Heat butter and olive oil in nonstick skillet. Coat beef
with flour and season with pepper and brown on both
sides. Place in soup kettle. In skillet sauté onions, carrot,
and minced garlic for 5 minutes. Add the vegetables to
the pot along with water, beef broth, herbs, and pepper.

Bring to boil and simmer for 1¹/₂ to 2 hours or until beef is coming off the bone. Add more water, if necessary. Strain broth into another pot. Slice meat and return desired amount to broth along with vegetables. Skim off any fat. Serve with crusty bread. Serves 6.

Calories	137	Protein	9 g.
Fat	9 g.	Carbohydrate	5 g.
Saturated Fat	3 g.	Sodium	32 mg.
Cholesterol	38 mg.	Potassium	401 mg.

LENTIL SOUP

1 tablespoon extra-virgin olive oil

1 medium onion, chopped

3 cloves garlic, crushed

1 carrot, shredded

1 green pepper, chopped

1 teaspoon oregano, dried

1 teaspoon cumin

1 ripe tomato, chopped

1 turnip, diced

1 cup lentils, washed

6 sun-dried tomatoes, snipped into pieces

6 cups low-sodium chicken or vegetable broth

Stalk of celery with leaves

Freshly ground pepper

2 bay leaves

Heat olive oil in soup kettle. Add onion, garlic, carrot, and pepper. Sauté until vegetables are soft. Add oregano, cumin, tomatoes, turnip, lentils, and sun-dried tomatoes. Stir carefully and add remaining ingredients. Simmer for

1¹/₂ hours, adding more broth or water, if necessary. Garnish with chopped tomato and celery leaves. Serves 6.

Calories 166	Protein. . . . . 9 g.
Fat . . . . 3 g.	Carbohydrate . . . . . 28 g.
Saturated Fat . . . . tr	Sodium. . . . . 33 mg.
Cholesterol. . . . . . . 5 mg.	Potassium . . . . 1,035 mg.

CONSOMMÉ JULIENNE

---

1 tablespoon unsalted butter

1 cup julienne carrot strips

¹/₂ cup julienne leek strips

¹/₂ cup finely shredded cabbage

¹/₄ cup thin onion slices

Pepper to taste

¹/₄ teaspoon basil

¹/₄ teaspoon dill weed

1 teaspoon sugar

3 cups low-sodium beef broth

Parsley, chopped

1 teaspoon low-fat sour cream (optional)

Melt butter in saucepan. Add vegetables, seasonings, and sugar. Cover and cook over a low heat for 5 minutes or until vegetables are tender. Add the beef broth and simmer for 5 minutes. Serve garnished with chopped parsley. If calories permit, add 1 teaspoon low-fat sour cream when consommé is served. Serves 4.

Calories 63	Protein. . . . . 1 g.
Fat . . . . 3 g.	Carbohydrate . . . . . . 9 g.
Saturated Fat. . . . . . . 2 g.	Sodium. . . . . 20 mg.
Cholesterol. . . . . . 12 mg.	Potassium . . . . . 526 mg.

BUTTERNUT SQUASH SOUP

1½ teaspoons unsalted butter

½ cup chopped onion

1 carrot, chopped

1 large butternut squash, peeled, seeded, and
    cubed

4 cups low-sodium chicken or vegetable stock

2 cups apple juice or cider

½ teaspoon allspice

½ teaspoon nutmeg

½ teaspoon cinnamon

3 tablespoons maple syrup

2 tablespoons lemon juice

1 cup nonfat plain yogurt

1½ cups finely chopped Granny Smith apples

In a large saucepan melt butter and sauté onion and carrot. Add squash and stock. Simmer, covered, for about 30 minutes or until the squash is tender. Puree in blender or food processor until smooth. Return the mixture to the kettle and add remaining ingredients. Heat thoroughly, but do not boil. Ladle in soup bowls. Garnish with grated apple peel and carrot. Serves 6.

Calories	188	Protein	4 g.
Fat	2 g.	Carbohydrate	43 g.
Saturated Fat	1 g.	Sodium	58 mg.
Cholesterol	7 mg.	Potassium	993 mg.

CURRIED APPLE SOUP

1 tablespoon butter
1 medium onion, chopped
1 celery stalk, chopped
6 eating apples (about 1½ pounds), washed,
    cored, and sliced
2 to 3 teaspoons curry powder
2 medium-size potatoes, peeled and chopped
5 cups low-sodium chicken broth
Freshly ground pepper
Chopped apple for garnish

In a large saucepan melt butter and sauté onion until soft. Add celery and apple and cook for a few more minutes. Add curry powder and continue to cook for another 10 minutes. Add potatoes and stock and cook until the vegetables are soft. Puree mixture in a blender or food processor. Reheat. Sprinkle with freshly ground pepper. Ladle into soup bowls and top with finely chopped apple. Serves 6.

Calories	153	Protein	1 g.
Fat	3 g.	Carbohydrate	34 g.
Saturated Fat	1 g.	Sodium	14 mg.
Cholesterol	9 mg.	Potassium	760 mg.

CREAM OF ASPARAGUS SOUP

1 lb. fresh asparagus
2 to 3 cups low-sodium chicken broth
2 scallions, thinly sliced
1 tablespoon fresh lemon juice
⅛ teaspoon cayenne
1 tablespoon fresh dill, finely chopped
½ cup plain nonfat yogurt

Cook the asparagus until just tender. Drain and let cool. Place the asparagus and the remaining ingredients in a blender or food processor and puree. May be served hot or cold. Serves 4.

Calories	49	Protein	4 g.
Fat	tr	Carbohydrate	9 g.
Saturated Fat	tr	Sodium	29 mg.
Cholesterol	4 mg.	Potassium	711 mg.

PUREE OF AVOCADO SOUP

2 avocados
1 tablespoon lemon juice
¼ teaspoon paprika
2 teaspoons chopped chives
1 teaspoon grated lemon rind
¼ teaspoon dill weed
¼ teaspoon oregano
2 teaspoons grated onions
2 cups milk

Peel, seed, and mash avocados. Add the rest of the ingredients. Heat in a double boiler. This is a thick soup, and can also be made with low-sodium dry milk if you wish to cut the count. Serves 4.

Calories	207	Protein	6 g.
Fat	16 g.	Carbohydrate	13 g.
Saturated Fat	3 g.	Sodium	72 mg.
Cholesterol	5 mg.	Potassium	755 mg.

CARROT SOUP

1 tablespoon unsalted butter

3 leeks, thinly sliced white part

1 lb. carrots, peeled and sliced thinly

2 to 3 teaspoons fresh grated ginger

4 cups low-sodium chicken stock

1 teaspoon dried tarragon

Ground pepper

Garnish choices: fresh dill, grated carrot,
    or mint leaves

In a saucepan melt butter and gently sauté leeks and carrots. Sprinkle with fresh ginger and add chicken stock. Simmer for 20 to 25 minutes or until carrots are tender. Puree cooked carrots in blender or food processor and return to broth. Stir thoroughly and add tarragon and ground pepper. Serve hot, garnished with fresh dill, grated carrot, or mint leaves. Serves 4 to 5.

Calories	140	Protein	3 g.
Fat	3 g.	Carbohydrate	27 g.
Saturated Fat	2 g.	Sodium	64 mg.
Cholesterol	13 mg.	Potassium	1,014 mg.

MUSHROOM SOUP

This is an adaptation of Mollie Katzen's Mushroom Bisque.

2 potatoes, peeled and quartered
2 cups low-sodium vegetable or chicken broth
1 tablespoon butter
1 large onion, chopped
2 cloves garlic, minced
1 stalk celery, chopped
1¼ lbs. mushrooms, chopped
¼ teaspoon thyme
¼ cup sherry
1 cup nonfat plain yogurt
Freshly ground pepper

In a medium saucepan combine potatoes and broth and simmer until potatoes are tender. Meanwhile in a large saucepan melt butter and sauté onion, garlic, and celery until they are soft. Add mushrooms and thyme and continue cooking until the vegetables are limp. Add sherry and simmer for 5 minutes. Remove 3 tablespoons of mushrooms for garnish. Puree in a blender or food processor both mixtures and combine with yogurt in the large saucepan to heat through. Sprinkle with black pepper. Ladle into soup bowls and garnish with reserved chopped mushrooms. (Chop more finely, if necessary.) Serves 6.

Calories	129	Protein	5 g.
Fat	2 g.	Carbohydrate	21 g.
Saturated Fat	1 g.	Sodium	44 mg.
Cholesterol	8 mg.	Potassium	823 mg.

CAULIFLOWER AND PIMENTO SOUP

1¹/₂ cups cooked cauliflower

2 tablespoons chopped pimento

3¹/₂ cups low-sodium chicken broth

¹/₂ onion, grated

1 to 2 teaspoons curry powder

1 garlic clove, crushed

2 teaspoons fresh horseradish, or horseradish
    preserved without salt

¹/₂ cup nonfat plain yogurt, at room temperature

Black pepper

Garlic powder

Slices of green or red pepper

Pimento slices

In a blender or food processor puree cauliflower and
pimento with a cup of broth. Transfer mixture to
saucepan and add remaining broth, onion, curry powder,
garlic, and horseradish. Simmer until soup is thickened
somewhat. Before serving, add yogurt and black pepper
and garlic powder to taste. (Only heat the yogurt until it
is just cooked through or it will separate.) Ladle into soup
bowls and garnish with chopped fresh green or red pepper and pimento. Serves 4.

*Note: This can be easily made with leftover Curried
Cauliflower with Garlic, in which case, adjust or eliminate curry powder, garlic, and horseradish.*

Calories	129	Protein	5 g.
Fat	2 g.	Carbohydrate	21 g.
Saturated Fat	1 g.	Sodium	44 mg.
Cholesterol	8 mg.	Potassium	823 mg.

TOMATO SOUP

1/2 cup finely chopped onion

1 tablespoon unsalted butter

2 cups canned low-sodium tomatoes

2 tablespoons white wine

1/4 teaspoon dill weed

1/4 teaspoon dried basil

1 tablespoon chopped fresh parsley

1 tablespoon low-fat sour cream

Sauté onion in butter until tender. Add tomatoes, wine, dill, basil, and parsley. Simmer 20 minutes. Puree in blender or food processor, if you like. Pour into serving dishes and top with sour cream. Serves 2.

Calories 141	Protein . . . . 3 g.
Fat . . . . 8 g.	Carbohydrate . . . . . 15 g.
Saturated Fat . . . . 5 g.	Sodium . . . . 39 mg.
Cholesterol . . . . . . 19 mg.	Potassium . . . . . 637 mg.

GEORGIAN BAY TOMATO SOUP

This recipe came from friends who made it over a campfire while on a canoe trip. That gives you an idea how easy it is.

2 finely chopped onions

5 thinly sliced garlic cloves

1 tablespoon olive oil

1 28-oz. can crushed tomatoes, no salt added

1/2 cup low-sodium peanut butter*

2 teaspoons cumin (or to taste)

¹/₂ teaspoon cayenne pepper

2 teaspoons chili powder

2 tablespoons red wine vinegar

1 teaspoon pepper

1 teaspoon sugar

2 cups water

Hot pepper sauce to taste

**Garnish (optional): chopped unsalted peanuts
    and minced onion**

Sauté onions and garlic in olive oil until soft. Add tomatoes, reducing heat to low. Stir in peanut butter thoroughly and then add all other ingredients, except garnish. Cook over a low heat at a bare simmer for 10 to 15 minutes. Soup burns easily, so don't let it boil. Ladle into bowls and add garnish, if desired. Serves 4.

*Use commercial, emulsified brand in all recipes that call for heating. Do not use the homemade peanut butter recipe we include in this book.

Calories 301	Protein. . . . . 13 g.
Fat . . . . 21 g.	Carbohydrate . . . . . 23 g.
Saturated Fat. . . . . . 3 g.	Sodium. . . . . 46 mg.
Cholesterol. . . . . . . 0 mg.	Potassium . . . . . 798 mg.

ZUCCHINI SOUP

This was adapted by M. E. Malone from *Gourmet Magazine*.

1 large leek, washed and finely chopped (use white and pale green parts only)

1 finely chopped small onion

3 shallots, chopped fine

3 cloves minced garlic

2 tablespoons extra-virgin olive oil

Freshly ground pepper to taste

1 large russet potato, peeled and cut into 1-inch pieces

1½ lbs. zucchini, sliced thin

3 cups low-sodium or homemade chicken broth

⅓ cup light cream

Juice from 1 lemon

Ice water for thinning soup

Sauté leek, onion, shallots, and garlic in olive oil, adding pepper to taste, until mixture is softened. Add potato, zucchini, and broth. Simmer mixture, covered, for 15 minutes or until potato is very tender. Puree mixture in a blender or food processor in batches until soup is smooth. Transfer to a bowl and add cream, lemon juice, and pepper. Chill soup at least 6 hours or overnight. Thin soup with ice water and season with additional lemon juice right before serving. Garnish with chopped chives, grated zucchini skin or grated lemon peel. Serves 6 to 8.

Calories	131	Protein	3 g.
Fat	8 g.	Carbohydrate	14 g.
Saturated Fat	2 g.	Sodium	20 mg.
Cholesterol	9 mg.	Potassium	454 mg.

WATERCRESS SOUP

4 large potatoes, peeled
1 bunch watercress, washed and chopped
Pepper to taste
½ teaspoon dried sage
1 teaspoon dried rosemary, crumbled
1 egg yolk
Juice of one lemon
Paprika
Parsley

Boil the potatoes until nearly done. Drain potatoes and reserve cooking water. Add watercress and pepper. Mash and strain through sieve. Put back into saucepan with enough of the potato water to make the desired consistency. Add sage and rosemary. Cook 20 minutes without boiling. Beat the egg yolk into the lemon juice and add slowly to the soup. Garnish with paprika and parsley. Serves 4.

Calories	122	Protein	3 g.
Fat	1 g.	Carbohydrate	26 g.
Saturated Fat	tr	Sodium	9 mg.
Cholesterol	36 mg.	Potassium	510 mg.

SUMMER VEGETABLE SOUP

2 tablespoons unsalted butter

2 tablespoons olive oil

3 garlic cloves, sliced

1 leek, sliced, white part only

2 medium onions, sliced

¾ cup each of green beans, zucchini, carrots, and broccoli

1½ cups white rose potatoes with skin, diced

2 tomatoes, skinned and chopped

Freshly ground pepper

6 cups low-sodium chicken broth

Heat butter and oil in kettle. Sauté garlic, leek, and onions briefly. Add remaining vegetables and steam with pepper for 20 minutes. Add chicken broth, bring to a boil, and simmer for 10 minutes. Let the soup cool about a half hour. Process the mixture in batches in a blender or food processor. Return to kettle and heat before serving, or refrigerate and serve cold. This freezes well. Serves 6 to 8.

Calories	171	Protein	3 g.
Fat	9 g.	Carbohydrate	22 g.
Saturated Fat	3 g.	Sodium	32 mg.
Cholesterol	16 mg.	Potassium	957 mg.

POTATO AND LEEK SOUP

This delicate soup may be served hot or cold.

1 tablespoon butter

3 to 4 leeks, sliced, white part only

5 to 6 medium potatoes, about 1 lb.

4 cups of low-sodium chicken broth

1½ cups of nonfat plain yogurt

**1 teaspoon dill weed, dried, or 1 tablespoon
    fresh dill**

1 teaspoon tarragon

Freshly ground pepper

Juice of ½ lemon

Melt butter in saucepan and sauté leeks until soft, about 10 minutes. Add potatoes, peeled and sliced, and chicken broth. Simmer, covered, for about 30 minutes or until tender. Puree small batches in blender or food processor and return to saucepan. Fold in yogurt, herbs, and pepper. Heat through, but do not boil. Refrigerate if serving cold. (This tastes better after the flavors have had a chance to blend.) Before serving stir in lemon juice. Garnish with clips of fresh dill, chives, or chopped red onion. Serves 6.

Calories	145	Protein	5 g.
Fat	2 g.	Carbohydrate	27 g.
Saturated Fat	1 g.	Sodium	59 mg.
Cholesterol	10 mg.	Potassium	794 mg.

GAZPACHO

5 ripe tomatoes
2 cloves garlic, crushed
1 small onion, chopped
1 cucumber, peeled and chopped
1/2 green pepper, chopped
1 carrot, grated
Freshly ground pepper
1 tablespoon fresh chopped fennel bulb or basil
   leaves
1 tablespoon olive oil
2 tablespoons red wine vinegar
1/2 cup ice water
Dash Tabasco sauce
Juice from one lemon

Finely chop one tomato. Add the other 4 tomatoes to
the blender or food processor and blend until pulpy. Add
the remaining ingredients, excluding lemon juice, and
blend until vegetables are coarsely chopped and combined. Stir in finely chopped tomato. Ladle into chilled
bowls and decorate with sprigs of fennel or basil. At the
last minute add a squeeze of fresh lemon to each bowl.
Serve with small bowls of extra chopped vegetables and
croutons made of low-sodium bread fried briefly in a little unsalted butter or olive oil. Serves 6.

Calories	63	Protein	2 g.
Fat	3 g.	Carbohydrate	10 g.
Saturated Fat	tr	Sodium	16 mg.
Cholesterol	tr	Potassium	409 mg.

COLD CUCUMBER AND MINT SOUP

5 cucumbers, peeled, cut in half, and seeded
1 large clove garlic, minced
1 to 1½ cups low-sodium chicken or vegetable
   broth
1 pint nonfat plain yogurt
½ teaspoon black pepper
1 cup fresh mint leaves, chopped
Juice from ½ lemon
Mint leaves for garnish

In a blender or food processor puree chopped cucumbers with garlic and 1 cup broth. Add yogurt, pepper, mint, and lemon juice. Continue to puree. Add more broth to achieve desired consistency. Refrigerate soup until thoroughly chilled. Ladle into soup bowls and garnish with mint leaves. Serves 4.

Calories 106		Protein . . . . 8 g.	
Fat . . . . 1 g.		Carbohydrate . . . . . 18 g.	
Saturated Fat . . . . tr		Sodium . . . . 96 mg.	
Cholesterol . . . . 4 mg.		Potassium . . . . . 841 mg.	

QUONQUONT FARM RASPBERRY SOUP

This is an adaptation of a recipe created by our local berry farm.

2 cups raspberries
½ cup sugar
½ cup nonfat plain yogurt
2 cups ice water
½ cup red wine

Puree the raspberries in a blender or food processor. Press through a sieve to remove seeds. In a bowl mix raspberries with sugar and yogurt. Add ice water and wine. Ladle into soup bowls and garnish with mint or raspberry leaves and whole raspberries. Serves 4.

Calories 157		Protein. . . . . .2 g.	
Fat. . . . . .tr		Carbohydrate . . . . . 34 g.	
Saturated Fat . . . . .tr		Sodium. . . . . 27 mg.	
Cholesterol. . . . . . 1 mg.		Potassium . . . . . 199 mg.	

FENNEL AND ROASTED PEPPER SOUP

---

4 red or green bell peppers

3 cloves minced garlic

1 bunch chopped leeks, white part only

4 sliced fennel bulbs

1 tablespoon extra-virgin olive oil

6 cups low-sodium chicken broth

¼ cup vermouth

**Garnish with: pimento strips and chopped
    parsley**

Freshly ground pepper to taste

Cut peppers in half. Remove seeds, core, and rind. Bake on foil-lined pan in 400-degree oven for about 30 minutes or until skin is blistered. Place in paper bag and let cool. Meanwhile, sauté garlic, leeks, and fennel in oil until soft. Slice peppers and add. Simmer mixture over a low heat for 20 minutes. Add broth and pepper, and simmer for another 30 minutes. Blend in small batches or puree in food processor until smooth. Reheat and add vermouth. Ladle into bowls and sprinkle with pimento strips and chopped parsley. Serves 6 to 8.

Calories 81	Protein. . . . . 1 g.
Fat . . . . 2 g.	Carbohydrate . . . . . 10 g.
Saturated Fat . . . . tr	Sodium. . . . . 19 mg.
Cholesterol. . . . . . . 5 mg.	Potassium . . . . . 687 mg.

MINESTRONE

2 large red onions, chopped
5 cloves garlic, chopped
3 carrots, peeled and chopped
3 large stalks celery, chopped
½ cup olive oil
1 medium-size head green cabbage, chopped
10 large kale leaves, chopped
½ teaspoon thyme
2 bay leaves
3 quarts water
1 28-oz. can plum tomatoes
1 16-oz. can chickpeas, no salt added
1 cup pasta shells
Black pepper, to taste

In a large stockpot, sauté the onions, garlic, carrots, and celery in the olive oil until onions are translucent. Add the cabbage, kale, thyme, and bay leaves and cook over medium-high heat for a minute or 2, stirring constantly. Add the water, tomatoes, chickpeas, pepper to taste, and bring to a boil. Lower the heat and simmer, covered, for 45 minutes. Add the pasta and cook 15 minutes more, or until the pasta is done. Makes 12 to 14 servings.

Calories 204	Protein. . . . . 6 g.
Fat . . . . 10 g.	Carbohydrate . . . . . 25 g.

| Saturated Fat. . . . . . . 1 g. | Sodium. . . . . 53 mg. |
| Cholesterol. . . . . . . 0 mg. | Potassium . . . . . 601 mg. |

OYSTER STEW

---

5 oysters
1 teaspoon unsalted butter
1 tablespoon low-sodium chili sauce
$\frac{1}{2}$ teaspoon lemon juice
Few grains cayenne
$\frac{1}{4}$ teaspoon paprika
$\frac{1}{4}$ cup oyster liquor
1 tablespoon cream
1 piece low-sodium toast

Place oysters, butter, chili sauce, lemon juice, cayenne, paprika, and oyster liquor in a deep pan. Cook about 1 minute, stirring constantly. Add cream, and when mixture comes to a boil, pour over toast placed in a soup plate. You may add grated fresh horseradish, if you wish. Serves 1.

Calories 253	Protein. . . . . 13 g.
Fat . . . . 11 g.	Carbohydrate . . . . . 25 g.
Saturated Fat. . . . . . . 5 g.	Sodium. . . . . 305 mg.
Cholesterol. . . . . 100 mg.	Potassium . . . . . 387 mg.

Pasta

We Americans have gone crazy for pasta, and our enthusiasm has brought an abundance of imported brands (in various shapes, sizes, flavors, and colors) to supermarket shelves. When using the dried variety, choose imported whole wheat for the greatest flavor. Excellent fresh pasta, made by specialty companies here, is also readily available. Cook pasta according to the directions on the package, and add a squeeze of lemon juice or flavored vinegar to the cooking water. And if you follow the recipes in this section, you'll never miss the salt!

Please note that, unless otherwise stated, all nutritional information refers to 1 serving size.

MAISIE'S MARINARA SAUCE

4 garlic cloves, minced
1 onion, chopped
2 to 3 tablespoons olive oil
1 28-oz. can crushed tomatoes
2 bay leaves
1 teaspoon dried basil
1 teaspoon dried oregano
Red pepper
Black pepper

In a skillet, sauté garlic and onion in olive oil until soft. Add crushed tomatoes, bay leaves, basil, and oregano. Add peppers to taste. Simmer for 30 minutes, stirring occasionally.

Total recipe:

Calories	528	Protein	10 g.
Fat	36 g.	Carbohydrate	50 g.
Saturated Fat	5 g.	Sodium	109 mg.
Cholesterol	0 mg.	Potassium	2,040 mg.

MAMA LONG'S VEGETABLE PASTA SAUCE

2 tablespoons olive oil
1 large red onion
5 garlic cloves, sliced
1 stalk celery, leaves included, chopped
1 green pepper, chopped
1 carrot, chopped

1 small potato, chopped
1 bunch of parsley
$^1/_2$ cup water
2 bay leaves
1 teaspoon dried basil, 2 teaspoons fresh
$^1/_2$ teaspoon oregano
$^1/_4$ teaspoon black pepper
1 28-oz. can Italian tomatoes, no salt added
1 small can tomato sauce, no salt added
1 can tomato paste, no salt added
$^1/_2$ cup red wine
1 teaspoon sugar (optional)

Heat olive oil in nonstick skillet. Sauté red onion and garlic until they are soft. In a blender or food processor combine celery, pepper, carrot, potato, parsley, and water and puree thoroughly. Add this mixture and remaining ingredients (except wine and sugar) to the skillet or to a saucepan and simmer for about 1 to $1^1/_2$ hours, stirring occasionally. then add the wine and simmer another $^1/_2$ hour. Before serving you may add sugar and freshly ground pepper. Serves 4.

Total recipe:

Calories	1,001	Protein	28 g.
Fat	32 g.	Carbohydrate	152 g.
Saturated Fat	5 g.	Sodium	427 mg.
Cholesterol	0 mg.	Potassium	5,825 mg.

CHICKEN AND RED PEPPER PASTA SAUCE

2 medium red bell peppers
1 tablespoon extra-virgin olive oil
1 small onion, finely chopped
2 medium garlic cloves, minced
½ lb. boneless chicken breasts, cut in chunks
¼ teaspoon black pepper
¼ teaspoon garlic powder
½ cup white wine
1 16-oz. can whole tomatoes, no salt added
1 tablespoon tomato paste, no salt added
1 teaspoon minced fresh basil
1 tablespoon fresh Italian parsley, chopped
1 teaspoon sugar
1 teaspoon finely chopped rosemary leaves,
    crumbled between fingers

Preheat oven to 500 degrees. Cut peppers in half, seed and core. Bake on foil-lined sheet for 25 minutes or until they're evenly blistered and browned. Remove from oven and cover with a towel. When cool enough to handle, peel and slice. In a nonstick skillet or large saucepan, heat olive oil and sauté onion and garlic. Add chicken, rubbed with black pepper and garlic powder, and cook for 5 to 7 minutes or until chicken begins to brown. Add wine, stirring and scraping to deglaze the pan. Add remaining ingredients. Simmer 20 to 25 minutes. Spoon over pasta of choice as soon as it's cooked and drained. Serves 4.

Calories	172	Protein	12 g.
Fat	6 g.	Carbohydrate	14 g.
Saturated Fat	1 g.	Sodium	43 mg.
Cholesterol	26 mg.	Potassium	561 mg.

SPAGHETTI BOLOGNESE

1 lb. ground lean beef
4 tablespoons olive oil
1 chopped onion
2 teaspoons minced parsley
6 chopped mushrooms
1 garlic clove
½ teaspoon basil
1 bay leaf
1 teaspoon sugar
½ teaspoon oregano
¼ teaspoon allspice
Pepper to taste
2 cups canned low-sodium tomatoes
1 lb. Italian-import spaghetti

Fry beef in hot oil until slightly brown. Drain and return to pan. Add onion, parsley, mushrooms, garlic, basil, bay leaf, sugar, oregano, allspice, and pepper. Sauté for 10 minutes. Add tomatoes. Simmer 1 hour. Remember: buy wheat flour pasta. It cooks tender without salt. Serves 6.

Calories	311	Protein	15 g.
Fat	25 g.	Carbohydrate	7 g.
Saturated Fat	8 g.	Sodium	65 mg.
Cholesterol	56 mg.	Potassium	479 mg.

PASTA WITH MUSHROOMS AND CAPERS

1 lb. rotini
2 tablespoons extra-virgin olive oil
2 cups fresh mushrooms, finely chopped
$\frac{1}{2}$ teaspoon thyme
$\frac{1}{2}$ cup nonfat plain yogurt, room temperature
1 tablespoon salt-free capers
1 tablespoon tomato paste with no salt added
2 tablespoons chopped parsley
2 whole scallions, chopped
Freshly ground pepper
Parsley for garnish
Nutmeg

Cook rotini in boiling water without salt. Drain. In a nonstick skillet heat olive oil and add mushrooms and thyme. Cook for 7 minutes. Add next 5 ingredients and heat through. Pour mixture over pasta and sprinkle with freshly ground pepper, chopped parsley, and nutmeg. Serves 4 to 5.

Calories	526	Protein	17 g.
Fat	9 g.	Carbohydrate	93 g.
Saturated Fat	1 g.	Sodium	29 mg.
Cholesterol	1 mg.	Potassium	348 mg.

PASTA WITH ROASTED PEPPERS AND SUN-DRIED TOMATOES

3 bell peppers, a mix of green, red, or yellow
$\frac{1}{2}$ lb. pasta shells or rotini
1 oz. sun-dried tomatoes (about 9), soaked in
    boiling water for about 5 minutes

¼ cup Greek olive oil
½ medium onion, chopped
¼ cup balsamic vinegar
¼ teaspoon black pepper

Preheat oven to 500 degrees. Cut peppers in half, seed and core. Place on foil-lined sheet and roast about 25 minutes until they are charred. Remove from oven and cover with a towel. When they are cool, peel and chop in thin slices. Reserve. Boil pasta according to package directions, without salt. Drain and rinse with cold water. Combine sun-dried tomatoes, olive oil, onion, vinegar, and pepper in blender or food processor and puree. Combine peppers and dressing with warm pasta. Refrigerate and bring to room temperature before serving. Serves 4 to 5.

Calories 408	Protein . . . . 9 g.
Fat . . . . 15 g.	Carbohydrate . . . . . 61 g.
Saturated Fat . . . . 2 g.	Sodium . . . . 15 mg.
Cholesterol . . . . 0 mg.	Potassium . . . . . 375 mg.

FRESH TOMATOES AND BASIL ON ANGEL HAIR PASTA

3 tablespoons extra-virgin olive oil
1 tablespoon balsamic vinegar
3 cloves garlic, pressed
½ cup fresh basil, chopped
4 cups chopped fresh tomatoes
½ cup pine nuts
Ground pepper
1 lb. angel hair pasta, cooked without salt

Combine olive oil, vinegar, garlic, and basil and puree in blender or food processor. Pour over chopped tomatoes and mix carefully. Add pine nuts and pepper. Spoon over plates of warm pasta. Serves 4.

Note: If your sodium count allows, sprinkle with Parmesan cheese.

Calories	658	Protein	18 g.
Fat	25 g.	Carbohydrate	97 g.
Saturated Fat	4 g.	Sodium	35 mg.
Cholesterol	0 mg.	Potassium	669 mg.

ROTINI WITH ZUCCHINI AND SUN-DRIED TOMATO SAUCE

1 tablespoon extra-virgin olive oil

1 medium onion, chopped

1 green pepper, seeded, washed, dried, chopped

1 small zucchini, grated

3 cloves garlic, minced

½ lb. rotini pasta

1 28-oz. can Italian tomatoes, no salt added

¼ cup red wine

1 oz. sun-dried tomatoes, snipped into pieces and reconstituted with boiling water for 5 minutes and drained

1 teaspoon sugar

2 tablespoons yogurt

6 fresh basil leaves (1 teaspoon dried)

Freshly ground pepper

In a nonstick skillet heat the olive oil and sauté onion, pepper, zucchini, and garlic until vegetables are soft.

Meanwhile, boil rotini until done.* While pasta is still warm, toss with vegetable mixture in casserole dish. In skillet heat canned tomatoes with wine. Puree sun-dried tomatoes with sugar, yogurt, and basil. Add to tomatoes in skillet and simmer until thickened, about 15 to 20 minutes. Pour over pasta and sprinkle with freshly ground pepper. Serves 6.

> *You may add lemon juice, bay leaf, or unsalted broth to pasta water.

Calories	236	Protein	8 g.
Fat	3 g.	Carbohydrate	44 g.
Saturated Fat	tr	Sodium	30 mg.
Cholesterol	tr	Potassium	550 mg.

LASAGNA WITH BROCCOLI

This dish is magic because you start off with un-cooked lasagna noodles and end up with a spicy vegetable version of an old favorite.

1 tablespoon olive oil

1 medium onion, sliced in rings

5 cloves garlic, sliced

2 Italian peppers, seeded and sliced

1/2 lb. broccoli, both stems and florets chopped

1 28-oz. can Italian tomatoes, no salt added

1/2 cup chopped parsley

1/2 cup chopped basil

1/4 teaspoon red pepper

1/4 teaspoon black pepper

10 lasagna noodles, uncooked

1 cup low-fat, low-sodium cottage cheese
1 oz. skim milk mozzarella, grated
Freshly ground pepper
1/2 teaspoon garlic powder

In a nonstick skillet heat olive oil and add onion and garlic. Sauté until soft and then add peppers and broccoli. Stir for about 1 minute and then add the tomatoes, parsley, basil, and the red and black pepper. Spray or rub an 8-by-8-inch pan with vegetable oil. Lay 5 noodles overlapping on the bottom of the pan. Spread half the vegetable mixture on top of the noodles. Spoon 1/2 cup of the cottage cheese over this. Next add another layer of noodles and the rest of the sauce. Mix the remaining cottage cheese with the grated mozzarella cheese and mix with pepper and garlic powder. Spread on top. Cover with aluminum foil and bake in a 350-degree oven for 1 to 1 1/4 hours or until noodles are tender. Serves 6.

Note: If you can afford the calories and sodium count, add a tablespoon of Parmesan cheese at the table.

Calories	296	Protein	15 g.
Fat	5 g.	Carbohydrate	50 g.
Saturated Fat	1 g.	Sodium	69 mg.
Cholesterol	5 mg.	Potassium	627 mg.

PASTA PRIMAVERA

1/2 lb. fresh linguine
2 tablespoons extra-virgin olive oil
2 tablespoons red wine vinegar
2 large tomatoes, chopped
1 bunch young arugula, coarsely chopped

Freshly ground pepper
2 cloves garlic, minced
1 small onion, chopped
3 scallions, sliced
$\frac{1}{2}$ lb. mushrooms, sliced
2 cups broccoli florets, steamed

Cook linguine in boiling water without salt until just tender. Drain. Immediately add 1 tablespoon olive oil and the vinegar, which have been pureed in blender or food processor with tomatoes and arugula. Toss with freshly ground pepper. In nonstick skillet heat the remaining olive oil and sauté garlic and onion until soft. Add scallions and mushrooms and continue cooking for about 5 minutes. Add steamed broccoli, heat through, and then pour vegetable mixture over pasta. Serves 4 to 5.

Calories	352	Protein	12 g.
Fat	9 g.	Carbohydrate	59 g.
Saturated Fat	1 g.	Sodium	37 mg.
Cholesterol	0 mg.	Potassium	761 mg.

ORZO WITH MUSHROOMS AND SUN-DRIED TOMATOES

Orzo is a pasta that looks like plump rice. It picks up flavors easily and should be embraced by anyone on a low-sodium diet.

$\frac{3}{4}$ cup orzo
3 quarts water
1 tablespoon extra-virgin olive oil
1 large chopped onion
3 cloves garlic, thinly sliced

½ lb. sliced mushrooms
¼ cup finely chopped sun-dried tomatoes,
    packed in oil
½ cup chopped fresh parsley
Freshly ground pepper

Cook orzo in rapidly boiling water until tender, about 10 minutes. Drain and reserve. Heat oil in non-stick skillet and sauté onion, garlic, and mushrooms until they are tender. Add sun-dried tomatoes, orzo, parsley, and pepper. Stir carefully and heat thoroughly. Serves 4.

For leftovers: Fill green peppers (with tops, mem-branes, and seeds removed) with orzo mixture. Place peppers in pan with ½ cup of water. Bake for 20 to 25 minutes.

Without green pepper:

Calories	268	Protein	8 g.
Fat	8 g.	Carbohydrate	43 g.
Saturated Fat	1 g.	Sodium	11 mg.
Cholesterol	0 mg.	Potassium	398 mg.

MISS BANGKOK NOODLES

This is a version of Thai-fried noodles, called street noodles because they are sold by vendors in the busiest sections of Bangkok or wherever the crowds gather all over Thailand. It's a far cry from the authentic dish, but it still tastes wonderful.

1 lb. Chinese or rice noodles
¼ teaspoon red pepper

¼ teaspoon black pepper

2 chicken breasts, sliced

1 tablespoon sesame oil

2 cloves garlic, crushed

1 tablespoon sugar

1 tablespoon low-sodium catsup

2 scallions, chopped

½ teaspoon low-sodium tamari sauce

½ cup unsalted peanuts, coarsely chopped

½ cup fresh cilantro, chopped

Bean sprouts

Additional chopped peanuts and scallions

Lemon slices

Cook noodles according to directions. Set aside. Rub red and black pepper into chicken. Heat oil and sauté chicken until cooked. Add garlic, sugar, catsup, scallions, and tamari sauce. With two forks, mix chicken and noodles. Then add peanuts and cilantro. Pile onto a large platter and surround with sprouts, chopped peanuts, scallions, and lemon slices. Serves 4.

Calories	516	Protein	16 g.
Fat	13 g.	Carbohydrate	84 g.
Saturated Fat	2 g.	Sodium	76 mg.
Cholesterol	33 mg.	Potassium	242 mg.

CHINESE NOODLES WITH PEANUT SAUCE

1 lb. Chinese-style noodles (or spaghetti)
1 tablespoon peanut oil
3 cloves garlic, minced
⅓ cup low-sodium peanut butter
⅓ cup low-sodium chicken broth
1 teaspoon low-sodium tamari or soy sauce
1 tablespoon sherry
1 tablespoon wine vinegar
2 teaspoons low-sodium chili sauce
1 teaspoon sugar
1 tablespoon toasted sesame seeds

Cook noodles or spaghetti according to package directions, without salt. Meanwhile combine the remaining ingredients by hand or in a blender or food processor. When noodles are cooked, drained, and still warm, toss with peanut sauce and sesame seeds. Serves 4 to 6.

Note: Chinese Noodles with Peanut Sauce is traditionally served with chopped raw vegetables such as green pepper, cucumber, bean sprouts, green onions, snow peas or radishes placed on the table in separate dishes.

Calories	561	Protein	5 g.
Fat	14 g.	Carbohydrate	104 g.
Saturated Fat	2 g.	Sodium	59 mg.
Cholesterol	tr	Potassium	176 mg.

Grains and Legumes

Grains and legumes are staples that really help the low-sodium cook serve meals that are tasty and healthy; they easily absorb a variety of flavors from the spices and herbs added to them, they contain beneficial amounts of fiber, and they are a surprisingly high protein source when served with rice. (Check our Salad section for additional grain and legume recipes.)

In Colonial times a family used to convey its hospitality to guests (and establish its status) by serving a great number of roasted meats at the table; on today's table, the once modest legume contributes a wealth all its own.

Please note that all nutritional information refers to 1 serving size.

BOB'S FAVORITE RICE

1 tablespoon extra-virgin olive oil
1 small onion, chopped
1 tablespoon pimentos, chopped
1 clove garlic, crushed
¼ teaspoon garlic powder
¼ teaspoon black pepper
1 cup white rice
2 cups low-sodium chicken broth

Heat oil in saucepan and sauté onion until it is soft. Add pimentos, garlic, garlic powder, pepper, and rice. Stir until rice is thoroughly coated. Add broth and bring to a boil. Reduce heat, cover, and simmer for about 25 minutes, or until rice is tender. Serves 4 to 5.

Calories	227	Protein	4 g.
Fat	4 g.	Carbohydrate	43 g.
Saturated Fat	1 g.	Sodium	7 mg.
Cholesterol	3 mg.	Potassium	329 mg.

OVEN-COOKED BROWN RICE WITH CUMIN

2 cups boiling water
1 cup brown rice
2 tablespoons lemon juice
1 tablespoon unsalted butter
2 teaspoons chopped parsley
⅛ teaspoon cumin

Mix ingredients and pour into greased casserole. Cover and bake 35 to 45 minutes in 350-degree oven. Serves 4.

Calories 213	Protein. . . . . 4 g.
Fat . . . . 3 g.	Carbohydrate . . . . . 41 g.
Saturated Fat. . . . . . . 2 g.	Sodium . . . . 7 mg.
Cholesterol. . . . . . . 8 mg.	Potassium . . . . . . 70 mg.

LEMON-PARSLEY RICE

¼ cup vegetable oil

3 tablespoons fresh parsley, minced

1 tablespoon lemon juice

Mix and pour over hot cooked rice. Serves 4.

Calories 291	Protein. . . . . 3 g.
Fat . . . . 14 g.	Carbohydrate . . . . . 38 g.
Saturated Fat. . . . . . . 2 g.	Sodium . . . . 7 mg.
Cholesterol. . . . . . . 0 mg.	Potassium . . . . . . 74 mg.

BROWN RICE PRIMAVERA

This is a colorful and fragrant dish for any time of year. It's best served at room temperature.

1 cup brown rice, cooked to package directions with 2 cups chicken broth

2 tablespoons red wine vinegar

4 tablespoons extra-virgin olive oil

Freshly ground pepper

1 tablespoon extra-virgin olive oil

1 large red onion, chopped

3 large cloves garlic, crushed

1 small zucchini, chopped

2 cups of broccoli florets
1 small red pepper, chopped
1 small green pepper, chopped
2 tablespoons minced fresh cilantro or to taste

Cook brown rice in chicken broth. Add vinegar, oil, and freshly ground pepper. Let stand at room temperature.

In nonstick frying pan heat olive oil and sauté onion until soft. Add garlic, zucchini, broccoli, and pepper and continue to sauté for 5 to 10 minutes or until vegetables are just tender. Carefully mix rice and vegetables, adding cilantro to taste. Add more ground pepper and garnish with 3 cilantro leaves. Serves 6.

Calories 247	Protein. . . . . 4 g.
Fat . . . . 12 g.	Carbohydrate . . . . . 32 g.
Saturated Fat. . . . . . . 2 g.	Sodium. . . . . 11 mg.
Cholesterol. . . . . . . 2 mg.	Potassium . . . . . 442 mg.

ORANGE-FLAVORED QUINOA

Good with duck, chicken, or pork dishes.

1 cup quinoa
1 cup water (cold)
1 cup orange juice
2 teaspoons grated orange rind
1 teaspoon unsalted butter

Combine quinoa, water, orange juice, orange rind, and butter in heavy 3-quart saucepan. Turn heat high until quinoa starts to boil. Stir once with fork. Reduce heat, cover, and simmer 12 to 14 minutes until liquid is absorbed. You may have to add a bit more orange juice if quinoa is not moist enough. Serves 4.

Calories 221	Protein. . . . . 4 g.
Fat . . . . 2 g.	Carbohydrate . . . . . 46 g.
Saturated Fat. . . . . . . 1 g.	Sodium . . . . 5 mg.
Cholesterol. . . . . . . 3 mg.	Potassium . . . . . 182 mg.

TOMATO AND BASIL RICE

1 cup rice

1 cup water (cold)

1 cup canned low-sodium tomato juice

1 tablespoon unsalted butter

2 teaspoons minced onion

½ teaspoon dried basil

Combine all ingredients in heavy 3-quart saucepan. Turn heat to high until rice starts to boil. Stir once with a fork. Reduce heat, cover, and simmer 12 to 14 minutes until liquid is absorbed. You may have to add a bit more tomato juice if rice is not moist enough. Serves 4.

Calories 222	Protein. . . . . 4 g.
Fat . . . . 3 g.	Carbohydrate . . . . . 43 g.
Saturated Fat. . . . . . . 2 g.	Sodium. . . . . 11 mg.
Cholesterol. . . . . . . 8 mg.	Potassium . . . . . 199 mg.

RISOTTO

Risotto is a delicious way to serve low-sodium rice. If your local supermarket does not carry Italian rice, your nearest specialty shop will or can order it. This is definitely worth whatever trouble is involved.

1 large onion, chopped

1½ teaspoons unsalted butter

1 tablespoon olive oil

1 cup Italian arborio rice

Freshly ground pepper

2 cups hot low-sodium chicken or beef broth, simmering

Grated low-sodium cheese to taste

Sauté onion in butter and oil until transparent. Add rice and ground pepper and sauté until grains are coated (2 to 3 minutes). Now add ½ cup of hot broth. Stir mixture over medium to medium-high heat until liquid is absorbed. (You must pay close attention to the rice during this process.) Then add another ½ cup of broth, stirring again until the liquid is absorbed. Repeat these steps until all the liquid is absorbed and the rice is tender. Expect this process to take about 30 minutes. Serve with a bowl of freshly grated cheese. Parmesan is traditional and best, if you can spare the sodium content. Serves 4.

Variations: This recipe is extremely receptive to experimentation. Midway during cooking you may add sautéed fresh or rehydrated dried chopped mushrooms, sun-dried tomatoes, currants, nuts, or herbs and spices such as oregano, basil, cumin, or saffron.

Calories	256	Protein	6 g.
Fat	6 g.	Carbohydrate	43 g.
Saturated Fat	2 g.	Sodium	19 mg.
Cholesterol	10 mg.	Potassium	341 mg.

SPICY BAKED BEANS

2 cups pea beans
1 bay leaf
$^1/_2$ cup white sugar
2 tablespoons brown sugar
$^3/_4$ cup chopped onion
2 teaspoons dry mustard
1 teaspoon low-sodium prepared mustard
2 teaspoons Worcestershire sauce
2 cups canned low-sodium tomatoes
$^1/_4$ teaspoon pepper
$^1/_4$ cup unsalted butter

Cook beans according to directions on package without salt but with a bay leaf. Drain, reserving bean water. Combine sugars, onion, mustards, Worcestershire sauce, tomatoes, and pepper. Add $1^1/_2$ cups of bean water. Pour into greased covered casserole. Dot with butter. Bake 6 to 8 hours in 250-degree oven. Add more water if beans become dry. Uncover for last hour of cooking. Serves 8.

Calories	286	Protein	11 g.
Fat	7 g.	Carbohydrate	47 g.
Saturated Fat	4 g.	Sodium	20 mg.
Cholesterol	16 mg.	Potassium	720 mg.

WHITE BEANS WITH KALE

Celery and kale have more sodium than most vegetables, but when combined with beans, which have virtually no sodium, the serving amounts are balanced.

1 lb. white beans
1 tablespoon extra-virgin olive oil
2 medium onions, chopped
1 carrot, sliced
1 stalk celery, sliced
3 to 4 garlic cloves, pressed
1 16-oz. can low-sodium tomatoes
3 to 4 cups low-sodium chicken broth
1 teaspoon ground cloves
2 crumbled bay leaves
Freshly ground pepper
1 to 2 cups fresh kale, chopped

Soak beans overnight or cover with boiling water and let sit for 4 hours. Rinse. In nonstick frying pan heat olive oil. Sauté onions, carrot, and celery until soft. In large pot mix beans, vegetables, garlic, tomatoes, chicken broth, cloves, bay leaves, and pepper. Simmer covered 2 to 3 hours or until tender. For the last $1/2$ hour add the chopped kale. Serves 8.

Calories	240	Protein	13 g.
Fat	3 g.	Carbohydrate	43 g.
Saturated Fat	1 g.	Sodium	27 mg.
Cholesterol	2 mg.	Potassium	945 mg.

BLACK BEANS WITH CILANTRO

Fresh cilantro, a great enhancer of low-sodium recipes, is available today in most supermarkets.

1 lb. bag of black beans
2 tablespoons olive oil
1 onion, chopped
1 large green pepper, chopped
4 to 6 garlic cloves, pressed
4 cups low-sodium chicken broth
1 tablespoon cumin
2 teaspoons cinnamon
2 tablespoons fresh, chopped cilantro

Soak beans in water overnight. Drain and rinse. Heat oil and sauté onion and peppers until soft. Add onions, peppers, and beans to large saucepan along with garlic, chicken broth, cumin, and cinnamon. Simmer for 2 to 3 hours until tender. Add chopped cilantro before serving. Serves 8.

Calories	221	Protein	12 g.
Fat	4 g.	Carbohydrate	35 g.
Saturated Fat	1 g.	Sodium	8 mg.
Cholesterol	3 mg.	Potassium	855 mg.

HOPPING JOHN

Northerners, as well, serve this traditional Southern dish on New Year's Day to bring good luck.

2 cups black-eyed peas, soaked overnight
      and drained
6 to 8 cups low-sodium beef broth
2 bay leaves
1 whole onion, stuck with 2 cloves
Freshly ground pepper
1½ cups uncooked rice
1 tablespoon unsalted butter
2 chopped onions
5 cloves garlic, sliced
1 chopped green pepper
1 teaspoon ground cloves
½ cup nonfat plain yogurt
2 cans stewed tomatoes, no salt added
1 teaspoon cayenne pepper
Optional: hot pepper sauce to taste

Combine black-eyed peas and broth in large saucepan. Add bay leaves, onion, and pepper. Cook black-eyed peas until tender, adding more broth if necessary. Drain peas and reserve about 3 cups of the liquid to use for cooking rice, according to package directions. While rice is cooking, melt butter in nonstick skillet and sauté onions, garlic, and green pepper until soft. Add drained black-eyed peas, pepper, and cloves. Gently mix in yogurt and heat through, without bringing to a boil. Heat stewed tomatoes separately and add cayenne pepper. Serve stewed tomatoes and rice on the side. Serves 4 to 6.

Calories	638	Protein	26 g.
Fat	6 g.	Carbohydrate	124 g.
Saturated Fat	2 g.	Sodium	76 mg.
Cholesterol	18 mg.	Potassium	2,251 mg.

Fish

If your town is blessed with a good fish market, shop there regularly. Fish wasn't meant to be shrink-wrapped or frozen, but to sit on a bed of chipped ice as soon after the catch as possible. Freshness is all, and more and more supermarkets are realizing this truth. It's very easy to detect freshness in fish: fresh fish will not smell fishy. Air freight has worked wonders, of course, but lobster still tastes best in Maine and Coho salmon in Seattle. Good fish demands very little help from the cook, especially when it's grilled or broiled. Lemon or lime juice, ground pepper, a judicious amount of sweet butter, fresh-clipped herbs, and a careful eye to avoid overcooking are the basics. Seek out a good fishmonger and don't be afraid to ask for guidance.

Please note that all nutritional information refers to 1 serving size.

FRESH FLOUNDER IN SHERRY

Sometimes brine is used in the washing and freezing of fish fillets. Be sure the fillets are cut from fresh whole fish.

1 lb. flounder fillets, cut into serving pieces
¹⁄₃ cup minced onions
¹⁄₂ cup sherry wine
8 medium mushrooms, chopped fine
¹⁄₄ cup water
Black pepper to taste

Place fish fillets in shallow greased baking dish. Sprinkle with onion, and add sherry, mushrooms, and water. Season with pepper. Bake in 325-degree oven until fish is tender. Serves 4.

Calories	153	Protein	22 g.
Fat	1 g.	Carbohydrate	5 g.
Saturated Fat	tr	Sodium	92 mg.
Cholesterol	58 mg.	Potassium	468 mg.

FILLETS OF FLOUNDER WITH DILL

2 lbs. fillets of flounder or other white fish
1 cup nonfat plain yogurt
3 tablespoons low-sodium mayonnaise
1 tablespoon white wine
1 tablespoon lemon juice
1 teaspoon snipped fresh dill
¹⁄₂ teaspoon curry powder

Arrange fillets in shallow oiled baking dish. Mix other ingredients and pour over all. Bake at 350 degrees for 35 minutes. You may add sautéed mushrooms and white grapes. Six servings.

Calories	175	Protein	23 g.
Fat	7 g.	Carbohydrate	3 g.
Saturated Fat	1 g.	Sodium	146 mg.
Cholesterol	60 mg.	Potassium	402 mg.

FILET OF SOLE WITH ORANGE JUICE

Granddaughter Melissa adapted this recipe from *The Silver Palate Cookbook.*

¾ cup orange juice
¾ cup white wine
1 lb. filets of sole
Freshly ground pepper
2 tablespoons Cointreau or cognac
2 teaspoons grated orange peel
1 tablespoon unsalted butter
2 leeks, white part only, sliced lengthwise
1 cup julienne carrots
1 cup julienne green beans
1 tablespoon fresh dill, chopped

In skillet combine orange juice and wine. Sprinkle the fish with pepper and poach for about 5 to 7 minutes or until done. Remove fish and keep warm. Add Cointreau or cognac and orange peel to poaching liquid and reduce by ¹/₂. Meanwhile, in a separate nonstick skillet melt butter and sauté leeks, carrots, and beans for about 5 minutes or until just tender. Place fish on platter, surround by vegetables, and pour sauce over individual filets. Chop fresh dill over all. Serves 4.

Calories 218	Protein. . . . . 22 g.
Fat . . . . 4 g.	Carbohydrate . . . . . 14 g.
Saturated Fat. . . . . . . 2 g.	Sodium. . . . . 107 mg.
Cholesterol. . . . . . 65 mg.	Potassium . . . . . 642 mg.

HADDOCK WITH WHITE WINE

2 lbs. haddock

¼ cup lemon juice

Pepper to taste

½ cup olive or vegetable oil

6 medium onions, sliced

2 garlic cloves, sliced

½ cup parsley, chopped

3 tomatoes, peeled, seeded, and sliced

¼ cup dry white wine, cider, or water

2 lemons, sliced

3 more tomatoes, sliced

Sprinkle fish with lemon juice and pepper. In a non-stick skillet heat oil and add onions, garlic, and parsley. Cook until onions are transparent. Add tomatoes and simmer 5 minutes. Add wine and cook 5 minutes longer. Place half the onion and tomato mixture in greased baking dish. Add fish, and cover with remaining mixture. Arrange lemon slices and the tomato slices over top and bake at 350 degrees until fish flakes—around 30 minutes. Serves 6.

Calories 343	Protein........... 24 g.
Fat .... 20 g.	Carbohydrate ..... 21 g.
Saturated Fat....... 3 g.	Sodium......... 92 mg.
Cholesterol...... 63 mg.	Potassium ..... 896 mg.

BROILED FRESH HADDOCK WITH LEMON SAUCE

2 lbs. fresh haddock

3 tablespoons lemon juice

Pepper to taste

1 tablespoon unsalted butter

1/4 cup olive or vegetable oil

1/2 teaspoon dry mustard

1 1/2 teaspoons water

Preheat the broiler. Cut the fish in serving pieces and place on oiled pan. Brush with one tablespoon of the lemon juice and season with pepper. Dot with butter, broil 7 to 10 minutes. While fish is cooking, combine the oil, mustard, water, and remaining lemon juice. Blend well. Heat and pour over fish. Serves 6.

Calories 195	Protein........... 21 g.
Fat .... 12 g.	Carbohydrate ...... 1 g.
Saturated Fat....... 3 g.	Sodium......... 74 mg.
Cholesterol...... 68 mg.	Potassium ..... 352 mg.

GRILLED TUNA WITH SALSA

1 lb. tuna steaks

Juice of 1 lime

1 clove garlic, chopped

Ground pepper

2 tablespoons olive oil

Salsa (see page 88)

Marinate tuna in lime juice, garlic, and pepper for 2 hours. Brush with olive oil and grill about 5 minutes on each side or until done. Serve with tomato or mango salsa. Serves 4.

Calories	226	Protein	27 g.
Fat	12 g.	Carbohydrate	1 g.
Saturated Fat	2 g.	Sodium	44 mg.
Cholesterol	43 mg.	Potassium	299 mg.

BLUEFISH WITH GINGER

This recipe was inspired by *Blues*, John Hersey's book on bluefish.

1 lb. bluefish

1 to 2 teaspoons grated fresh ginger

1 garlic clove, minced

Freshly ground pepper

2 teaspoons grated lemon peel

3 tablespoons low-sodium mayonnaise

Preheat oven to 400 degrees. Lay fish in lightly oiled baking pan. Rub ginger, garlic, pepper, and lemon peel into flesh of fish. Cover with mayonnaise. Bake fish in oven for about 20 minutes, or until done. Serves 4.

Calories	186	Protein	17 g.
Fat	13 g.	Carbohydrate	1 g.
Saturated Fat	2 g.	Sodium	93 mg.
Cholesterol	53 mg.	Potassium	331 mg.

RED SNAPPER MARGARITA

Michael Janeway says the secret to his recipe is tequila. "It's what gives it that bite."

4 fillets of red snapper

¼ cup extra-virgin olive oil

¼ cup tequila

1 teaspoon low-sodium tamari or soy sauce

4 cloves garlic, minced

1 to 3 tablespoons finely chopped ginger

**1 tablespoon grated lime zest (or grated zest from
    2 whole limes)**

1 tablespoon scallions or shallots, chopped

¼ teaspoon cayenne pepper

1 tablespoon chopped fresh basil

Mix all ingredients and pour over fish. Let marinate for at least 3 hours in the refrigerator. Grill skin side down for 5 minutes inside fish grill. Flip and grill for 5 minutes on the other side or until done. Serves 4.

Calories	190	Protein	23 g.
Fat	8 g.	Carbohydrate	1 g.
Saturated Fat	1 g.	Sodium	71 mg.
Cholesterol	40 mg.	Potassium	467 mg.

BROILED SWORDFISH

This recipe comes from Italy, and it is a real favorite of ours. Swordfish should be moist, and this surely is.

Juice of 2 lemons
1 teaspoon fresh mint or ¹/₂ teaspoon dried mint, chopped
¹/₄ cup olive oil
2 teaspoons oregano
Pepper to taste
2 lbs. swordfish (fresh or frozen)

Blend well lemon juice, mint, oil, oregano, and pepper. Brush fish with approximately ¹/₃ of the mixture. Place on preheated broiler rack about 4 inches below flame. Broil 5 minutes or until slightly brown, turn, brush again with mixture. Broil about 7 minutes or until done. Brush again with mixture before serving. Serve hot. Serves 6.

Calories	217	Protein	22 g.
Fat	13 g.	Carbohydrate	2 g.
Saturated Fat	2 g.	Sodium	98 mg.
Cholesterol	43 mg.	Potassium	342 mg.

BROILED FRESH SALMON STEAKS

The ancient Romans marching across France gave the salmon its name. They named this historic fish *salmo,* the leaper, in admiration for its strength and agility.

4 salmon steaks
4 tablespoons lime juice

1 tablespoon unsalted butter

Pepper to taste

4 teaspoons tarragon

$1/2$ cup dry white wine or dry vermouth

Place salmon in shallow baking pan. Sprinkle with half the lime juice and dot with butter. Season with pepper and half the tarragon. Pour wine or vermouth around but not over steaks. Broil for 10 to 15 minutes, basting twice the last 5 minutes. Turn salmon, season with remaining ingredients, and broil 5 minutes longer. Baste twice more. Serve with sauce poured over fish. Serves 4.

Calories	238	Protein	24 g.
Fat	12 g.	Carbohydrate	3 g.
Saturated Fat	3 g.	Sodium	59 mg.
Cholesterol	82 mg.	Potassium	409 mg.

SAUTÉED SALMON STEAKS

2 lbs. salmon steaks

2 tablespoons dry mustard mixed with enough water to make paste

$1/4$ cup unsalted butter

$1/4$ cup apple cider or juice (if not cider season)

Spread salmon steaks with mustard. Melt butter in skillet. Add cider or apple juice. Poach steaks 5 minutes on each side or until done. Cider is excellent in the cooking of any fish. Serves 6.

Calories	194	Protein	24 g.
Fat	9 g.	Carbohydrate	2 g.
Saturated Fat	2 g.	Sodium	51 mg.
Cholesterol	47 mg.	Potassium	490 mg.

FISH STEW WITH LEMONGRASS

The small amounts of shrimp and scallops in this recipe should not add too significantly to your sodium count. Lemongrass is available in gourmet shops and some supermarkets and imparts a subtle lemony flavor to this dish.

$\frac{1}{4}$ lb. shrimp, shelled and rinsed

$\frac{1}{4}$ lb. scallops

Juice of one lime

Cayenne pepper or no-salt Cajun seasoning, to taste

2 chopped onions

5 cloves garlic, finely sliced

1 tablespoon extra-virgin olive oil

1 28-oz. can crushed tomatoes, no salt added

$\frac{1}{2}$ cup white wine

1 lb. white fish in season, sliced in chunks

4 to 5 sticks dried lemongrass

1 tablespoon chopped fresh tarragon or 1 teaspoon dried

$\frac{1}{2}$ cup chopped fresh parsley

Freshly ground pepper to taste

2 tablespoons lemon juice

Sprinkle shrimp and scallops with lime juice. Rub cayenne pepper or Cajun seasoning into shrimp. Let sit for a few minutes. In a nonstick skillet sauté onions and garlic in olive oil until they are soft. Add tomatoes and heat thoroughly. Add wine and bring to a simmer. Then add the white fish. Cook for about 5 minutes and add shrimp, scallop, and cayenne pepper mixture, and lemongrass. Stir carefully and watch the shrimp. Do not overcook. Shrimp are done when just pink. Right before serving add tarragon, parsley, and pepper. Stir in lemon juice. Serve at once with rice. Serves 5.

> Note: If you wish to omit the scallops and shrimp, simply add the lime juice and flavoring to the white fish before cooking.

Calories	244	Protein	29 g.
Fat	5 g.	Carbohydrate	17 g.
Saturated Fat	1 g.	Sodium	175 mg.
Cholesterol	88 mg.	Potassium	933 mg.

BAKED OYSTERS

A craving for oysters may be indulged occasionally if your doctor says so, but watch out for the number you serve. Each oyster has approximately 10 milligrams sodium. Taking the scientific route, you could use 5 oysters per serving, which keeps the sodium content well within the allowed serving of a piece of meat. Oysters cheered Ted more than any other food, and that was good medicine, too.

For each serving:

5 oysters

2 teaspoons unsalted butter

1 teaspoon chopped parsley

Freshly ground black pepper to taste

Remove oysters from shells and drain them. Place each oyster back on the half shell with a tiny piece of un-salted butter on top. Place in baking pan, sprinkle with parsley and pepper, bake in 400-degree oven for 6 to 8 minutes. Serves 1.

Sauce

1 tablespoon unsalted butter

Juice of one lemon

2 teaspoons grated onion

¼ teaspoon tarragon vinegar

⅛ teaspoon dry mustard

Melt the butter, stir in the other ingredients, and pour over oysters. Serve hot. Serves 1.

Baked oysters

Calories	122	Protein	5 g.
Fat	10 g.	Carbohydrate	3 g.
Saturated Fat	6 g.	Sodium	81 mg.
Cholesterol	61 mg.	Potassium	174 mg.

Sauce

Calories	118	Protein	1 g.
Fat	12 g.	Carbohydrate	5 g.
Saturated Fat	7 g.	Sodium	2 mg.
Cholesterol	31 mg.	Potassium	73 mg.

SHRIMP SALAD

---

12 low-sodium canned shrimp, cut up

1 tablespoon dry white wine

1 teaspoon chopped parsley

1 teaspoon lemon juice

1 tablespoon low-sodium mayonnaise

Soak shrimp in wine for $1/2$ hour. Remove shrimp and mix with other ingredients. Serve on lettuce leaves. Serves 1.

Calories	29	Protein	3 g.
Fat	1 g.	Carbohydrate	2 g.
Saturated Fat	0 g.	Sodium	83 mg.
Cholesterol	21 mg.	Potassium	96 mg.

Meats

There are three ingredients that enhance the natural flavor of meat and recur in our favorite recipes—lemon juice, garlic, and freshly ground pepper. Use them to taste, and don't be afraid of the garlic.

Searing meat—quickly browning it in oil in a skillet—before baking or roasting it slowly, is a technique that keeps it tender, juicy, and tasty. Grilling has a similar effect, especially if you can lower the heat of your grill after the initial browning. When prepared by these simple methods, top-quality cuts of meat—like fillet of beef and pork tenderloin—offer delicate taste and a delectable texture. For more ordinary cuts of meat, make sure you think about taste before cooking. Marinating, experimenting with rubs, basting, and stewing in herbed and spiced liquids are good ways to add needed flavor.

Please note that all nutritional information refers to one serving size.

TRADITIONAL MEAT LOAF

1½ lbs. ground lean beef (You may substitute ½ lb.
    ground turkey for ½ lb. ground beef.)
1 medium onion, chopped fine
½ cup wheat germ or low-sodium bread crumbs
1 cup canned low-sodium stewed tomatoes
1 egg
2 teaspoons chopped parsley
1 tablespoon olive oil or vegetable oil
1 teaspoon basil
1 teaspoon oregano
1 teaspoon sugar
⅛ teaspoon garlic powder
¼ teaspoon allspice
¼ teaspoon pepper
1 tablespoon chopped green pepper

In a large bowl mix all ingredients thoroughly. Form in
an oval loaf and bake for 1 hour at 350 degrees. Serves 6.
Variation: Instead of bread crumbs or wheat germ,
substitute oatmeal.

Calories 306	Protein. . . . . 24 g.
Fat . . . . 19 g.	Carbohydrate . . . . . 10 g.
Saturated Fat. . . . . . . 7 g.	Sodium. . . . . 80 mg.
Cholesterol. . . . . 105 mg.	Potassium . . . . . 477 mg.

APPLESAUCE MEAT LOAF

The herb allspice is redolent with the flavors of cloves, cinnamon, and nutmeg; it actually comes from the small fruit of an evergreen in the myrtle family.

1½ lbs. ground lean beef (You may substitute ¾ lb. ground turkey for ¾ lb. ground beef.)

1 egg, beaten

2 tablespoons chopped onion

1 teaspoon allspice

1 cup applesauce

Combine all ingredients. Pack into a greased loaf pan.

Topping

1 apple, pared, cored, and cut in rings

¼ cup brown sugar

⅛ teaspoon cloves

1 tablespoon water

1 teaspoon mustard

Press apple rings on top of loaf. Mix sugar, cloves, water, and mustard and pour on top. Bake at 350 degrees for 1 hour and 15 minutes. Serves 8.

Calories	224	Protein	16 g.
Fat	12 g.	Carbohydrate	13 g.
Saturated Fat	5 g.	Sodium	58 mg.
Cholesterol	79 mg.	Potassium	261 mg.

HERBED HAMBURGERS

2 lbs. ground lean beef
1 tablespoon olive oil or unsalted butter
½ cup finely chopped onion
½ teaspoon garlic powder or 1 clove minced
    garlic
1 tablespoon chopped fresh parsley
¼ teaspoon marjoram
¼ teaspoon basil
2 tablespoons lemon juice
2 teaspoons cold water

Mix all ingredients and make patties. Broil, grill, or pan-fry. A chopped tomato may be added to mixture. Makes 10 hamburgers.

Calories 192	Protein . . . . 15 g.
Fat . . . . 13 g.	Carbohydrate . . . . . . 1 g.
Saturated Fat . . . . 5 g.	Sodium . . . . 50 mg.
Cholesterol . . . . . . 56 mg.	Potassium . . . . . 215 mg.

OLD-FASHIONED BEEF POT ROAST

1 tablespoon flour
¼ teaspoon ground pepper
½ teaspoon allspice
3 lbs. lean beef
1½ tablespoons vegetable oil
1 pint boiling water or low-sodium stock
2 onions
2 cloves

Mix the flour with pepper and allspice and dredge meat with the mixture. Melt the oil in a heavy pan. Brown meat on all sides, then add the boiling water or stock, onions, and cloves. Cover and allow to simmer for about 3 hours or until meat is tender. One half hour before meat is finished, potatoes may be added. Serves 6.

Variation: Substitute 1^1/$_2$ cups prune juice for water or stock and add 8 whole prunes and 4 whole cloves to pot, then simmer.

Variation Two: Substitute 1 cup Burgundy for water and 1 small can low-sodium tomatoes, 1 carrot, and ^{1}/$_2$ teaspoon basil to pot then simmer.

Calories	397	Protein	19 g.
Fat	33 g.	Carbohydrate	4 g.
Saturated Fat	13 g.	Sodium	59 mg.
Cholesterol	78 mg.	Potassium	251 mg.

STEAK AU POIVRE WITH COGNAC

Filet mignon and rib eye are the best cuts for this recipe.

1 lb. boneless steak
Freshly ground pepper
Oil for grill pan
2 tablespoons cognac

Rub steak thickly with fresh pepper. Wipe ridged pan with oil and grill until done to your taste. Just before serving, spoon cognac over meat and let it heat through. Serves 4.

Calories	204	Protein	24 g.
Fat	10 g.	Carbohydrate	tr

Saturated Fat....... 4 g.		Sodium........ 59 mg.	
Cholesterol...... 68 mg.		Potassium ..... 337 mg.	

GRILLED STEAK SALAD

The warm olive oil and fresh basil combine with the garlic to make a heavenly flavor.

1 large head of Boston lettuce
1 ripe tomato, cut in ½-inch wedges
3 tablespoons extra-virgin olive oil
5 cloves garlic, sliced
¼ cup fresh basil, chopped
1 tablespoon balsamic vinegar
¾ lb. flank steak
Freshly ground pepper
¼ teaspoon garlic powder
1 Bermuda onion, sliced
Basil leaves

Put prepared lettuce in bowl and add tomato. Heat 1 tablespoon of olive oil and sauté garlic. When garlic is soft, remove pan from heat, cool slightly, and stir in basil. After it has wilted add remaining oil and the vinegar. Whisk thoroughly. Use this dressing while it's warm to toss salad after steak is cooked and sliced. Rub flank steak with pepper and garlic powder and grill or broil until done to your taste. Cut in thin slices on the diagonal. Lay strips over freshly tossed salad and garnish with onion slices and basil leaves. Serves 4.

Calories 288		Protein........... 28 g.	
Fat .... 16 g.		Carbohydrate ...... 8 g.	

Saturated Fat. . . . . . . 3 g.	Sodium. . . . . 61 mg.
Cholesterol. . . . . . 71 mg.	Potassium . . . . . 630 mg.

BEEF BURGUNDY

---

3 lbs. lean round steak cut in ½-inch chunks

3 tablespoons flour

¼ teaspoon pepper

1 tablespoon unsalted butter

2 medium onions, chopped fine

½ cup leeks or scallions, chopped coarse

½ cup carrots, sliced

1 tablespoon fresh parsley, chopped

1 tablespoon chives, minced

1 clove garlic, crushed

1 tablespoon olive oil

2 tablespoons cognac

1½ cups Burgundy wine

Dredge meat in flour and pepper. In a nonstick skillet sauté in hot butter until very brown. Transfer meat, drained, to casserole. Add vegetables, garlic, and olive oil to remaining fat in skillet, brown lightly, stirring constantly. Flame cognac in a soup ladle and pour over beef. Add seasonings and vegetables. Pour over enough wine to cover the casserole. Bake at 350 degrees for 3 hours. Serve with parsley potatoes or butter noodles. Serves 8.

Calories 437	Protein. . . . . 19 g.
Fat . . . . 31 g.	Carbohydrate . . . . . . 9 g.
Saturated Fat. . . . . 13 g.	Sodium. . . . . 64 mg.
Cholesterol. . . . . . 78 mg.	Potassium . . . . . 339 mg.

ESTOUFFADE OF BEEF

$1/2$ lb. pea beans
1 bay leaf
$1/2$ teaspoon cumin
2 lbs. round steak, cut in 6 pieces
1 tablespoon unsalted butter
2 cups red wine
4 tomatoes, finely chopped
2 onions, finely chopped
2 carrots, finely chopped
2 cloves garlic
Pepper to taste
$1/2$ teaspoon thyme
$1/2$ teaspoon marjoram
2 tablespoons cornstarch

Cook beans with bay leaf and cumin according to directions on package but without salt. In a heavy pot, brown beef in butter. Add wine, vegetables, garlic, and seasonings. Cover and simmer for 2 to $2^1/2$ hours or until tender. You might want to add a little more wine. Place beef over beans on platter. Strain liquid into a saucepan, thicken, with cornstarch mixed with a little water, over low heat. Pour over beef. Serves 6.

Calories	577	Protein	27 g.
Fat	32 g.	Carbohydrate	32 g.
Saturated Fat	14 g.	Sodium	83 mg.
Cholesterol	83 mg.	Potassium	958 mg.

CHILI

1 lb. dried kidney beans
1 cup chopped onion
1 tablespoon parsley, chopped
1 teaspoon cumin
1 tablespoon fennel, chopped
Pepper to taste
1 cup canned low-sodium tomatoes
2 cloves garlic, minced
1 teaspoon dried basil or 1 tablespoon fresh
2 tablespoons rum
1 lb. ground lean beef, sautéed

Wash beans and let them soak overnight. Drain. Put beans in heavy kettle, cover with water, add onion, parsley, cumin, fennel, and pepper. Simmer 1¹/₂ hours. Drain, if necessary. Put in bean pot with tomatoes, garlic, basil, rum, and sautéed beef. Bake 1 hour in 300-degree oven. This is good served with a little dab of sour cream. Serves 6.

Calories 407	Protein 30 g.
Fat 11 g.	Carbohydrate 46 g.
Saturated Fat 4 g.	Sodium 52 mg.
Cholesterol 47 mg.	Potassium 1,033 mg.

SAUERBRATEN

2 cups vinegar
2 cups water or low-sodium beef broth
3 bay leaves
10 peppercorns

8 whole cloves

1 medium onion, sliced

4 lbs. beef pot roast

2 tablespoons flour

2 tablespoons vegetable oil

Combine vinegar, water, bay leaves, peppercorns, cloves, and onion. Bring to boil. Place meat in bowl. Pour hot mixture over meat.

Cover and marinate in refrigerator for 2 days. Turn occasionally. Remove meat, drain, and rub with flour. Brown on all sides in hot oil. Add marinade. Place in iron pot or ovenproof casserole. Cover and bring to boil. Then reduce heat and simmer 2 to 3 hours. Serves 8.

Calories	273	Protein	27 g.
Fat	16 g.	Carbohydrate	7 g.
Saturated Fat	6 g.	Sodium	64 mg.
Cholesterol	90 mg.	Potassium	311 mg.

ROAST LEG OF LAMB

Leg of lamb (4 to 5 lbs.)

1 clove garlic, thinly sliced

Juice of 1 lemon

1 teaspoon flour

Freshly ground black pepper to taste

Insert thin slices of garlic under skin of lamb on each side, and rub with lemon juice. Dredge with flour and season with freshly ground black pepper. Place the meat skin side down in a roasting pan. Serve with Pineapple Sauce. Serves 6.

Calories 163	Protein. . . . . 24 g.
Fat . . . . 7 g.	Carbohydrate . . . . . . 0 g.
Saturated Fat. . . . . . . 2 g.	Sodium. . . . . 58 mg.
Cholesterol. . . . . 76 mg.	Potassium . . . . . 287 mg.

Pineapple Sauce

³/₄ cup crushed canned pineapple

¹/₂ cup pineapple juice

¹/₄ cup sugar

¹/₄ teaspoon allspice

¹/₄ teaspoon prepared mustard

³/₄ cup water

2 tablespoons fresh mint

Place the pineapple, pineapple juice, sugar, allspice, mustard, and water in a saucepan and cook about 10 minutes over a slow fire until the sauce thickens. Cool and add mint. Chill before serving. Makes about 2 cups.

Calories 352	Protein. . . . . 1 g.
Fat . . . . tr	Carbohydrate . . . . . 91 g.
Saturated Fat . . . . tr	Sodium. . . . . 26 mg.
Cholesterol. . . . . . . 0 mg.	Potassium . . . . . 377 mg.

ROAST LAMB FIBONACCI

This dish is named for the Italian mathematician who discovered a numerical sequence, 0, 1, 1, 2, 3, 5, 8, 13, etc., that appears everywhere in nature and art. The number of garlic cloves in this recipe takes our example of the sequence one step further.

8 cloves garlic, peeled and slivered

Leg of lamb (5 to 7 lbs.)

2 teaspoons crumbled rosemary leaves

1 teaspoon thyme

Freshly ground pepper

2 teaspoons low-sodium mustard

2 tablespoons extra-virgin olive oil

21 unpeeled, whole garlic cloves

1 tablespoon flour

$1/2$ to $3/4$ cup water

Preheat oven to 350 degrees. Insert slivers of garlic all over lamb. Sprinkle with rosemary (make sure you crumble it in your fingers), thyme, and ground pepper. Spread mustard over entire lamb and then rub with 1 tablespoon of olive oil. In large roasting pan sauté the 21 garlic cloves in 1 tablespoon of olive oil on low heat for about 5 minutes. Spread the cloves evenly over the pan and lay the leg of lamb on top. Cover with aluminum foil and roast for 1 hour. Uncover and continue to roast until lamb is done to taste (about 18 minutes to the pound.) Pour off the fat. Add 1 tablespoon flour and blend in thoroughly. Then mix in water and heat until thickened. Serve gravy in a separate dish. Serves 10.

Calories	261	Protein	22 g.
Fat	17 g.	Carbohydrate	4 g.
Saturated Fat	6 g.	Sodium	58 mg.
Cholesterol	79 mg.	Potassium	307 mg.

LAMB SHISH KEBAB

Bamboo skewers are widely available. Just soak them in water for several hours before threading on the meat and vegetables.

Juice of 1 lemon
2 large cloves garlic, crushed
1 teaspoon ground ginger
1 teaspoon freshly grated ginger
¼ teaspoon ground pepper
½ teaspoon low-sodium tamari or soy sauce
¾ lb. lamb, cut in 1½-inch cubes
1 tablespoon extra-virgin olive oil
1 large onion, cut in 8 pieces
1 green pepper, cut in chunks
1 small zucchini, cut in chunks

Make a marinade by combining lemon juice, garlic, ginger, pepper, and tamari. Pour over lamb and let marinate in refrigerator for about 2 hours or overnight. Before making the kebabs, rub olive oil over meat. Thread skewers alternating vegetables and lamb, spooning extra marinade over all. Barbecue over hot coals or broil, turning frequently, until done. Makes 4 kebabs.

Calories 224		Protein . . . . 25 g.	
Fat . . . . 10 g.		Carbohydrate . . . . . . 8 g.	
Saturated Fat . . . . 3 g.		Sodium . . . . 72 mg.	
Cholesterol . . . . . . 76 mg.		Potassium . . . . . 476 mg.	

CURRY OF LAMB

1½ lbs. lean lamb, cut in 1-inch cubes
1 tablespoon flour
⅛ teaspoon pepper
1 tablespoon unsalted butter
1½ cups hot water or low-sodium beef broth
2 tablespoons curry powder
1 teaspoon sugar
1 cup orange juice

Dredge lamb in flour and pepper. Heat butter and brown meat. Add water or broth and cook 1½ hours. Combine flour and pepper mixture, curry, and sugar; mix to smooth paste with orange juice in a small bowl. Add to lamb, stirring constantly. Cook until thickened. Serves 6.

Calories 225	Protein. . . . . 25 g.
Fat . . . . 10 g.	Carbohydrate . . . . . . 7 g.
Saturated Fat. . . . . . . 4 g.	Sodium. . . . . 67 mg.
Cholesterol. . . . . . 83 mg.	Potassium . . . . . 390 mg.

MOROCCAN LAMB

1 tablespoon olive oil
1 teaspoon unsalted butter
1½ lbs. lean lamb, cut in 1-inch cubes
2 chopped onions
5 cloves garlic, minced
1 tablespoon flour
1 28-oz. can crushed tomatoes, no salt added
1 cup low-sodium chicken broth

1 teaspoon cumin

1 tablespoon chopped fresh cilantro

1 teaspoon cinnamon

1/2 teaspoon cardamom

1/2 teaspoon cayenne pepper

Freshly ground pepper

1/2 cup raisins

In a large, flameproof casserole heat oil and butter and sauté lamb until it is nicely browned. Remove from heat and, in remaining fat, sauté onions and garlic until they are soft. Add lamb, stir in flour, and blend well. Add tomatoes and remaining ingredients, except for raisins and pepper. Simmer on the stove, covered, for 1 1/2 to 2 hours, or until tender. Add freshly ground pepper and raisins. Serve with couscous. Serves 5 to 6.

Calories	315	Protein	27 g.
Fat	12 g.	Carbohydrate	26 g.
Saturated Fat	4 g.	Sodium	90 mg.
Cholesterol	81 mg.	Potassium	945 mg.

EGGPLANT STUFFED WITH LAMB

1 large eggplant

1 cup chopped onions

1 cup chopped fresh mushrooms

1 1/4 teaspoons basil

1/2 teaspoon oregano

1/4 teaspoon pepper

2 tablespoons unsalted butter

1 lb. ground lamb

4 tablespoons canned low-sodium tomato paste

$^1\!/_4$ to $^1\!/_2$ cup low-sodium dry bread crumbs or
  wheat germ

1 tablespoon fresh parsley, chopped

1 tablespoon fresh mint, chopped

Wash eggplant, wrap it in aluminum foil, and bake 50 minutes. Cut in half, remove pulp to within $^1\!/_2$ inch of the outer skin, and mash pulp. Sauté onions, mushrooms, and seasonings in the butter and add to eggplant pulp. Add the meat, tomato paste, and bread crumbs or wheat germ. Mix well and cook until meat loses its pink color. Spoon mixture into the eggplant shells and place in casserole. Bake 15 to 20 minutes. Garnish with parsley and mint. Serve with nonfat plain yogurt and pita bread. Four servings.

Calories	484	Protein	24 g.
Fat	34 g.	Carbohydrate	24 g.
Saturated Fat	15 g.	Sodium	88 mg.
Cholesterol	99 mg.	Potassium	1,078 mg.

PORK CHOPS AND RICE

4 3-oz. boneless pork chops

8 tablespoons uncooked rice

1 cup boiling water

$^1\!/_2$ teaspoon rosemary

$^1\!/_2$ teaspoon sage

1 teaspoon sugar

8 slices tomato

$^1\!/_2$ green pepper, sliced

$^1\!/_2$ teaspoon basil

Pepper to taste
4 teaspoons unsalted butter

Brown chops in frying pan or skillet. Remove to a casserole and put uncooked rice around chops. Pour fat off frying pan and add boiling water to frying pan. Add rosemary, sage, and sugar. Pour over chops and rice. Add sliced tomatoes and green pepper. Sprinkle with basil and pepper. Dot with butter. Cover, bake about 30 minutes or until rice is cooked and meat is tender. Serves 4.

Calories 329	Protein . . . . 26 g.
Fat . . . . 15 g.	Carbohydrate . . . . . 22 g.
Saturated Fat . . . . 5 g.	Sodium . . . . 70 mg.
Cholesterol . . . . . 85 mg.	Potassium . . . . . 476 mg.

PORK CHOPS WITH CRANBERRIES

6 3-oz. boneless pork chops
2 cups cranberries, ground
1/2 cup honey
1/2 teaspoon allspice
1/2 teaspoon ground cloves

Brown chops quickly on both sides in nonstick frying pan. Place chops in bottom of greased baking dish. Combine cranberries, honey, allspice, and cloves. Spread mixture on chops. Cover and bake for about 45 minutes at 350 degrees. Serves 6.

Calories 323	Protein . . . . 24 g.
Fat . . . . 13 g.	Carbohydrate . . . . . 28 g.
Saturated Fat . . . . 5 g.	Sodium . . . . 66 mg.
Cholesterol . . . . . 81 mg.	Potassium . . . . . 400 mg.

PORK MEDALLIONS IN PESTO

This succulent dish was adapted from a recipe from the Reveries Restaurant in County Sligo, Ireland.

4 pork medallions (about 1 lb. total weight)
$1/4$ teaspoon black pepper
$1/4$ teaspoon garlic powder
2 tablespoons extra-virgin olive oil
1 medium onion, chopped
3 garlic cloves, minced
4 tomatoes, seeded and finely chopped
$1/2$ cup fresh basil, chopped
$1/2$ cup low-sodium bread crumbs
$1/2$ cup white wine
1 cup chicken stock
2 tablespoons nonfat plain yogurt
2 tablespoons toasted pine nuts

Preheat oven to 350 degrees. Rub pork medallions with black pepper and garlic powder and place in baking pan. In a nonstick skillet heat 1 tablespoon of olive oil and sauté onion and $1/3$ of garlic until soft. Add tomatoes, $1/4$ cup of basil, and bread crumbs. Mix thoroughly. Divide mixture into 4 equal parts and spread on top of each medallion. Bake for 20 to 30 minutes or until done. While pork is baking heat the other tablespoon of olive oil in the skillet and sauté the remaining garlic. Add wine, chicken stock, and remaining basil and simmer until reduced by half. Remove liquid to blender or food processor, add yogurt, and puree. Reheat, with pine nuts, but do not boil. When pork is cooked, spread sauce on serving platter and place medallions on top. Serves 4.

Calories	309	Protein	28 g.
Fat	13 g.	Carbohydrate	18 g.
Saturated Fat	3 g.	Sodium	78 mg.
Cholesterol	80 mg.	Potassium	988 mg.

ROAST LOIN OF PORK

6 lbs. pork loin roast

Pepper to taste

¼ teaspoon paprika

2 carrots

1 large onion

2 cloves garlic

1 cup water

1 cup dry Sauterne

2 whole cloves

Juice of 1 lemon

2 tablespoons currant jelly

1 teaspoon dry mustard

2 tablespoons flour

Season loin with pepper and paprika and place in roasting pan. Pare carrots, onion, and garlic and cut in small pieces. Place in pan with pork and ¼ cup water and roast 3 hours in 350-degree oven.

Remove roast to platter and keep hot. Place roasting pan on top of stove, add the remaining water, wine, cloves, lemon juice, jelly, and mustard. Let boil for 20 minutes. Strain sauce, pressing as many vegetables as

possible through sieve. Stir in flour to thicken. Pour over
pork. Serves 10.

Calories 255	Protein. . . . . 25 g.
Fat . . . . 11 g.	Carbohydrate . . . . . . 8 g.
Saturated Fat. . . . . . . 4 g.	Sodium. . . . . 66 mg.
Cholesterol. . . . . . 77 mg.	Potassium . . . . . 395 mg.

Roast pork is good basted with:

1 cup Burgundy

1 clove garlic

¼ teaspoon rosemary

¼ teaspoon dill

Calories 255	Protein. . . . . 25 g.
Fat . . . . 11 g.	Carbohydrate . . . . . . 8 g.
Saturated Fat. . . . . . . 4 g.	Sodium. . . . . 66 mg.
Cholesterol. . . . . 77 mg.	Potassium . . . . . 395 mg.

SPARERIBS WITH PINEAPPLE SAUCE

2 lbs. spareribs

2 cups canned pineapple chunks with liquid

1 cup water

2 tablespoons cornstarch

3 tablespoons wine vinegar

2 tablespoons sugar

¼ cup pineapple juice

Fry spareribs in a skillet. When cooked, remove and
let them drain on paper towels. Pour off fat and place
spareribs and pineapple back into skillet. Simmer 5 minutes. Cook water and cornstarch in double boiler. Stir un-

til thick. Add vinegar, sugar, and pineapple juice. Serve over spareribs. Serves 3.

Calories 455	Protein . . . . 26 g.
Fat . . . . 26 g.	Carbohydrate . . . . . 30 g.
Saturated Fat . . . . . 10 g.	Sodium . . . . 84 mg.
Cholesterol . . . . . 103 mg.	Potassium . . . . . . 511 mg.

VEAL WITH NOODLES

2 lbs. shoulder veal

6 whole allspice

½ bay leaf

½ teaspoon rosemary

1 clove garlic

1 lb. package Italian imported noodles

1½ tablespoons unsalted butter

2 medium onions, chopped

½ green pepper, diced

8 medium-size mushrooms

2 teaspoons flour

¼ cup cold water

Cover meat with boiling water, add seasonings and garlic, and cook until tender. Remove meat and cut into 3-inch cubes. Strain stock, heat to boiling, add noodles, and cook until tender. Melt butter in pan. Sauté onions, pepper, and mushrooms until soft but not brown. Blend in flour, then add cold water and stir until sauce reaches a smooth consistency. Place alternate layers of noodles, meat, and sauce in greased baking dish. Bake 50 to 60 minutes. Serves 6.

Calories 485	Protein. . . . . 39 g.
Fat . . . . 11 g.	Carbohydrate . . . . . 55 g.
Saturated Fat. . . . . . . 4 g.	Sodium. . . . . 100 mg.
Cholesterol. . . . . 183 mg.	Potassium . . . . . 492 mg.

BAKED VEAL CHOPS WITH TOMATO

In medieval times the herb sage was thought to pro-
long life, reduce sorrow, and increase wisdom.

2 tablespoons flour
6 3-oz. veal chops
1½ cups sliced onions
⅛ teaspoon pepper
½ teaspoon sage
½ teaspoon rosemary
½ cup white wine
½ cup water
1 cup canned low-sodium tomatoes
½ teaspoon basil

Flour the chops and pan-broil them until slightly
browned. Cover with onions, pepper, sage, rosemary,
wine, and water. Put on the lid and simmer for 15 minutes. Add tomatoes and basil and bake for 30 minutes at
400 degrees. Serves 6.

Calories 182	Protein. . . . . 23 g.
Fat . . . . 5 g.	Carbohydrate . . . . . . 8 g.
Saturated Fat. . . . . . . 1 g.	Sodium. . . . . 69 mg.
Cholesterol. . . . . . 81 mg.	Potassium . . . . . 409 mg.

VEAL CHOPS WITH WHITE WINE

6 3-oz. veal chops
1 clove garlic
Pepper to taste
1 onion, chopped
1 tablespoon parsley, chopped
2 tablespoons shallots, chopped
1 tablespoon unsalted butter
1½ tablespoons flour
1 cup white wine

Rub chops with garlic and pepper. Brown chops in iron pot or ovenproof dish and keep hot. Sauté onion, parsley, and shallots in butter. When they are soft, stir in flour and blend well. Add wine and cook until sauce is thickened, stirring constantly. Pour sauce over chops. Cover iron pot with buttered wax paper and bake in moderate oven for 25 minutes. Remove paper and cook 10 minutes longer in 350-degree oven. Serves 6.

Calories 196	Protein . . . . 23 g.
Fat . . . . 7 g.	Carbohydrate . . . . . . 4 g.
Saturated Fat . . . . 2 g.	Sodium . . . . 65 mg.
Cholesterol . . . . . . 86 mg.	Potassium . . . . . 315 mg.

VEAL CHOPS WITH PARSLEY AND GARLIC

$^1/_2$ cup minced parsley

2 cloves garlic

2 tablespoons olive oil

Juice from $^1/_2$ lemon

4 3-oz. boneless veal chops

Mash parsley and garlic to a paste with mortar and pestle (or wooden salad spoon and bowl). Add olive oil and lemon juice. Marinate chops in mixture for 2 hours. Lift chops from marinade and grill them in a hot skillet until tender. Serves 4.

Calories	217	Protein	27 g.
Fat	11 g.	Carbohydrate	1 mg.
Saturated Fat	2 g.	Sodium	79 mg.
Cholesterol	100 mg.	Potassium	344 mg.

VEAL STEW

3 lbs. lean veal, cut in 2-inch cubes, rubbed with black pepper and garlic powder

1 tablespoon olive oil

2 cups canned low-sodium tomatoes

1 bay leaf

1 tablespoon fresh parsley, minced

1 teaspoon rosemary, crumbled

$^1/_2$ teaspoon basil

$^1/_2$ teaspoon thyme

3 cloves garlic, crushed

2 bulbs fennel, sliced

1 carrot, sliced

1 onion, chopped

$^1/_2$ cup uncooked rice

In a nonstick skillet brown meat in oil. Add tomatoes, bay leaf, parsley, rosemary, basil, and thyme and cook $1^1/_2$ hours or until tender. Skim off fat. Sauté garlic, fennel, carrot, and onion. When vegetables are soft add rice and cook $^1/_2$ hour. Serves 8.

Calories	242	Protein	27 g.
Fat	8 g.	Carbohydrate	15 g.
Saturated Fat	3 g.	Sodium	103 mg.
Cholesterol	106 mg.	Potassium	577 mg.

VENISON STEW

2 lbs. venison stew meat

1 teaspoon pepper

1 teaspoon dried oregano

1 teaspoon garlic powder

1 tablespoon flour

2 tablespoons cooking oil

2 large cloves garlic, crushed

3 large onions, coarsely chopped

2 medium carrots, sliced

1 bay leaf

$^1/_2$ cup red wine

3 cups low-sodium beef broth

6 potatoes, peeled and sliced

2 tablespoons cornstarch

Season stew meat with pepper, oregano, and garlic powder. Dust with flour. Heat oil in large casserole. Sauté meat until browned. Add garlic, onions, carrots, bay leaf, wine, and broth. Simmer, covered, for about 1¹/₂ hours or until venison is tender. Add potatoes and cook another 30 minutes, or until potatoes are tender. Mix cornstarch with an equal amount of water. Stir into stew until mixture has thickened. Serves 8 to 10.

Calories	287	Protein	27 g.
Fat	6 g.	Carbohydrate	29 g.
Saturated Fat	tr	Sodium	74 mg.
Cholesterol	2 mg.	Potassium	937 mg.

Poultry and Game

Chicken really benefits from flavors imparted before the cooking process begins—so many of the recipes that follow feature marinades. Experiment with herbs and spices you add to the liquid. We suggest a few combinations: crumbled rosemary, marjoram, and sage; cumin, ginger, and turmeric; tarragon, dill, and thyme; oregano, basil, and cayenne pepper. The Condiments and Sauces section offers additional marinade recipes, basting sauces, and herb butters.

Try rubbing combinations of dried herbs and spices directly into the meat several hours before cooking—these "rubs" infuse the dish with a rich, but subtle taste. Add a squeeze of lemon juice and an extra sprinkle of fresh herbs right before serving to keep the flavors at their fullest.

Please note that all nutritional information refers to 1 serving size.

ROAST CHICKEN

1 4-lb. roasting chicken
3 tablespoons unsalted butter
1 teaspoon dried tarragon
1 tablespoon lemon juice
Piece of lemon peel

Have chicken at room temperature. Rub chicken with 2 tablespoons of the butter, tarragon, and lemon juice. Place 1 tablespoon of butter and lemon peel inside the chicken. Roast chicken uncovered in oven at 300 degrees until tender, basting often. Chicken requires 30 to 35 minutes per pound. Instead of lemon peel and butter, a piece of low-sodium bread fried in unsalted butter and rubbed with garlic may be substituted. Serves 6.

Variation: Put a green pepper or onion in the cavity of the chicken before roasting.

Calories	219	Protein	25 g.
Fat	12 g.	Carbohydrate	tr
Saturated Fat	5 g.	Sodium	61 mg.
Cholesterol	88 mg.	Potassium	213 mg.

BROILED CHICKEN

1 2-lb. broiler, quartered
1 clove garlic
Pepper to taste
$1/2$ teaspoon tarragon, thyme, or rosemary
1 cup hot water
2 tablespoons unsalted butter

Rub chicken with garlic. Brown quickly on both sides under hot broiler. Place chicken in baking dish and season with pepper and tarragon. Bake in 350-degree oven and baste with hot water and butter until tender. Serves 4.

Calories 220		Protein. . . . . 26 g.	
Fat . . . . 12 g.		Carbohydrate . . . . . . 1 g.	
Saturated Fat. . . . . . 5 g.		Sodium. . . . . 63 mg.	
Cholesterol. . . . . 88 mg.		Potassium . . . . 220 mg.	

CHICKEN WITH ALMOND RICE

---

2 whole chicken breasts

6 tablespoons olive oil

2 tablespoons minced onion

8 mushrooms, sliced

1 tablespoon lemon juice

1½ cups low-sodium chicken-flavored broth

Pepper to taste

¾ cup uncooked rice

⅓ cup slivered blanched unsalted almonds

Preheat the oven to 300 degrees. Brown chicken breasts in oil. Remove and drain on paper towels. Sauté onion in oil remaining in pan. Add mushrooms and lemon juice and sauté 3 minutes longer. Add chicken-bouillon mixture, pepper, and rice. Bring to a boil and simmer 3 minutes more. Stir in almonds. Place rice mixture in oiled casserole. Top with chicken. Cover and bake 45 minutes. Serves 4.

Calories 545	Protein. . . . . 31 g.
Fat . . . . 32 g.	Carbohydrate . . . . . 33 g.
Saturated Fat. . . . . . . 5 g.	Sodium. . . . . 66 mg.
Cholesterol. . . . . . 74 mg.	Potassium . . . . . 640 mg.

HERB CHICKEN

---

1 chicken, 3 to 3½ lbs., cut in pieces

1 teaspoon marjoram

1 teaspoon thyme

1 tablespoon chopped parsley

Freshly ground black pepper

4 tablespoons unsalted butter

Wash and dry chicken. Place in greased low baking dish, and sprinkle with marjoram and thyme. Let stand 1 hour. Sprinkle with parsley and pepper. Dot with butter. Bake in 400-degree oven for 35 to 45 minutes or until tender. Breast meat has less sodium. For company, heat pineapple chunks and place under chicken. Serves 4.

Herb chicken/breast:

Calories 271	Protein. . . . . 26 g.
Fat . . . . 18 g.	Carbohydrate . . . . . . 1 g.
Saturated Fat. . . . . . . 9 g.	Sodium. . . . . 62 mg.
Cholesterol. . . . . 103 mg.	Potassium . . . . . 222 mg.

Herb chicken/leg:

Calories 301	Protein. . . . . 22 g.
Fat . . . . 23 g.	Carbohydrate . . . . . . 1 g.
Saturated Fat. . . . . . 10 g.	Sodium. . . . . 76 mg.
Cholesterol. . . . . 110 mg.	Potassium . . . . . 205 mg.

CHICKEN CACCIATORE

3 whole chicken breasts, split
¼ cup olive oil
1 onion, chopped fine
2 tablespoons chopped green pepper
½ cup dry white wine
1 bay leaf
¼ teaspoon rosemary
¼ teaspoon basil
4 fresh tomatoes cut in small pieces or 2 cups
    canned low-sodium tomatoes
1 clove garlic, minced
Pepper to taste

Sauté chicken in olive oil for about 20 minutes or until brown. Remove to platter. Cook onion and green pepper until transparent. Stir in wine, add remaining ingredients, and cook for about 15 minutes or until tender. Serves 6.

Calories	286	Protein	26 g.
Fat	16 g.	Carbohydrate	6 g.
Saturated Fat	3 g.	Sodium	72 mg.
Cholesterol	72 mg.	Potassium	441 mg.

CHICKEN MARENGO

Marengo is the name of a village in Italy where Napoleon defeated the Austrians on June 14, 1800. Maybe this recipe explains why Napoleon said, "An army marches on its stomach."

1 4-lb. frying chicken cut up in serving pieces

4 tablespoons olive oil or vegetable oil

2 tablespoons flour

$\frac{1}{2}$ cup water

$\frac{1}{2}$ cup dry white wine

1 garlic clove, minced

Small bay leaf

$\frac{1}{4}$ teaspoon thyme

2 tablespoons chopped parsley

1 tablespoon canned low-sodium tomato paste
  (or fresh tomatoes may be used)

8 large mushrooms

Pepper to taste

Sauté chicken in oil in deep pan. Turn frequently so it is golden brown and crisp. Remove chicken. Stir flour in drippings. Add water and wine, and blend well. Add garlic, herbs, tomato paste, and mushrooms. Season with pepper. Replace chicken in sauce, cover pan, and simmer 1 hour.

In place of wine, water, and tomato paste, 2 cups of canned low-sodium tomatoes may be used. Serves 6.

Calories	280	Protein	26 g.
Fat	16 g.	Carbohydrate	4 g.
Saturated Fat	3 g.	Sodium	65 mg.
Cholesterol	72 mg.	Potassium	351 mg.

CHICKEN IN SOUR CREAM WITH PAPRIKA

In 1937, Professor Albert von Szent-Gyorgyi, a Hungarian scientist, discovered Vitamin C in paprika and won the Nobel Prize for his research.

This dish is good enough for your most elegant guest.

1 2½-lb. frying chicken cut into serving pieces
¼ cup olive oil
¼ cup flour
½ teaspoon pepper
¼ cup finely chopped onion
¼ teaspoon thyme
2 teaspoons paprika
4 tablespoons light sour cream

Wash and dry chicken. Heat oil in a skillet. Mix flour and pepper. Dredge chicken. Sauté the chicken in the oil until brown. Remove and drain. Sauté the onion in the oil until tender. Return chicken to pan and sprinkle with thyme. Cover and cook gently 30 minutes until done. Remove chicken and sprinkle with paprika. Deglaze pan with sour cream, and pour over the chicken. Serves 4.

Calories	371	Protein	28 g.
Fat	22 g.	Carbohydrate	14 g.
Saturated Fat	5 g.	Sodium	67 mg.
Cholesterol	78 mg.	Potassium	288 mg.

CHICKEN BREASTS WITH LIME JUICE

This is simple and luscious.

2 whole boned and skinned chicken breasts, halved
½ to 1 teaspoon Cajun seasoning, without salt
½ teaspoon garlic powder

1/4 teaspoon black pepper

Juice from 1 lime

1 1/2 teaspoons unsalted butter

1 tablespoon olive oil

1/2 cup white wine

1 large tomato, skinned, seeded, and chopped

Lime slices

Wash and pat dry chicken breasts. Rub with Cajun seasoning, garlic powder, and pepper. Dip in juice of 1/2 lime. Melt butter and oil and sauté chicken pieces, basting with any leftover juice as it is cooking. Add wine and tomato and simmer until chicken is done. Before serving, pour over the juice from the other half of the lime and garnish with lime slices. Serves 4.

Calories	232	Protein	24 g.
Fat	11 g.	Carbohydrate	3 g.
Saturated Fat	3 g.	Sodium	59 mg.
Cholesterol	68 mg.	Potassium	291 mg.

ROAST CHICKEN WITH 40 CLOVES OF GARLIC

This dish gets high marks from young and old. It is much easier than it sounds and much less demanding than you might imagine. You'll only need about 4 small bulbs and the garlic flavor is delicate and mellow. You don't have to peel 40 garlic cloves, only separate them. It's easy enough for a weekday night and sumptuous enough for a special occasion.

Freshly ground pepper

1 teaspoon Bell's salt-free seasoning or a mixture of rosemary, thyme, oregano, and sage

3- to 4-lb. roasting chicken
1 tablespoon extra-virgin olive oil
40 cloves of garlic (about 4 small heads)
1¹/₂ cups white wine
1 carrot, sliced
Fresh chopped parsley

Preheat oven to 350 degrees. Rub pepper and seasoning over entire roasting chicken. In a nonstick frying pan, heat oil and gently sauté chicken for 5 minutes on each side. Remove. Add garlic and brown another 5 minutes. In the bottom of a heavy casserole or roasting pan with lid, spread the garlic cloves. Set the chicken on top. Add the wine and sliced carrot. Cover and bake for about an hour or until the juices run clear. Remove the chicken from the pan. Cook the sauce down for about 5 minutes on top of the stove. Pour some over the chicken, sprinkle with chopped parsley, and serve the rest of the sauce separately. Serves 5 to 6.

Calories	314	Protein	25 g.
Fat	14 g.	Carbohydrate	10 g.
Saturated Fat	4 g.	Sodium	83 mg.
Cholesterol	91 mg.	Potassium	369 mg.

GREEN VEGETABLES, CHICKEN IN PEANUT SAUCE

Adapted from *Cooking Thai Food in American Kitchens* by Maulee Pinsuvana, Registration No. Ai 16112, Bangkok, Thailand, 1976 (USA printing).

1 slice ginger root, peeled and chopped

2 cloves garlic, crushed

1 teaspoon curry powder

½ cup plus 1 tablespoon nonfat plain yogurt (mixed with 1 tablespoon cornstarch)

1 tablespoon unsalted butter

1 cup sliced chicken breast

1 tablespoon peanut oil

½ red onion, sliced

2 tablespoons commercial unsalted peanut butter

1 tablespoon sugar

1 tablespoon low-sodium chili powder

Angostura bitters

1 cup chopped spinach

1 bunch chopped scallions

Unsalted peanuts, chopped

Mix ginger, garlic, curry powder, 1 tablespoon yogurt, and melted butter together. Pour over chicken slices and marinate for 1 hour. Heat oil in nonstick skillet. Brown onion until soft. Over low heat add peanut butter, sugar, chili powder, remaining yogurt, and a sprinkling of bitters. Stir-fry for 1 minute. Remove from heat. In boiling water cook spinach and scallions for 3 minutes. Drain. Place in a ring on serving platter. Brown chicken breast in skillet until cooked through. Arrange on spinach and scallions. Pour the peanut sauce over the chicken and sprinkle with roasted peanuts. Serves 4 to 5.

Note: In Thai cooking coconut milk is a staple. It comes in a low-sodium variety. You may substitute it for the yogurt if you like.

Calories 197	Protein . . . . 14 g.
Fat . . . . 13 g.	Carbohydrate . . . . . . 9 g.
Saturated Fat . . . . 2 g.	Sodium . . . . 51 mg.
Cholesterol . . . . . . 20 mg.	Potassium . . . . . 371 mg.

BRUNSWICK STEW

This is adapted from a favorite Southern dish that serves a crowd and freezes well.

1 3-lb. frying chicken, cut up

¼ teaspoon ground pepper

⅛ teaspoon red pepper

½ teaspoon garlic powder

¼ teaspoon cumin powder

1 tablespoon canola oil

1½ teaspoons unsalted butter

2 large onions, chopped

6 cups low-sodium chicken broth

2 bay leaves

4 medium tomatoes, chopped

4 medium potatoes, diced

4 ears of freshly cut corn (or 1 package frozen corn)

1 long Italian pepper, seeded, rinsed, and chopped

Wash and dry chicken. Rub with peppers, garlic, and cumin. In a nonstick skillet sauté chicken in oil until golden. Remove to larger pot. In skillet melt butter and sauté onions until soft. Add to chicken, cover with broth, and add bay leaves. Cook until meat is tender. (Add more broth if necessary.) Add remaining ingredients and cook until vegetables are tender and mixture is thick. Serves 8.

Calories 291	Protein........... 26 g.
Fat .... 9 g.	Carbohydrate ..... 27 g.
Saturated Fat....... 2 g.	Sodium......... 79 mg.
Cholesterol...... 76 mg.	Potassium ..... 969 mg.

CHICKEN DIABLE

½ teaspoon garlic powder

¼ teaspoon pepper

1 teaspoon curry

½ teaspoon mace

3 lbs. chicken breasts, washed and dried

Juice of one lemon

2 tablespoons unsalted butter

½ cup honey

1 tablespoon low-sodium mustard

Mix together garlic powder, pepper, curry, and mace and rub into chicken pieces. Coat both sides of the chicken with lemon juice and let marinate. Melt butter and stir in honey and mustard. Place chicken skin side up in a roasting pan and pour the butter mixture over all. Bake covered in 350-degree oven for 30 minutes. Remove cover and bake for another 30 minutes or until done. Serves 4.

Calories 361	Protein . . . . 26 g.
Fat . . . . 13 g.	Carbohydrate . . . . . 36 g.
Saturated Fat . . . . . . 6 g.	Sodium . . . . 64 mg.
Cholesterol . . . . . 89 mg.	Potassium . . . . . 265 mg.

CHICKEN FAJITAS AMARILLO

This recipe comes from T. Boone Pickens's kitchen.

Juice of 4 to 5 limes
2 to 4 garlic cloves, pressed
2 jalapeño peppers, seeded and chopped*
Handful of fresh cilantro, chopped
1 12-oz. bottle of Mexican beer (domestic will do)
2 lbs. boneless chicken
Freshly ground lemon pepper

Mix lime juice, garlic, peppers, cilantro, and beer. Pour over chicken. Marinate for 6 to 8 hours. Sprinkle chicken with lemon pepper, then grill or broil, basting with marinade, until done. Slice and serve with heated flour tortillas, made without salt.

Remember to use gloves

Garnishes

Salsa
Plain nonfat yogurt or light sour cream
Chopped onion
Chopped tomato
Green, red, and yellow pepper sautéed in 1 tablespoon canola oil

Hot Sauce:

Chop 1 onion, 1 jalapeño pepper, seeded, and $1/2$ tomato in blender or food processor.
Serves 6 to 8.

Chicken fajitas:

Calories 180	Protein. . . . . 25 g.
Fat . . . . 6 g.	Carbohydrate . . . . . . 3 g.
Saturated Fat. . . . . . . 2 g.	Sodium. . . . . 75 mg.
Cholesterol. . . . . . 76 mg.	Potassium . . . . . 253 mg.

Low-sodium flour tortillas:

Calories 105	Protein. . . . . 3 g.
Fat . . . . 3 g.	Carbohydrate . . . . . 19 g.
Saturated Fat . . . . tr	Sodium. . . . . tr
Cholesterol. . . . . . . 0 mg.	Potassium . . . . . . 35 mg.

GINGER CHICKEN WITH PEARS

Sheila Lukins and Julee Rosso inspired this recipe. They use quail instead of chicken breasts.

1 to 1⅓ lbs. boneless chicken breasts
1–2 tablespoons freshly grated ginger
¼ teaspoon black pepper
¼ teaspoon garlic powder
¼ teaspoon ground cloves
2 pears, cored and sliced in long wedges
2 cloves garlic, crushed
Juice of one lemon
½ cup sherry
½ cup currants
1½ teaspoons unsalted butter

1 tablespoon cornstarch

½ cup orange juice

Cut chicken in strips and rub with ginger, pepper, garlic powder, and cloves. Combine chicken, pears, garlic, lemon juice, sherry, and currants. Marinate for several hours or overnight. Heat butter and sauté chicken pieces until browned on each side. Add marinade and cover. Simmer for about 10 minutes or until chicken and pears are done. Remove chicken and pears to serving platter. Mix cornstarch and orange juice until smooth. Add to pan and stir until sauce has thickened. Pour over chicken and pears. Serves 4.

Calories	295	Protein	24 g.
Fat	8 g.	Carbohydrate	24 g.
Saturated Fat	3 g.	Sodium	55 mg.
Cholesterol	68 mg.	Potassium	408 mg.

CORNISH HENS WITH PRUNES

Fancy and very easy.

2 Cornish hens, 1 to 1½ lbs. each

8 dried prunes, soaked all night or heated in microwave for 2 minutes in water to cover

Freshly ground pepper

½ cup orange juice

2 tablespoons honey

2 tablespoons balsamic vinegar

½ teaspoon Kikkoman lite soy sauce

1 teaspoon dried, crumbled rosemary

1 large clove garlic, crushed

Garnish: grated orange peel, chopped fresh parsley

Wash and dry Cornish hens. Fill each cavity with 4 prunes and sprinkle skin with freshly ground pepper. Mix orange juice, honey, vinegar, soy sauce, rosemary, and garlic. Pour over hens and let stand for 30 minutes. In 375-degree oven bake hens for about 45 minutes, or until juices run clear when pricked. Baste every 10 to 15 minutes. Cut each hen in half. Pour sauce over all and sprinkle with grated orange peel and chopped parsley. Serves 4.

Calories	289	Protein	24 g.
Fat	12 g.	Carbohydrate	23 g.
Saturated Fat	3 g.	Sodium	92 mg.
Cholesterol	92 mg.	Potassium	360 mg.

JODY MCKENZIE'S CURRIED CHICKEN SALAD

The poaching method leaves the chicken amazingly tender and moist.

2 whole chicken breasts, poached, skinned, and chopped, about 4 cups

Water to cover

1 teaspoon tarragon

1 onion, chopped

1 celery rib with leaves

1 carrot, sliced

2 large cloves garlic, sliced

Ground pepper

Juice of 1 lemon

1 cup Granny Smith apples, cored and chopped finely

1 cup chopped walnuts (roasted for 10 minutes at 350 degrees)

¼ cup mayonnaise (low-sodium, low-fat)
¼ cup nonfat plain yogurt
2 to 3 teaspoons curry powder
Garnish: lettuce leaves, dill sprigs

In saucepan place chicken, enough water to cover it, and the next 6 ingredients. Bring to a boil, cover, and turn off heat. Let sit for 1 hour. Remove chicken from broth. (Save broth in refrigerator for immediate use or freeze in 1-cup yogurt containers.) Skin, bone, and slice chicken. Toss chicken with lemon juice. Add chopped apple and walnuts. Mix together mayonnaise, yogurt, and curry powder. Serve on lettuce leaves and decorate with sprigs of dill. Serves 6 to 8.

Variation: Add grapes and pineapple and substitute almonds for walnuts.

Calories 383		Protein. . . . . 29 g.	
Fat . . . . 27 g.		Carbohydrate . . . . . . 8 g.	
Saturated Fat. . . . . . . 4 g.		Sodium. . . . . 112 mg.	
Cholesterol. . . . . 80 mg.		Potassium . . . . . 338 mg.	

CURRIED TURKEY

This is an unusually good dish for leftover turkey. Use the white meat because the sodium content is less than the dark. Serve with rice cooked with orange juice.

3 tablespoons unsalted butter
2 cups turkey (cooked and cubed)
1 can pineapple chunks (drained)
1 tablespoon curry powder
2½ tablespoons flour

¾ **cup milk**

¾ **cup low-sodium broth**

2 teaspoons lemon juice

2 ripe halved avocados (dipped in lemon juice)

Melt butter in a flat saucepan and add turkey and pineapple. Sprinkle mixture with curry powder, flour, broth, and milk. Cook 5 minutes, stirring constantly. Add lemon juice. Fill avocado halves with mixture. Bake 30 minutes at 350 to 375 degrees. Garnish with peach or apricot. Watch the calories! Serves 4.

Calories 444	Protein . . . . 26 g.
Fat . . . . 28 g.	Carbohydrate . . . . . 24 g.
Saturated Fat . . . . . 10 g.	Sodium . . . . 81 mg.
Cholesterol . . . . . 80 mg.	Potassium . . . . 1,054 mg.

TURKEY WITH PEPPERS AND POTATOES

The flavor of roasted vegetables and the crunch of grated potatoes give the turkey its moist, delicious taste.

1 lb. turkey tenderloins

Juice of 1 lime

Garlic powder

Ground pepper to taste

1 small onion, grated

1 red pepper, finely chopped

4 small potatoes, peeled and grated

2 tablespoons extra-virgin olive oil

3 cloves garlic, crushed

1 oz. low-sodium Swiss cheese, grated

In oiled baking dish spread turkey pieces. Sprinkle with lime juice, garlic powder, and ground pepper. Spread onions and peppers on top of each turkey slice. Mix grated potatoes with ground pepper, olive oil, and garlic. Pile on top of turkey, covering vegetables carefully. Bake in a hot oven, about 475 degrees, for 25 minutes. Check frequently to see that it is browning nicely. Sprinkle with cheese and place under broiler for a few minutes to complete browning. Serves 4.

Calories 326	Protein . . . . 30 g.
Fat . . . . 12 g.	Carbohydrate . . . . . 23 g.
Saturated Fat . . . . 3 g.	Sodium . . . . 81 mg.
Cholesterol . . . . . 69 mg.	Potassium . . . . . 657 mg.

JAN DIZZARD'S TURKEY FILLETS

Jan is a hunter, and when he was placed on a low-sodium diet, he found that the strategy for doing without salt involved making reductions. ("I cook down bones of any critter I can get my hands on.") Using a packet of low-sodium broth with a quarter of the water can do in a pinch.

½ cup herbed (no salt) bread crumbs

1 1-lb. package of turkey medallions

2 tablespoons olive oil

1 small onion or two shallots, chopped fine

4 to 6 shiitake mushrooms, stems removed, chopped

½ to 1 cup dry white wine

¼ cup turkey reduction or concentrated chicken broth

Place bread crumbs on wax paper or baking sheet and coat the fillets by pressing them onto the crumbs. Let rest. In a nonstick pan heat 1 tablespoon of the oil until hot (but not smoking). Brown the fillets for 2 minutes or so to a side. When browned, remove from the pan and turn the heat to low. Add the remaining oil, onions, and mushrooms. Stir to keep the browned bread crumbs and cooking juices from burning. When onions and mushrooms begin to wilt, add wine and deglaze the pan. Raise heat and reduce liquid by half. Add the reduction or concentrated broth, stir to blend, turn heat to low. Return fillets to pan, cover, and let simmer until cooked through—about 10 to 15 minutes. Serve and spoon sauce over fillets. Serves 4.

Calories	247	Protein	23 g.
Fat	10 g.	Carbohydrate	11 g.
Saturated Fat	2 g.	Sodium	48 mg.
Cholesterol	50 mg.	Potassium	375 mg.

TURKEY SALAD

¾ lb. turkey medallions

Water to cover

1 onion, chopped

1 celery stalk, chopped

1 carrot, chopped

1 teaspoon tarragon

⅓ cup nonfat plain yogurt

1 tablespoon low-sodium mayonnaise

2 tablespoons honey

Juice and grated peel of 1 lime

Freshly ground pepper
2 ripe peaches, peeled and sliced
1 cup green grapes, sliced
Lettuce leaves

In a large skillet or medium saucepan place turkey medallions and cover with water. Add onion, celery, carrot, and tarragon. Bring to boil, cover, and turn off heat. Let sit for 1 hour. Remove turkey from broth and cut into chunks. (Refrigerate or freeze broth for another use.) Combine yogurt, mayonnaise, honey, lime, and freshly ground pepper. Toss with warm turkey. Refrigerate until chilled through. Add peaches and grapes. Arrange salad on lettuce leaves. Serves 4.

Calories	285	Protein	27 g.
Fat	8 g.	Carbohydrate	28 g.
Saturated Fat	2 g.	Sodium	106 mg.
Cholesterol	66 mg.	Potassium	623 mg.

SAVORY DUCK

1 5-lb. duck, cut up
2 tablespoons flour
3 tablespoons olive oil
Pepper to taste
1 medium onion, chopped fine
3 tablespoons chopped fresh parsley
1/8 teaspoon rosemary
1 teaspoon thyme
1 clove garlic, minced
1 cup red wine

Dredge the duck with flour and sear well in oil. Remove pieces to a casserole and season with pepper. Add onion, parsley, rosemary, thyme, and garlic. Pour wine over duck. Cover casserole. Place in 350-degree oven and cook 2 hours. Serves 6.

Calories	398	Protein	17 g.
Fat	31 g.	Carbohydrate	6 g.
Saturated Fat	9 mg.	Sodium	54 mg.
Cholesterol	71 mg.	Potassium	267 mg.

ROAST DUCKLING

1 5-lb. Long Island duckling

1 clove garlic

4 carrots

8 medium onions

1 orange

3 tablespoons currant jelly

Rub duckling with garlic. Place in uncovered pan and bake 20 to 30 minutes per pound in 350-degree oven, basting every 10 minutes. Remove duckling to heated pan. Skim off excess fat from duck juices. Reduce juices over high heat to ¼ the original quantity. Slice carrots and onions and simmer in gravy. Cut orange rind in strips, boil in a little water a few minutes. Set aside. Squeeze the juice of an orange in the duck gravy. Add currant jelly, mixing well. Garnish duck with orange rind and serve with carrots and onions. Serves 6.

Calories	401	Protein	19 g.
Fat	25 g.	Carbohydrate	27 g.
Saturated Fat	8 g.	Sodium	73 mg.
Cholesterol	71 mg.	Potassium	615 mg.

RABBIT IN GUINNESS

Plan to make this several hours or a day ahead so the flavors have a chance to mingle.

1 3-lb. rabbit, cut up
Freshly ground pepper
Flour
1 tablespoon canola oil
1 tablespoon unsalted butter
2 medium onions, chopped
3 to 4 cloves garlic, pressed
1 tablespoon brown sugar
1 12-oz. bottle of Guinness (or other stout)
2 to 3 cups of low-sodium chicken stock
2 crumbled bay leaves
1 teaspoon dried rosemary
1 tablespoon juniper berries
2 tablespooons cornstarch
2 tablespoons cider vinegar
Fresh parsley

Season rabbit pieces with freshly ground pepper. Roll in flour. Heat oil and butter in nonstick frying pan. Sauté rabbit pieces until each side is golden brown. Remove rabbit pieces. Sauté onions until transparent. Place rabbit, onions, garlic, brown sugar, and stout in a casserole or roasting pan with lid. Add chicken stock, bay leaves, rosemary, and juniper berries. Cover and simmer for about $1^1/_2$ hours, or until the rabbit is tender. Let sit or refrigerate if rabbit is being served the next day. Before serving, reheat, then remove rabbit. In a bowl mix cornstarch and vinegar until cornstarch is dissolved. Add a bit of hot broth, mix until smooth, then stir into pot. (If thickening is still needed, add additional cornstarch and vinegar.) Keep rabbit warm in sauce. Add more ground pepper if needed. Serve rabbit on platter, ladled with sauce and sprinkled with fresh parsley. Serves 6.

Calories	296	Protein	27 g.
Fat	12 g.	Carbohydrate	16 g.
Saturated Fat	4 g.	Sodium	39 mg.
Cholesterol	81 mg.	Potassium	550 mg.

A fresh, crisp salad can really pull a meal together—
and if the greens are enhanced with colorful raw veggies,
that salad is as good for the soul as it is for the body. Try
some of the once unfamiliar varieties that are commonly
available today. Most supermarkets sell prewashed salad
blends that combine and contrast tastes and textures—
look for the mixtures with small, individual leaves rather
than torn pieces of larger leaves. As you shop for dressing, remember that processed, bottled brands too often
drench our salads in excess amounts of sodium. For a
dramatic change, try sprinkling greens with nothing but
minced garlic and sesame seeds. Remember that the simplest dressing is sometimes the best: oil, vinegar, a twist
of the pepper mill, maybe a pinch of dry mustard or
fresh-snipped chives.

Experiment with herb and wine vinegars, or lemon
and lime juice until you find a combination that best suits
the meal and your taste. Use extra-virgin olive oil for its
superior flavor and its benefit to your health. As one of
the oils containing significant amounts of monounsaturated fats (along with canola, hazelnut, peanut, and
sesame) olive oil lowers cholesterol and other harmful
fats and has also been found to lower blood pressure. The
oil pressed from the olive fruit is not high in sodium—it's

the salty brine, which the fruit absorbs as it soaks in its preservative, that makes the olive itself off-limits for anyone on a salt-free diet.

Unless otherwise noted, please be aware that all nutritional information refers to 1 serving size.

GREEN SALAD

Rub salad bowl with garlic clove. Add crispy greens and sprinkle with oregano or tarragon. Mix with olive or vegetable oil and vinegar. Add a little sugar if you like.

COLORFUL VEGETABLE CHOPS

One night a friend served a salad that was made up of nothing but finely chopped green vegetables with a light vinaigrette. This gave birth to "chops"—not only green, but red, yellow, and white! Following are suggested ingredients for various chops. Use proportions to your own taste.

Green Chop

Scallions
Green peppers
Celery (limit, if necessary, to 1 rib)
Unpeeled zucchini
Broccoli stems

Red Chop

Bermuda onion
Radishes
Red peppers
Tomatoes

White Chop

White radishes
Jicama

Peeled and seeded cucumber
Vidalia onion
Fennel bulb

Yellow/Orange Chop

Orange peppers
Yellow tomatoes
Unpeeled summer squash
Rutabaga

VINAIGRETTE

**2 tablespoons vinegar (balsamic for the red chop,
    basil-flavored for green chop, and orange juice for
    yellow/orange chop)**
2 tablespoons extra-virgin olive oil
1 teaspoon honey

Entire recipe:

Calories 264	Protein. . . . . 0 g.
Fat . . . . 27 g.	Carbohydrate . . . . . . 7 g.
Saturated Fat. . . . . . . 4 g.	Sodium . . . . 1 mg.
Cholesterol. . . . . . . 0 mg.	Potassium . . . . 8 mg.

CAESAR SALAD

---

1 clove garlic
4 tablespoons olive oil
3 tablespoons wine vinegar
1/8 teaspoon dry mustard
1/8 teaspoon onion powder

1 teaspoon sugar

Pepper to taste

1 bunch romaine lettuce, washed

1 egg beaten

Rub salad bowl with garlic clove, add olive oil, vinegar, and seasonings. Stir around, then add romaine torn into medium-size pieces. Stir some more. Now add the egg and stir with salad fork and spoon. Serves 8.

Calories 77		Protein. . . . . 1 g.	
Fat . . . . 7 g.		Carbohydrate . . . . . . 2 g.	
Saturated Fat. . . . . . . 1 g.		Sodium. . . . . 10 mg.	
Cholesterol. . . . . . 27 mg.		Potassium . . . . . . 92 mg.	

WATERCRESS, JICAMA, AND ORANGE SALAD

2 bunches watercress, washed and chopped

1 medium jicama, peeled and sliced

2 oranges, peeled and divided into sections or 2 cans mandarin oranges, drained

1 small Vidalia onion, thinly sliced

¼ cup nonfat plain yogurt

¼ cup orange juice

1 tablespoon honey

1 teaspoon low-sodium mustard

¼ cup finely chopped fresh mint

¼ cup toasted walnuts, chopped

Arrange watercress, jicama, orange, and onion slices on 6 plates. Combine yogurt, orange juice, honey, mustard, and mint in blender or food processor and puree. Drizzle over each salad. Top with chopped walnuts. Serves 6.

Variation: Experiment with other fruits, such as pomegranate, star fruit, and persimmon.

Calories	88	Protein	1 g.
Fat	3 g.	Carbohydrate	14 g.
Saturated Fat	tr	Sodium	15 mg.
Cholesterol	0 mg.	Potassium	257 mg.

BELGIAN ENDIVE AND PINK GRAPEFRUIT SALAD

2 ruby red grapefruits, peeled, pith and seeds removed, separated into sections

4 small heads of Belgian endive

2 scallions, thinly sliced

2 tablespoons prepared low-sodium mustard

3 tablespoons white wine vinegar

1 tablespoon reserved red grapefruit juice

7 tablespoons walnut oil

1/2 tablespoon minced Italian parsley

Fresh ground pepper to taste

Cut grapefruit sections into thirds, crosswise, and place in bowl. Cut ends from heads of Belgian endive and remove and set aside 4 outer leaves from each head. Slice remaining endive crosswise into 1/4-inch slices. Drain grapefruit, reserving 1 tablespoon juice for salad dressing. Mix sliced endive, scallions, and grapefruit. Toss and set aside while preparing vinaigrette.

Whisk mustard, vinegar, and grapefruit juice together. Gradually add the oil in a slow, steady stream. Whisk in parsley and add pepper to taste. Toss endive mixture with enough dressing to lightly coat and marinate.

Arrange 4 outer leaves of endive on each plate. Divide endive and grapefruit salad into 4 portions and spoon in the middle of leaves. Drizzle additional dressing over uncovered portion of leaves. Serves 4.

Calories	53	Protein	2 g.
Fat	1 g.	Carbohydrate	14 g.
Saturated Fat	tr	Sodium	14 mg.
Cholesterol	0 mg.	Potassium	378 mg.

RASPBERRY AND ORANGE SALAD

1 cup fresh raspberries

1 small can drained mandarin oranges

1 sliced onion

2 tablespoons raspberry syrup

2 tablespoons balsamic vinegar

2 tablespoons olive oil

Assorted greens (Boston lettuce, spinach, endive)

Mix all ingredients together, except lettuce, and let sit at room temperature for about 1 hour. Arrange lettuce on individual plates and divide raspberry mixture among each. Serves 5.

Variation: Add toasted almonds.

Calories	120	Protein	1 g.
Fat	6 g.	Carbohydrate	18 g.
Saturated Fat	1 g.	Sodium	11 mg.
Cholesterol	0 mg.	Potassium	173 mg.

WALDORF SALAD

1 apple, chopped

1 banana, sliced

Juice of 1 lime

1 cup green seedless grapes, sliced

1 rib celery, chopped

½ cup walnut meats, chopped

2 tablespoons orange juice

½ cup low-sodium mayonnaise

Mix apple and banana and add lime juice. Add grapes, celery, and walnuts. Stir orange juice into mayonnaise and gently toss with remaining ingredients. Serves 6.

Calories 250	Protein. . . . . 2 g.
Fat . . . . 22 g.	Carbohydrate . . . . . 14 g.
Saturated Fat. . . . . . . 2 g.	Sodium. . . . . 81 mg.
Cholesterol. . . . . . 6 mg.	Potassium . . . . . 231 mg.

CHERRY ORCHARD MOLD

1½ tablespoons unflavored gelatin

1 cup orange juice

1 cup cherry juice

½ cup sugar

¾ cup sherry wine

1 tablespoon lemon juice

1 cup canned bing cherries

Dissolve gelatin in ½ cup orange juice. Bring cherry juice and remaining orange juice to boil, add gelatin mixture, sugar, sherry, and lemon juice. Mix until dissolved. Add cherries. Pour in mold and chill. Serves 6.

Calories 170	Protein. . . . . 3 g.
Fat. . . . . tr	Carbohydrate . . . 34 mg.
Saturated Fat . . . . tr	Sodium . . . . 6 mg.
Cholesterol. . . . . . . 0 mg.	Potassium . . . . . 261 mg.

CRANBERRY RING

2 cups cranberries

1½ cups cold water

1 cup sugar

⅛ teaspoon mace

1 tablespoon unflavored gelatin

½ cup chopped walnuts

Wash cranberries in a medium saucepan. Add 1 cup cold water, cook until tender. Add sugar and mace and cook 5 minutes. Soften gelatin in ¹/₂ cup cold water, dissolve in hot cranberries. Chill until mixture begins to thicken. Add nuts and mix. Pour into oiled mold. Chill until firm. Serves 6.

Variation: For the holidays, garnish the ring with kiwi disks to form a decorated wreath.

Calories 206	Protein. . . . . 4 g.
Fat . . . . 6 g.	Carbohydrate . . . . . 38 g.
Saturated Fat . . . . tr	Sodium . . . . 4 mg.
Cholesterol. . . . . . . 0 mg.	Potassium. . . . . 111 mg.

CAJUN CARROT SALAD

This classic Southern dish lends itself to countless variations. Make sure you let it sit for 24 hours. It lasts for days.

- 4 quarts water
- 3 tablespoons sugar
- 2 lbs. carrots, sliced in rounds
- ½ cup lemon juice
- ¾ cup cider or tarragon vinegar
- 1 tablespoon low-sodium prepared mustard
- 1 teaspoon freshly ground pepper
- 3 cloves garlic, pressed
- 2 teaspoons dried tarragon
- ½ cup canola oil
- 1 red and 1 green pepper or 2 green peppers, chopped
- 2 Bermuda onions, chopped

In a large, 8-quart pot, bring water and 1 tablespoon of the sugar to a full boil. Add carrots and cook for about 10 minutes, until just tender. Rinse quickly in a colander under cold water. In a 2-quart bowl mix lemon juice, vinegar, 2 tablespoons sugar, mustard, ground pepper, garlic, and tarragon. Whisk in oil until well blended. Add carrots, peppers, and onions. Toss gently. Cover. Refrigerate for 1 to 3 days. Serves 8 to 10.

Calories	199	Protein	2 g.
Fat	14 g.	Carbohydrate	20 g.
Saturated Fat	1 g.	Sodium	42 mg.
Cholesterol	0 mg.	Potassium	507 mg.

CAROL'S CORN SALAD

Strikingly beautiful to look at, as well as delicious to taste.

1 large (28-oz.) bag frozen corn, blanched and
    drained
1 Bermuda onion, chopped
1 sweet green pepper, seeded, chopped
1 red pepper, seeded, chopped
1 shredded carrot
1 fresh jalapeño pepper, seeded and chopped*
½ cup cider or white vinegar
2 tablespoons fresh cilantro, minced
Freshly ground pepper

Mix all ingredients carefully in a medium bowl. Cover and refrigerate until well chilled. Before serving garnish with cilantro leaves. Serves 8 to 10.

Remember to wear plastic gloves when chopping jalapeño.

Calories 105	Protein. . . . . 3 g.
Fat . . . . 1 g.	Carbohydrate . . . . . 26 g.
Saturated Fat . . . . tr	Sodium . . . . 3 mg.
Cholesterol. . . . . . . 0 mg.	Potassium . . . . . 354 mg.

COLESLAW

1 head of cabbage
⅓ cup vinegar
½ teaspoon pepper

¼ teaspoon dill weed
¼ teaspoon tarragon
¼ teaspoon chervil
4 tablespoons low-fat sour cream
4 tablespoons low-sodium mayonnaise
Paprika
Parsley

Scoop out the center section of the cabbage, leaving only a shell. Shred the center section and soak in ice water for 30 minutes. Drain and dry thoroughly, add vinegar and seasonings. Toss and let marinate for an hour. Drain again, squeezing cabbage slightly to remove any excess liquid. Pour sour cream and mayonnaise over cabbage and toss lightly. Place slaw in chilled shell of cabbage. Garnish with paprika and parsley. Serves 8.

Calories	95	Protein	2 g.
Fat	8 g.	Carbohydrate	7 g.
Saturated Fat	1 g.	Sodium	52 mg.
Cholesterol	5 mg.	Potassium	307 mg.

PINEAPPLE COLESLAW

2 cups shredded cabbage
1 cup crushed pineapple, drained
1 small green pepper, cut fine
4 tablespoons low-sodium mayonnaise
½ tablespoon vinegar
⅛ teaspoon pepper
¼ teaspoon dill seed

Combine cabbage, pineapple, and green pepper. Mix well. Mix mayonnaise with vinegar, pepper, and dill seed. Combine with cabbage mixture. Serves 6.

Calories 94	Protein. . . . . 1 g.
Fat . . . . 8 g.	Carbohydrate . . . . . . 6 g.
Saturated Fat. . . . . . . 1 g.	Sodium. . . . . 43 mg.
Cholesterol. . . . . . 3 mg.	Potassium . . . . . 160 mg.

FRENCH DRESSING

½ cup olive or other vegetable oil

1¾ teaspoons paprika

1 teaspoon dry mustard

1½ cloves garlic

½ teaspoon basil

⅛ teaspoon pepper

1 tablespoon chopped onions or chives

3 tablespoons cider vinegar

2 tablespoons lemon juice

2 tablespoons chopped fresh parsley

Combine all ingredients. Let sit in covered jar in refrigerator at least 12 hours before serving. Shake before using.

Total recipe:

Calories. 1,002	Protein. . . . . 2 g.
Fat . . . . 110 g.	Carbohydrate . . . . . 12 g.
Saturated Fat. . . . . . 15 g.	Sodium . . . . 5 g.
Cholesterol. . . . . . . 0 mg.	Potassium . . . . . 267 mg.

Tablespoonful:

Calories 77	Protein . . . . tr
Fat . . . . 8 g.	Carbohydrate . . . . . . 1 g.
Saturated Fat. . . . . . . 1 g.	Sodium. . . . . tr
Cholesterol. . . . . . . 0 mg.	Potassium . . . . . . 21 mg.

TED'S FAVORITE DRESSING

¼ **cup honey**
¼ **cup olive oil**
¼ **cup wine or cider vinegar**
1 **clove garlic, minced**

Place all the ingredients in a covered jar, shake well, and refrigerate before serving.

Total recipe:

Calories 742	Protein . . . . tr
Fat . . . . 54 g.	Carbohydrate . . . . . 73 g.
Saturated Fat. . . . . . . 7 g.	Sodium . . . . 5 mg.
Cholesterol. . . . . . . 0 mg.	Potassium. . . . . . 116 mg.

Tablespoonful:

Calories 62	Protein . . . . tr
Fat . . . . 5 g.	Carbohydrate . . . . . . 6 g.
Saturated Fat. . . . . . . 1 g.	Sodium . . . . tr
Cholesterol. . . . . . . 0 mg.	Potassium . . . . . . 10 mg.

RANCH DRESSING OR DIP

¾ **cup plain nonfat yogurt**
¼ **cup low-sodium mayonnaise**
2 **tablespoons cider vinegar**
2 **tablespoons chopped scallions**
2 **crushed garlic cloves**
1 **teaspoon dried tarragon**
2 **tablespoons chopped fresh parsley**
1 **teaspoon low-sodium mustard**
Freshly ground pepper

Combine ingredients thoroughly. Makes 1¹/₄ cups.

Tablespoonful:

Calories 27	Protein. . . . . 1 g.
Fat . . . . 2 g.	Carbohydrate . . . . . . 1 g.
Saturated Fat . . . . tr	Sodium. . . . . 18 mg.
Cholesterol. . . . . . 1 mg.	Potassium . . . . . . 33 mg.

LOW-SODIUM COTTAGE CHEESE SALAD DRESSING

---

1 cup low-sodium cottage cheese

**¹/₄ cup diced fresh tomatoes or ¹/₂ apple,
cut up fine**

1¹/₂ teaspoon vinegar

¹/₂ teaspoon sugar

¹/₂ teaspoon paprika

Few grains cayenne

¹/₄ teaspoon allspice

¹/₂ teaspoon dill weed

¹/₈ teaspoon garlic powder

¹/₈ teaspoon caraway seed

Combine all ingredients and mix well. Moisten with low-sodium mayonnaise if you wish. A good addition is two tablespoons of plain yogurt.

Total recipe:

Calories 215	Protein. . . . . 29 g.
Fat . . . . 2 g.	Carbohydrate . . . . . 18 g.
Saturated Fat. . . . . . . 1 g.	Sodium. . . . . 189 mg.
Cholesterol. . . . . . 11 mg.	Potassium . . . . . 438 mg.

Tablespoonful:

Calories 11	Protein. . . . . 1 g.
Fat. . . . . tr	Carbohydrate . . . . . . 1 g.
Saturated Fat . . . . tr	Sodium . . . . 9 mg.
Cholesterol. . . . . . 1 mg.	Potassium . . . . . . 22 mg.

SPECIAL RUSSIAN DRESSING

4 tablespoons low-sodium mayonnaise

1 tablespoon low-sodium catsup

1 teaspoon tarragon vinegar

1 teaspoon chives, chopped

Total recipe:

Calories 425	Protein . . . . tr
Fat . . . . 48 g.	Carbohydrate . . . . . . 2 g.
Saturated Fat. . . . . . 4 g.	Sodium. . . . . . . 310 mg.
Cholesterol. . . . . 17 mg.	Potassium . . . . . . 85 mg.

Tablespoonful:

Calories 85	Protein . . . . tr
Fat . . . . 10 g.	Carbohydrate . . . . . . 1 g.
Saturated Fat. . . . . . 1 g.	Sodium. . . . . 62 mg.
Cholesterol. . . . . . 3 mg.	Potassium . . . . . . 17 mg.

POTATO SALAD

Make this an hour or so before serving. This will give
the herbs a chance to meld.

4 medium-size new potatoes

1 medium chopped onion

1 tablespoon chopped green pepper

¼ cup diced cucumber

1 hard-boiled egg, chopped

4 slices low-sodium cucumber pickles

1 tablespoon fresh chopped parsley

$\frac{1}{2}$ teaspoon tarragon

$\frac{1}{4}$ teaspoon celery seed

$\frac{1}{2}$ teaspoon oregano

$\frac{1}{8}$ teaspoon garlic powder

Pepper to taste

4 tablespoons low-sodium mayonnaise

1 tablespoon vinegar or dry white wine

Cook new potatoes whole in skin, then peel and dice. While they are still warm, mix the potatoes with onion, green pepper, cucumber, egg, pickles, parsley, tarragon, celery seed, oregano, garlic powder, and pepper. Mix mayonnaise and vinegar or wine, and add to potato mixture. Mix well. Chill salad thoroughly. Serves 6.

Calories 146		Protein. . . . . 3 g.	
Fat . . . . 9 g.		Carbohydrate . . . . . 15 g.	
Saturated Fat. . . . . . . 1 g.		Sodium. . . . . 51 mg.	
Cholesterol. . . . . 38 mg.		Potassium . . . . . 300 mg.	

LEMON NEW POTATO SALAD

16 to 24 new potatoes

$\frac{1}{2}$ to $\frac{3}{4}$ cup fresh lemon juice

12 fresh scallions, chopped

$\frac{1}{2}$ cup chopped fresh mint

Freshly ground pepper

1 egg, beaten

2 garlic cloves

Boil potatoes until just tender. Drain. Cut if large, but leave on skins. While still warm, stir in lemon juice, scallions, mint, and pepper. Mix and chill. Add beaten egg mixed with crushed garlic. Mix and chill again. Add more lemon or pepper to taste. Garnish with a sprig of parsley.

Calories	201	Protein	5 g.
Fat	1 g.	Carbohydrate	45 g.
Saturated Fat	tr	Sodium	22 mg.
Cholesterol	36 mg.	Potassium	871 mg.

BLACK BEAN SALAD

1 lb. uncooked black beans

1¹/₂ cups fresh corn kernels, about 3 ears (frozen corn, blanched and drained may be used)

1¹/₂ cups chopped tomato

³/₄ cup chopped scallions

¹/₃ cup minced fresh cilantro

2 tablespoons chopped pimento

¹/₄ cup lemon juice

¹/₄ cup olive oil

Soak beans overnight and cook in water to cover until beans are tender, about 1¹/₂ hours. Drain and rinse. In bowl combine warm beans, corn, and remaining ingredients. Refrigerate several hours and serve at room temperature. Serves 8.

Calories	293	Protein	4 g.
Fat	15 g.	Carbohydrate	40 g.
Saturated Fat	2 g.	Sodium	20 mg.
Cholesterol	0 mg.	Potassium	643 mg.

WILD RICE SALAD

This recipe was inspired by Diane Rossen Worthington. It delights the eye and is especially good to bring to a friend's house for a summer potluck.

1 cup wild rice blend
2 cups low-sodium chicken or vegetable broth
1 small onion, grated
1 medium Bermuda onion, chopped
2 carrots, chopped
1 small zucchini, grated
2 oranges, peeled and chopped
¼ cup lemon juice
¼ cup lime juice
3 cloves garlic, pressed
1 tablespoon each of fresh chives, parsley,
    and mint
¼ teaspoon cayenne pepper
Freshly ground pepper
¼ cup olive oil
Optional: white raisins and grapes

Cook rice according to package directions, substituting broth for water. While the rice is still warm, toss with vegetables and chopped orange. Mix together all other ingredients and pour over rice and vegetables, carefully blending. This will keep for several hours in the refrigerator, but bring to room temperature before serving. Cut orange peel into 5 triangles and arrange with parsley or cilantro in a circle on top of rice. Serves 6.

Calories 239	Protein............ 5 g.
Fat .... 10 g.	Carbohydrate ..... 36 g.
Saturated Fat....... 1 g.	Sodium......... 14 mg.
Cholesterol....... 2 mg.	Potassium ..... 523 mg.

WILD RICE AND CORN SALAD

This is great as an accompaniment to grilled meats or just by itself.

1 cup wild rice

²/₃ cup cider vinegar

¼ cup extra-virgin olive oil

1 tablespoon honey

1 tablespoon low-sodium Dijon mustard

1½ cups corn kernels

1 tablespoon jalapeño pepper, chopped fine

2 scallions, chopped

¾ cup chopped tomatoes

1 bunch cilantro, finely chopped

Cook wild rice according to package directions. While rice is still warm add vinegar and oil, combined with honey and mustard. Mix thoroughly. Add remaining ingredients. Serve at room temperature. Serves 6 to 8.

Calories 238	Protein............ 6 g.
Fat .... 10 g.	Carbohydrate ..... 36 g.
Saturated Fat....... 1 g.	Sodium......... 13 mg.
Cholesterol....... 0 mg.	Potassium ..... 317 mg.

TABOULI

This eastern Mediterranean dish is popularly served at summer picnics, but makes a welcome addition to midwinter menus.

1 cup dry bulgur wheat
Juice of 2 lemons
6 cloves garlic, pressed
1 bunch of green onions
1 cup chopped parsley
$1/2$ cup chopped fresh mint
2 large tomatoes, chopped
1 cucumber, peeled and diced
$1/4$ extra-virgin olive oil
Freshly ground pepper

Soak the dry bulgur wheat in boiling water to cover (about 7 cups) for 1 to 2 hours, or until water is absorbed. Drain in a sieve or colander, pressing out all moisture. In a bowl carefully mix the rest of the ingredients and chill well. The flavor of tabouli improves with time. Serves 6.

Calories 192		Protein. . . . . 4 g.	
Fat . . . . 10 g.		Carbohydrate . . . . . 25 g.	
Saturated Fat. . . . . . . 1 g.		Sodium. . . . . 16 mg.	
Cholesterol. . . . . . . 0 mg.		Potassium . . . . . 395 mg.	

COUSCOUS SALAD

2 cups low-sodium chicken broth
1 cup quick-cooking couscous
2 medium tomatoes, chopped

1 cup cucumber, diced

6 green onions, chopped

1 cup cooked garbanzo beans, no salt added

1 cup parsley, chopped

¹/₄ teaspoon pepper

¹/₄ cup olive oil

³/₄ cup fresh lemon juice

¹/₂ teaspoon garlic powder

1 teaspoon low-sodium mustard

1 tablespoon minced fresh mint

Bring chicken broth to a boil and add couscous. Cover, remove from heat, and let stand for about 15 minutes or until all water has been absorbed. Toss with fork and add remaining ingredients. Mix carefully. Serves 8.

Calories	199	Protein	6 g.
Fat	8 g.	Carbohydrate	29 g.
Saturated Fat	1 g.	Sodium	13 mg.
Cholesterol	1 mg.	Potassium	401 mg.

CITRUS COUSCOUS

1 teaspoon olive oil

1 lb. sliced mushrooms

1 small chopped onion

1 tablespoon cumin

Cayenne pepper to taste

1 cup couscous

1 tablespoon grated lemon zest

1 tablespoon grated orange zest

⅓ cup dried apricots

½ cup chopped parsley

½ cup chopped mint

1 large chopped tomato

1 can water chestnuts

½ cup toasted pine nuts

Heat oil in large nonstick frying pan and sauté mushrooms and onion to soften. Add cumin and cayenne pepper. Follow package directions for making couscous. Add water to onions and mushrooms and bring to boil. Stir in couscous, orange and lemon rind, and apricots. Cover and turn off heat. Add parsley, mint, tomato, water chestnuts, and pine nuts. Serves 4.

Calories	381	Protein	12 g.
Fat	15 g.	Carbohydrate	57 g.
Saturated Fat	2 g.	Sodium	34 mg.
Cholesterol	0 mg.	Potassium	954 mg.

KASHA SALAD

A recipe is like a folktale, the way it is passed along. This salad began in Mollie Katzen's *Moosewood Cookbook* as Sri Wasano's Infamous Indonesian Rice Salad. It ended up in Texas at a popular restaurant as Kasha Salad and was brought to New England by a Texas friend. This was surely like a seed traveling on the wind.

1 cup kasha (buckwheat groats)

2 cups water or broth

3 tablespoons peanut oil

3 tablespoons sesame oil

½ cup orange juice

2 large cloves garlic, crushed

½ teaspoon low-sodium tamari

½ teaspoon cayenne pepper

2 tablespoons cider vinegar

1 can chopped fresh pineapple

3 scallions, chopped

1 stalk celery, chopped

1 small red pepper, chopped

1 small green or yellow pepper, chopped

1 cup fresh bean sprouts

½ cup raisins

1 cup coarsely chopped unsalted peanuts

2 tablespoons sesame seeds, toasted

Optional: 1 can water chestnuts, rinsed

Spread kasha on foil-lined pan and toast in 350-degree oven for 10 minutes. Then add kasha to boiling water or broth. Lower heat and cook for about 25 minutes or until tender, stirring to keep kasha from sticking to pan. Spoon into bowl and add oils, orange juice, garlic, tamari, pepper, vinegar, and pineapple. Refrigerate. When cold, add remaining ingredients, stirring gently with 2 forks. Serves 8 to 10.

Total recipe:

Calories 236	Protein . . . . 6 g.
Fat . . . . 14 g.	Carbohydrate . . . . . 26 g.
Saturated Fat . . . . 2 g.	Sodium . . . . 26 mg.
Cholesterol . . . . 1 mg.	Potassium . . . . . 387 mg.

BLACK-EYED PEAS AND ARUGULA SALAD

1 lb. black-eyed peas
6 cups low-sodium chicken broth
2 tablespoons extra-virgin olive oil
2 tablespoons red wine vinegar
3 cloves garlic, crushed
1 tablespoon low-sodium mustard
1 tablespoon honey
¼ teaspoon cloves
⅛ teaspoon red pepper
Freshly ground pepper
1 Bermuda onion, chopped
2 cups fresh spring arugula, washed, dried, and
    finely chopped

Wash and pick over black-eyed peas. Drain. Soak in fresh water overnight and drain again. In a large pot, combine beans and chicken broth. Bring to a boil and then simmer for about 1 hour or until tender. Drain. While still warm add a dressing made of oil, vinegar, garlic, mustard, honey, cloves, and peppers. Mix dressing carefully with black-eyed peas and add onion and arugula. Serves 8.

Calories 192	Protein. . . . . 5 g.
Fat . . . . 4 g.	Carbohydrate . . . . . 35 g.
Saturated Fat. . . . . . . 1 g.	Sodium. . . . . 14 mg.
Cholesterol. . . . . . . 4 mg.	Potassium . . . . 1,011 mg.

SOUTHWESTERN MACARONI SALAD

This dish goes well with barbecued chicken or ribs.

1 lb. small elbow macaroni
²/₃ cup cider vinegar
1 cup chopped celery
1 small chopped green pepper
1 small chopped red pepper
6 scallions, minced
1 jalapeño pepper, seeded and chopped
¼ cup canola oil
3 dashes low-sodium Worcestershire sauce
3 dashes hot pepper sauce
½ teaspoon fresh ground pepper
1 15-oz. can low-sodium black-eyed peas, rinsed
    and drained
1½ cups fresh corn kernels, or 12 oz. canned or
    frozen corn, salt-free

Cook macaroni al dente according to package directions. Drain and pour into large bowl. Immediately pour
cider vinegar over hot macaroni and stir. Let stand while
chopping vegetables. Add chopped vegetables and remaining ingredients. Mix well. Serve at room temperature, or refrigerate. Keeps overnight to serve cold the next
day. Serves 12 as a side dish.

Calories	237	Protein	8 g.
Fat	6 g.	Carbohydrate	41 g.
Saturated Fat	1 g.	Sodium	126 mg.
Cholesterol	0 mg.	Potassium	291 mg.

Vegetables

Elma always valued the flavor, texture, and increased vitamin value of "lovely, fresh vegetables," and she filled her book with many suggestions for enhancing—without salt—the sweet and tender specimens she chose at our local farm stand. Today our groceries and produce marts carry vegetables imported from faraway places as well as an abundance of locally grown favorites. We can also choose from a vastly increased selection of fresh herbs and seasonings that Elma didn't always have at her disposal. We encourage you to be versatile and experiment with your vegetable preparation. For example, the contrasting colors in a crisp stir-fry will add visual appeal to your plate and variety to your daily vitamin requirements.

Please note that all nutritional information is for 1 serving size.

POACHED ARTICHOKES

Artichokes have more sodium than most vegetables but should nevertheless be enjoyed from time to time. Choose artichokes that squeak when you squeeze them. This recipe, inspired by Martha Rose Shulman, makes butter dunking sauce unnecessary.

4 medium artichokes

2 to 3 teaspoons crushed rosemary

3 cloves garlic, minced

1 medium sliced onion

1 lemon, sliced in rounds

1 cup white wine

½ cup water

2 bay leaves

1 tablespoon olive oil

Freshly ground pepper

Cut the stem off at the base of each artichoke. With scissors clip off the point of each leaf. Cut about ¹/₂ inch off the top of each artichoke. Mix rosemary and minced garlic cloves and divide between the 4 artichokes, placing mixture between layers of leaves. Put remaining ingredients in deep, wide saucepan and add artichokes. Bring to a simmer, cover, and cook for 45 to 50 minutes, or until leaves are very tender. Serves 4.

Calories 137	Protein. . . . . 5 g.
Fat . . . . 4 g.	Carbohydrate . . . . . 20 g.
Saturated Fat. . . . . . . 1 g.	Sodium. . . . . 119 mg.
Cholesterol. . . . . . . 0 mg.	Potassium . . . . . 541 mg.

ASPARAGUS WITH MARJORAM

2 lbs. asparagus
4 tablespoons unsalted butter
Pepper to taste
¼ teaspoon marjoram
1 tablespoon fresh parsley, minced
Juice of one lemon

Steam the asparagus until just tender. Mix melted butter with pepper, marjoram, parsley, and lemon juice. Pour sauce on asparagus. If you'd like, you may wrap the asparagus in groups of 4 or 5 with pimento strips. Serves 6.

Calories 105	Protein . . . . 4 g.
Fat . . . . 8 g.	Carbohydrate . . . . . . 7 g.
Saturated Fat . . . . . . 5 g.	Sodium . . . . 7 mg.
Cholesterol . . . . . . 21 mg.	Potassium . . . . . 451 mg.

STRING BEANS WITH TOMATO

1 lb. string beans
½ cup hot water
2 tablespoons olive or vegetable oil
1 small onion, chopped
1 clove garlic, minced
1 large tomato
1 tablespoon white wine
1 tablespoon green pepper, chopped
1 tablespoon parsley, minced
½ teaspoon marjoram
⅛ teaspoon cinnamon or allspice

Cut string beans in half. Place in saucepan. Add hot water. Cover and cook until just tender. In separate pan heat oil. Add onion and garlic to oil. Cook over a low flame for 10 minutes. Peel tomato and cut pieces into oil and onion mixture. Add wine, pepper, herbs, and spices. Simmer 10 minutes, add beans, stir, cover, and cook 10 minutes more. Serves 4.

Calories	122	Protein	3 g.
Fat	7 g.	Carbohydrate	14 g.
Saturated Fat	1 g.	Sodium	10 mg.
Cholesterol	0 mg.	Potassium	500 mg.

MINTED STRING BEANS

The mint family has over 25 species, and all are used for flavorings and medicines. The most common are spearmint and peppermint.

1 lb. string beans
¼ cup sugar
Hot bean liquor
1 tablespoon vinegar
1½ tablespoons unsalted butter
½ tablespoon flour
1 teaspoon dried mint

Wash beans and cut them in julienne strips. Cook in a small amount of boiling water until just tender. Save liquor.

Sauce

Put sugar in heavy frying pan and add bean liquor and vinegar. Cook until sugar is dissolved. In nonstick skillet, melt butter, blend in flour and mint, and add hot liquid, slowly, stirring constantly. Cook until thickened. Pour over beans. Serves 4.

Calories	129	Protein	2 g.
Fat	5 g.	Carbohydrate	22 g.
Saturated Fat	3 mg.	Sodium	5 mg.
Cholesterol	12 mg.	Potassium	337 mg.

BEETS

Beets are most delicious when they are baked with their skins on and top intact.

One medium-size beet per person.

Wrap each beet separately in foil and bake at 300 degrees for about an hour. Serve right from foil with a dollop of plain nonfat yogurt or combine with recipe below.

Calories	22	Protein	1 g.
Fat	tr	Carbohydrate	4 g.
Saturated Fat	tr	Sodium	34 mg.
Cholesterol	tr	Potassium	197 mg.

BEETS WITH ONIONS AND HONEY

The old *Farm Journal Cookbook* offers this recipe for beets.

2 teaspoons unsalted butter

1 tablespoon cider vinegar

2 tablespoons honey

1 tablespoon orange juice

1 small onion, sliced and separated into rings

5 cooked beets, peeled and sliced

In a saucepan combine butter, vinegar, honey, and orange juice. Add onions and beets. Simmer until heated through, about 5 minutes. Onions should remain crisp. Serves 4 to 5.

Calories 78		Protein. . . . . 1 g.	
Fat . . . . 2 g.		Carbohydrate . . . . . 15 g.	
Saturated Fat. . . . . . . 1 g.		Sodium. . . . . 32 mg.	
Cholesterol. . . . . . . 6 mg.		Potassium . . . . . 240 mg.	

BROCCOLI WITH LEMON

1 lb. broccoli

2 teaspoons sugar

½ teaspoon paprika

½ teaspoon dried mustard

2 tablespoons lemon juice

1 tablespoon unsalted butter

Trim, split, and wash broccoli stalks. Cook in a little boiling water about 10 minutes. Blend sugar, paprika, and mustard in a bowl. Add lemon juice and melted butter. Mix well and pour over broccoli. Serves 4.

Calories 91		Protein. . . . . 3 g.	
Fat . . . . 7 g.		Carbohydrate . . . . . . 8 g.	
Saturated Fat. . . . . . . 4 g.		Sodium. . . . . 24 mg.	
Cholesterol. . . . . 17 mg.		Potassium . . . . . 278 mg.	

BROCCOLI WITH WALNUTS

1 bunch broccoli

1 tablespoon walnut oil

2 cloves garlic, pressed

¼ cup chopped walnuts

Cut broccoli florets from stem and steam them in a small amount of water until they turn bright green and begin to be tender. Drain. Heat walnut oil at a low temperature in that same pan, add garlic and walnuts, and toast for about 5 minutes. Toss with broccoli. Serves 4.

Calories	105	Protein	4 g.
Fat	8 g.	Carbohydrate	6 g.
Saturated Fat	1 g.	Sodium	25 mg.
Cholesterol	0 mg.	Potassium	330 mg.

BROCCOLI IN OLIVE OIL

This is great hot or cold.

1 bunch broccoli
1 tablespoon extra-virgin olive oil
2 cloves garlic, crushed
½ teaspoon oregano
Juice of ½ lemon

Cut broccoli florets from stem and steam them in a small amount of water until they turn bright green and begin to be tender. Drain. Heat olive oil in nonstick skillet, add garlic, and then toss with broccoli. Sprinkle with oregano and add lemon juice. Serves 4.

Calories	59	Protein	3 g.
Fat	4 g.	Carbohydrate	6 g.
Saturated Fat	1 g.	Sodium	24 mg.
Cholesterol	0 mg.	Potassium	302 mg.

BRUSSELS SPROUTS

Pull off wilted leaves. Soak sprouts 10 minutes in cold water, then drain. Gash stem, drop in boiling water. Reduce heat and simmer 10 minutes. There are 18 sprouts per pound in the fresh vegetable department. Allow 4 to 5 per serving.

During the last 5 minutes of cooking time add one of the following combinations:

1. ¼ teaspoon dill (ground or seed)
   ¼ teaspoon dry mustard
2. ¼ teaspoon nutmeg
   ¼ teaspoon caraway seed
3. ¼ teaspoon basil
   ¼ teaspoon dry mustard

Brussels sprouts may be topped with unsalted butter, a dash of lemon juice, or vinegar. For a wonderful topping, mix nutmeg with sour cream. Serves 4.

Calories	44	Protein	3 g.
Fat	1 g.	Carbohydrate	10 g.
Saturated Fat	0 g.	Sodium	24 mg.
Cholesterol	0 mg.	Potassium	360 mg.

CABBAGE

Place cabbage in boiling water, and allow to simmer for 7 to 10 minutes.

These herb combinations can be used:

1. ¼ teaspoon fennel
   ¼ teaspoon nutmeg

2. ¹/₄ teaspoon oregano
   ¹/₄ teaspoon dry mustard
3. ¹/₄ teaspoon caraway seed
   ¹/₄ teaspoon dill (ground or seed)
4. ¹/₄ teaspoon savory
   ¹/₄ teaspoon cumin seed or tarragon

Cabbage may be topped with unsalted butter. If you can stand the calories or sodium count and your doctor approves, a little sour cream is very good. Vinegar and lemon juice and cabbage go well, too. Garnish with parsley. Serves 4.

Calories	30	Protein	1 g.
Fat	tr	Carbohydrate	7 g.
Saturated Fat	tr	Sodium	28 mg.
Cholesterol	0 mg.	Potassium	297 mg.

RED CABBAGE

This recipe was awarded a prize by the *London Daily Express* on Christmas 1927.

1 head of red cabbage
1 tablespoon unsalted butter
Pepper to taste
¹/₂ teaspoon nutmeg
1 tablespoon sugar
1 medium onion, chopped
2 cups hot water
2 apples, sliced
4 whole cloves
1 tablespoon vinegar
2 tablespoons raspberry or currant jelly

Slice cabbage. Heat butter in saucepan. Add cabbage, pepper, nutmeg, sugar, and onion. Sauté until soft. Then add hot water, apples, cloves, and vinegar. Cover and cook slowly until tender. The final touch is a topping of currant or raspberry jelly.

Calories 31	Protein . . . . 1 g.
Fat . . . . 2 g.	Carbohydrate . . . . . 16 g.
Saturated Fat . . . . 1 g.	Sodium . . . . 12 mg.
Cholesterol . . . . 4 mg.	Potassium . . . . . 214 mg.

SWEET AND SOUR RED CABBAGE

2 cups red cabbage

1/2 teaspoon cornstarch

2 teaspoons water

1/8 cup vinegar

1 tablespoon sugar

1/4 teaspoon tarragon

Shred cabbage coarsely. Cover in boiling water and cook 7 to 10 minutes. Drain all but 1/2 cup water. Add cornstarch mixed with 2 teaspoons of water, vinegar, sugar, and tarragon. Cook a few minutes. Serves 4.

Calories 46	Protein . . . . 1 g.
Fat . . . . tr	Carbohydrate . . . . . 12 g.
Saturated Fat . . . . tr	Sodium . . . . 4 mg.
Cholesterol . . . . 0 mg.	Potassium . . . . . . 76 mg.

CURRIED CAULIFLOWER WITH GARLIC

If you have any of this cauliflower left over, it makes a great, quick soup. (See Cauliflower and Pimento Soup on page 108.)

1 large head of cauliflower, cut into florets

2 teaspoons unsalted butter

2 cloves garlic, crushed

2 teaspoons curry powder

1 tablespoon horseradish, freshly grated or preserved without salt

½ cup nonfat plain yogurt, at room temperature, mixed with 2 teaspoons of cornstarch

Freshly ground black pepper

Fresh dill or dried dill weed

Cook cauliflower florets in boiling water until tender, about 10 to 15 minutes. Drain. In same pot melt butter and heat garlic, curry powder, horseradish, and yogurt. Add cooked cauliflower and sprinkle with freshly ground black pepper and chopped fresh dill or dill weed. Serves 6.

Calories	42	Protein	2 g.
Fat	2 g.	Carbohydrate	5 g.
Saturated Fat	1 g.	Sodium	21 mg.
Cholesterol	4 mg.	Potassium	269 mg.

CARROTS

Cook peeled carrots in small amount of boiling water for about 10 minutes or until tender. After 5 minutes of cooking time add any of the following combinations:

1. **Parsley, lemon juice, and unsalted butter**
2. **Bay leaf and thyme or dill weed (add to water while carrots are cooking)**
3. **Curry powder and freshly grated ginger**
4. **Brown sugar and cinnamon**
5. **Honey and allspice, cinnamon, or nutmeg**

Calories 35		Protein. . . . . 1 g.	
Fat. . . . . tr		Carbohydrate . . . . . . 8 g.	
Saturated Fat . . . . tr		Sodium. . . . . 52 mg.	
Cholesterol. . . . . . . 0 mg.		Potassium . . . . . 177 mg.	

LIMA BEANS

1 lb. fresh lima beans
¼ teaspoon sage
1 tablespoon unsalted butter
3 teaspoons lemon juice
1 tablespoon chopped parsley

Cook lima beans in an inch of boiling water, covered. Simmer for 20 minutes. (One pound serves 4.) After 10 minutes of cooking time add sage. When tender add unsalted butter, lemon juice, and chopped parsley. If permitted, a little sour cream is divine. Remember: Frozen lima beans are generally salted.

Fresh stewed tomatoes, onions, or sautéed mushrooms may be added. 4 servings.

Variation: Substitute 2 teaspoons chives and ground black pepper for chopped parsley.

Calories 156	Protein. . . . . 7 g.
Fat . . . . 6 g.	Carbohydrate . . . . 19 g.
Saturated Fat. . . . . . 4 g.	Sodium . . . . 3 mg.
Cholesterol. . . . . 17 mg.	Potassium . . . . . 457 mg.

MUSHROOMS WITH THYME

1 lb. mushrooms

2 tablespoons water

3 tablespoons olive oil

1 clove garlic, minced

1 teaspoon vinegar

Pepper to taste

1 teaspoon dried thyme

Wash and cut mushrooms in large pieces. Heat water and oil in frying pan. Add garlic, vinegar, pepper, and thyme. Stir well and cook slowly about 15 minutes. Serves 4.

Calories 120	Protein. . . . . 2 g.
Fat . . . . 11 g.	Carbohydrate . . . . . . 6 g.
Saturated Fat. . . . . . 1 g.	Sodium . . . . 3 mg.
Cholesterol. . . . . . . 0 mg.	Potassium . . . . . 393 mg.

MUSHROOMS AMHERST

These mushrooms were first served to us by a professor at Amherst College.

20 medium-size mushroom caps
1 tablespoon unsalted butter
Powdered garlic
Powdered onion
Marjoram
Pepper to taste
¼ pint low-fat sour cream
1½ tablespoons finely chopped parsley
**3 small finely chopped green onions, tops and
    bottoms**

Sauté the mushroom caps in the butter slowly, so that the mushroom juice combines with the butter. Sprinkle liberally with powdered garlic, powdered onion, marjoram, and pepper. Sprinkle them again when you turn them. In the meantime combine the sour cream, parsley, and onions. When the mushrooms are brown and tender (10 to 15 minutes) take the pan off the heat and add half of the sour-cream mixture. With a spatula, scrape the brown butter and mushroom juice from the bottom of the pan and stir it in with the sour cream until you have a smooth, golden sauce. Serve immediately.

Use as a side dish on rice, potatoes, or meat, or on a slice of low-sodium bread for a luncheon dish. Serves 4.

Calories 183	Protein. . . . . 3 g.
Fat . . . . 18 g.	Carbohydrate . . . . . . 5 g.
Saturated Fat. . . . . . 11 g.	Sodium. . . . . 20 mg.
Cholesterol. . . . . . 44 mg.	Potassium . . . . . 284 mg.

SHIITAKE MUSHROOMS AND SNOW PEAS

1 cup fresh shiitake mushrooms
1 tablespoon sesame oil
1 bunch scallions, cut in 2-inch pieces
3 cloves garlic, minced
1 teaspoon minced fresh ginger
1 lb. snow peas, washed and trimmed
½ cup fresh chopped parsley
1 tablespoon toasted sesame seeds
1 can water chestnuts, drained and sliced

Soak mushrooms in warm water to cover for 30 minutes. Drain and remove stems. Cut into small pieces. Heat oil in nonstick skillet. Sauté mushrooms, scallions, and garlic in oil until soft. Add ginger and snow peas. Cook, stirring frequently, for about 2 minutes. Add parsley, sesame seeds, and water chestnuts and heat through. Serves 4 to 5.

Calories	131	Protein	5 g.
Fat	5 g.	Carbohydrate	20 g.
Saturated Fat	1 g.	Sodium	11 mg.
Cholesterol	0 mg.	Potassium	434 mg.

OKRA AND TOMATOES

This recipe was adapted from Martha Rose Shulman's book *Fast Vegetarian Feasts*.

1 tablespoon olive oil
1 large chopped onion

3 minced garlic cloves

1 lb. okra, trimmed and sliced ¼-inch thick

2 tablespoons wine or cider vinegar

2 to 3 tablespoons white wine

1 lb. sliced ripe tomatoes or 1 28-oz. can crushed
   tomatoes, no salt added

1 teaspoon dried basil or 1 tablespoon chopped
   fresh

1 teaspoon dried oregano

Freshly ground pepper

Heat oil in nonstick skillet and sauté onion and garlic until soft. Add okra and 1 tablespoon vinegar and
sauté until the okra turns bright green, about 5 minutes.
Add 2 tablespoons wine, tomatoes, and herbs. Season
with remaining vinegar, wine, and ground pepper.
Serves 4 to 6.

Calories	108	Protein	3 g.
Fat	4 g.	Carbohydrate	17 g.
Saturated Fat	1 g.	Sodium	17 g.
Cholesterol	0 mg.	Potassium	635 mg.

WAYS WITH ONIONS

You can boil onions or steam or even roast them.
Take your choice. If you want to boil, place the peeled
onions in a pan, cover with boiling water, and cook 30 to
45 minutes. If you like to steam, place unpeeled onions
on a rack over hot water. Cover the pan and steam for 30
to 45 minutes. Then you have to peel. If you boil, you
can peel onions under hot running water. Here's your
chance to use salt—and the only time in this book—rub

your hands with salt or vinegar. No odor. To roast, wrap onions in foil and place in 350-degree oven for 30 to 40 minutes.

Interesting flavor combinations for onions are: basil, marjoram, and thyme; or coriander and caraway seed.

Always pepper to taste. Add melted unsalted butter.

Baked Onions and Apples

2 medium-to-large onions sliced ½-inch thick

4 cups apple rings, ¼-inch thick

½ cup sugar

¼ teaspoon nutmeg

¼ teaspoon thyme

1 teaspoon grated lemon rind

2 tablespoons lemon juice

2 tablespoons unsalted butter

Place a layer of sliced onions in an oiled baking dish. Cover onions with a layer of apple rings, which should be cored but not peeled. Mix together the sugar, nutmeg, thyme, and lemon rind, and sprinkle over the apples. Repeat the process until onions and apples are used up. Pour over the top the lemon juice and melted butter and then bake for 1 hour in 350-degree oven. Serves 4.

Calories	281	Protein	1 g.
Fat	12 g.	Carbohydrate	47 g.
Saturated Fat	7 g.	Sodium	3 mg.
Cholesterol	31 mg.	Potassium	220 mg.

Roasted Bermuda Onion in Foil

1 Bermuda onion

1 teaspoon unsalted butter

2 teaspoons sherry

⅛ teaspoon thyme

Core onion as you would an apple, but be careful not to go all the way through. Fill cavity with butter, sherry, and thyme. Wrap in 2 thicknesses of aluminum foil. You may cook onion over charcoal or in oven at 350 degrees until tender. Serves 1.

Calories	106	Protein	2 g.
Fat	4 g.	Carbohydrate	14 g.
Saturated Fat	3 g.	Sodium	5 mg.
Cholesterol	11 mg.	Potassium	221 mg.

Glazed Onions

3 lbs. white onions, peeled

4 teaspoons sugar

1 teaspoon dry mustard

3 tablespoons unsalted butter

½ teaspoon thyme

Paprika

Cook onions in water until tender (20 to 30 minutes). Drain and put in shallow baking dish. Combine sugar, mustard, butter, and thyme. Spread mixture on onions. Sprinkle with paprika. Bake at 325 degrees for 20 minutes. Baste occasionally. Serves 8.

Calories	154	Protein	2 g.
Fat	10 g.	Carbohydrate	17 g.
Saturated Fat	6 g.	Sodium	6 mg.
Cholesterol	25 mg.	Potassium	246 mg.

Caramelized Onions

This recipe came from Adlard's restaurant in London via *Bon Appétit*. It makes a great accompaniment to roasted lamb or pork.

1 tablespoon olive oil
3 large onions, sliced in rings
1 tablespoon brown sugar
2 teaspoons white sugar
1 cup red wine
¼ cup balsamic vinegar
Freshly ground pepper

Heat oil in a large saucepan. Add onions and cook over medium-high heat until golden brown, stirring frequently, about 10 minutes. Reduce heat to medium. Sprinkle sugars over onions and sauté 5 minutes more. Increase heat to high. Add wine and vinegar and boil until almost no liquid remains in pan, about 10 minutes. Season with pepper. Serves 4.

Calories	122	Protein	1 g.
Fat	4 g.	Carbohydrate	17 g.
Saturated Fat	1 g.	Sodium	7 mg.
Cholesterol	0 mg.	Potassium	222 mg.

HERBED PEAS

Remember to use only fresh peas. Frozen peas are usually salted. Never take chances. Two lbs. of unhulled peas fill about 2 cups and serve 4.

2 tablespoons unsalted butter
2 lbs. fresh peas

6 scallions

1 tablespoon fresh chopped parsley

¼ teaspoon marjoram

¼ teaspoon rosemary

⅛ teaspoon thyme

½ teaspoon sugar

2 tablespoons cream

Melt butter in heavy skillet. Add peas, scallions, and all ingredients except cream. Cook covered until peas are tender, add cream, and heat thoroughly.

Calories 194	Protein. . . . . 5 g.
Fat . . . . 15 g.	Carbohydrate . . . . . 12 g.
Saturated Fat. . . . . . . 9 g.	Sodium. . . . . 12 mg.
Cholesterol. . . . . . 41 mg.	Potassium . . . . . 224 mg.

PEA PODS AND MUSHROOMS

1 lb. fresh pea pods

Lettuce leaf

½ lb. mushrooms, sliced

1 clove garlic, minced

2 tablespoons vegetable oil

⅓ cup liquor from peas

Pepper

Parsley

Cook peas with lettuce leaf. Drain, reserving ⅓ cup liquor. In nonstick skillet, sauté mushrooms and garlic in oil. Remove mushrooms and add to peas. Add to skillet the liquor from the peas and the mushrooms. Season with pepper, pour over peas, and garnish with chopped parsley if you wish. Serves 4.

Calories 143	Protein . . . . 5 g.
Fat . . . . 7 g.	Carbohydrate . . . . . 15 g.
Saturated Fat . . . . 1 g.	Sodium . . . . 5 mg.
Cholesterol . . . . 0 mg.	Potassium . . . . . 388 mg.

SWIFT RIVER SQUASH

A New England inn served this lovely dish in the dead of winter.

2 butternut squash

1 tablespoon unsalted butter

6 tablespoons maple syrup

36 walnuts, roasted for 5 to 10 minutes at 350 degrees

1 teaspoon nutmeg

Cut squash in half crosswise and scrape away seeds. Place skin side down in shallow roasting pan with about an inch of water. Bake in 350-degree oven for 45 to 60 minutes, adding water when necessary. When flesh is tender, remove. Melt butter in skillet with syrup, walnuts, and nutmeg. Divide squash into 6 pieces and spread mixture evenly over each piece. Mash lightly. Sprinkle with nutmeg. Serves 6.

Calories 203	Protein . . . . 3 g.
Fat . . . . 10 g.	Carbohydrate . . . . . 31 g.
Saturated Fat . . . . 2 g.	Sodium . . . . 27 mg.
Cholesterol . . . . 6 mg.	Potassium . . . . . 429 mg.

BASIL CRUSTED TOMATOES

4 medium tomatoes
1 tablespoon wheat germ
1 tablespoon unsalted butter
Pepper to taste
1 teaspoon basil
1 teaspoon sugar

Cut off stem ends and cut each tomato in half. Place the tomato halves in baking dish. In a small bowl mix wheat germ, butter, pepper, basil, and sugar. Sprinkle on top of tomatoes. Cover and bake at 375 degrees for about 30 minutes or until tomatoes are soft. Serves 4.

Calories 64	Protein. . . . . 2 g.
Fat . . . . 4 g.	Carbohydrate . . . . . . 8 g.
Saturated Fat. . . . . . . 2 g.	Sodium. . . . . 12 mg.
Cholesterol. . . . . . . 8 mg.	Potassium . . . . . 303 mg.

RATATOUILLE

Peeled eggplant is often sprinkled with salt to bring bitter juices to the surface. You can achieve the same result without salt, however, by parboiling the eggplant before proceeding with this recipe.

1 eggplant (peeled, cubed, and boiled for 5 minutes, then drained)
Flour
1 tablespoon olive oil
3 zucchini, cut in 1-inch cubes
2 medium onions, chopped

2 peppers (1 red and 1 green, if possible), seeded
   and chopped

2 cups mushrooms, sliced

2 15-oz. cans of tomatoes (no salt added) or 2 lbs.
   fresh, chopped

2 tablespoons low-sodium tomato paste

5 cloves garlic, minced

1 teaspoon basil

2 teaspoons oregano

2 tablespoons fresh parsley, chopped

Freshly ground pepper

Toss eggplant in flour. Heat olive oil in nonstick skillet and sauté eggplant until soft, about 5 minutes. Set aside in casserole dish. Do the same with the zucchini and add to the eggplant. Sauté the onions until soft, then add peppers and mushrooms. Add mixture to casserole along with chopped tomatoes, tomato paste, garlic, and herbs. Grind fresh pepper over all. Bake covered in a hot oven (400 degrees) for 15 minutes. Turn oven to 325 and continue baking for 1 hour. Serves 6.

Note: If sodium and fat amounts allow, add grated mozzarella before baking or Parmesan cheese at the table.

Calories 136	Protein. . . . . 4 g.
Fat . . . . 3 g.	Carbohydrate . . . . . 26 g.
Saturated Fat. . . . . . . 1 g.	Sodium. . . . . 27 mg.
Cholesterol. . . . . . . 0 mg.	Potassium . . . . 1,011 mg.

TOMATOES IN YOGURT SAUCE

1 tablespoon olive oil

1 onion, chopped

1 green pepper, sliced in strips

4 medium tomatoes, sliced

1 teaspoon dried basil or 2 teaspoons fresh basil

3 cloves garlic, pressed

¼ cup wine

½ cup nonfat, plain yogurt

Pimento

In a nonstick skillet heat 1 tablespoon olive oil. Sauté onions and peppers until just soft. Add tomatoes, basil, and garlic and heat through. Pour wine over mixture and bring to a simmer. Reduce heat and add yogurt. Sprinkle with chopped parsley and garnish with pimento strips. Serves 4.

Calories	107	Protein	4 g.
Fat	4 g.	Carbohydrate	14 g.
Saturated Fat	1 g.	Sodium	36 mg.
Cholesterol	1 mg.	Potassium	478 mg.

TOMATOES IN FOIL

4 large tomatoes

Pepper to taste

8 teaspoons unsalted butter

¼ cup chopped parsley

⅓ cup chopped green onions including tops, or
⅓ cup onions

1 teaspoon basil
1 teaspoon tarragon
1 clove garlic, minced

Cut tomatoes crosswise into halves. Sprinkle with pepper, top each with 1 teaspoon butter. Mix remaining ingredients and mound equally on each tomato half. Set tomatoes on 2 pieces of aluminum foil. Wrap and seal tightly. Grill on charcoal or bake in oven until soft, approximately 20 minutes. Serves 4.

Calories	120	Protein	2 g.
Fat	9 g.	Carbohydrate	11 g.
Saturated Fat	5 g.	Sodium	20 mg.
Cholesterol	22 mg.	Potassium	476 mg.

MARINATED ZUCCHINI

A wonderful pickle substitute.

4 medium zucchini
1/8 cup olive oil
1 clove garlic, chopped
1 teaspoon basil
1 teaspoon oregano
1 tablespoon chopped fresh parsley
1/4 teaspoon pepper
1/4 cup vinegar

Cut zucchini into 1-inch slices. Sauté in hot oil until light brown, and drain on absorbent paper. In a casserole place 1 layer of zucchini. Dot with chopped garlic, basil, oregano, and parsley. Sprinkle with pepper. Repeat until all zucchini are used. Boil vinegar 5 minutes and pour over squash. Let marinate at least 12 hours. Drain and serve. Can be kept for over a week in refrigerator. Serves 8.

Calories	45	Protein	1 g.
Fat	3 g.	Carbohydrate	4 g.
Saturated Fat	1 g.	Sodium	3 mg.
Cholesterol	0 mg.	Potassium	216 mg.

MAGIC ZUCCHINI

This is almost too easy.

2 large zucchini
Olive oil
Oregano
Optional: garlic powder

Cut zucchini half lengthwise. Rub zucchini with olive oil, oregano, and optional garlic powder. Place on foil-lined pan and broil for about 8 minutes or until lightly browned. Slice in chunks and serve. Serves 4.

Calories	31	Protein	1 g.
Fat	1 g.	Carbohydrate	5 g.
Saturated Fat	tr	Sodium	4 mg.
Cholesterol	0 mg.	Potassium	334 mg.

STUFFED ZUCCHINI

2 medium zucchini
1 tablespoon extra-virgin olive oil
1 large finely chopped onion

2 cloves garlic, thinly sliced
¼ lb. finely chopped mushrooms
4 to 5 chopped sun-dried tomatoes, packed in oil
¼ teaspoon dried thyme
Freshly ground pepper

Slice off ends of zucchini and cut in half lengthwise. Scoop out centers and chop. Place boats in oiled baking pan. In nonstick skillet sauté onion and garlic in oil until soft. Add mushrooms and tomatoes (which may be chopped in food processor or blender) along with chopped zucchini. Add thyme and pepper. Pile mixture in zucchini boats, cover with foil, and bake in 350-degree oven for 20 to 25 minutes. Serves 4.

Calories	106	Protein	2 g.
Fat	7 g.	Carbohydrate	10 g.
Saturated Fat	1 g.	Sodium	9 mg.
Cholesterol	0 mg.	Potassium	420 mg.

BAKED SLICED POTATO

Scrub and dry a medium-size Idaho potato. Cut ¼-inch vertical slices, but don't cut through to bottom of potato. Place thin slices of onion between potato slices. Brush with unsalted butter, season with dash of pepper, garlic powder, mint, or rosemary. Wrap each potato in aluminum foil. Bake over hot charcoal fire or in a 450-degree oven for 45 to 60 minutes. Serves 1.

Calories	336	Protein	5 g.
Fat	12 g.	Carbohydrate	54 g.
Saturated Fat	2 g.	Sodium	18 mg.
Cholesterol	0 mg.	Potassium	910 mg.

STUFFED BAKED POTATOES

2 baking potatoes
1 tablespoon unsalted butter
Pepper to taste
4 tablespoons milk

Bake potatoes in hot oven, 450 degrees, for 45 to 60 minutes. Remove potatoes from oven and cut in halves lengthwise. Scoop out the contents with a teaspoon. Mash, add butter, pepper, and milk. Beat until fluffy, pile lightly into shells, bake at 450 degrees for 15 minutes. Serves 4.

Choose one of the following combinations for Stuffed Baked Potatoes:

1. ½ tablespoon low-sodium grated cheese
2. 1 teaspoon grated onion
3. 1 teaspoon chopped chives
4. 2 mushrooms sautéed and cut into pieces
5. ½ teaspoon curry powder or ½ teaspoon nutmeg
6. 1 tablespoon sour cream, 1 teaspoon chives, and 1 teaspoon grated onion

Calories 106		Protein. . . . . 2 g.	
Fat . . . . 3 g.		Carbohydrate . . . . . 18 g.	
Saturated Fat. . . . . . . 2 g.		Sodium. . . . . 12 mg.	
Cholesterol. . . . . . . 9 mg.		Potassium . . . . . 330 mg.	

MASHED POTATOES

4 medium-size potatoes
1 small onion, minced

2 cloves garlic, minced
1 bay leaf
¼ teaspoon rosemary
2 teaspoons chopped parsley
1 tablespoon unsalted butter
3 tablespoons hot milk
⅛ teaspoon mace

Cook potatoes in saucepan in enough boiling water to which have been added onion, garlic, bay leaf, rosemary, and parsley. Cover and cook 20 to 30 minutes, or until tender. Remove bay leaf. Drain, mash, and add butter, hot milk, and mace. Beat until creamy. Garnish with parsley. Serves 4.

Calories 155	Protein . . . . 3 g.
Fat . . . . 3 g.	Carbohydrate . . . . . 30 g.
Saturated Fat . . . . . . 2 g.	Sodium . . . . 14 mg.
Cholesterol . . . . . . 9 mg.	Potassium . . . . . 491 mg.

BOILED NEW POTATOES

Ah! Spring.

16 new potatoes, peeled or unpeeled
2 teaspoons chopped parsley
½ teaspoon dried mint or 1 tablespoon fresh
2 tablespoons unsalted butter
¼ teaspoon nutmeg

Cook potatoes with parsley and mint in boiling water in covered saucepan for 20 to 30 minutes. Serve with melted butter and nutmeg. Serves 4.

Calories 228	Protein. . . . . 4 g.
Fat . . . . 6 g.	Carbohydrate . . . . . 41 g.
Saturated Fat. . . . . . . 4 g.	Sodium . . . . 9 mg.
Cholesterol. . . . . 17 mg.	Potassium . . . . . 763 mg.

PARSLEY POTATOES

Parsley has been appreciated since the Middle Ages as a seasoning and a garnish in cooking. It contains Vitamins A and C, plus iron and iodine. So eat your garnish.

4 tablespoons unsalted butter

1 clove garlic

1/8 teaspoon thyme

1/8 teaspoon rosemary

1/8 teaspoon tarragon

1/8 teaspoon dry mustard

2 teaspoons chopped parsley

Pepper to taste

1/2 teaspoon lemon juice

4 medium-size peeled potatoes, cooked

Melt butter. Add garlic. Remove from heat and let stand 5 to 10 minutes. Add thyme, rosemary, tarragon, mustard, parsley, pepper, and lemon juice. Let stand for at least 1/2 hour. Strain, reheat, and serve on hot potatoes. Serves 4.

Calories 248	Protein. . . . . 3 g.
Fat . . . . 12 g.	Carbohydrate . . . . . 34 g.
Saturated Fat. . . . . . . 7 g.	Sodium. . . . . 10 mg.
Cholesterol. . . . . . 31 mg.	Potassium . . . . . 621 mg.

ROASTED POTATOES WITH ROSEMARY AND GARLIC

4 red or California new potatoes

2 tablespoons olive oil

$\frac{1}{2}$ teaspoon thyme

$\frac{1}{2}$ teaspoon rosemary, crumbled

Pepper to taste

4 cloves unpeeled garlic

1 bay leaf

Start oven at 450 degrees. Quarter potatoes and place in casserole that has been coated with olive oil. Sprinkle thyme, rosemary, and pepper over potatoes. Toss in garlic cloves and bay leaf. Bake 40 minutes, turning occasionally, until potatoes are tender. Squeeze garlic pulp onto potatoes. Serves 4.

Calories	193	Protein	3 g.
Fat	5 g.	Carbohydrate	35 g.
Saturated Fat	3 g.	Sodium	8 mg.
Cholesterol	12 mg.	Potassium	460 mg.

HASH BROWN POTATOES

2 cups diced cooked potatoes

4 tablespoons finely chopped onion

4 teaspoons flour

Pepper to taste

$\frac{1}{4}$ teaspoon rosemary

2 tablespoons milk

2 tablespoons vegetable or olive oil

$\frac{1}{8}$ teaspoon nutmeg

Combine potatoes and onion. In a separate bowl mix flour, pepper, and rosemary. Slowly blend in milk. Combine with the potato and onion mixture. Heat oil in heavy frying pan. Spread potato mixture evenly in the pan, making 1 large cake that does not touch the sides. Cook over medium heat until the underside is brown. Cut into 4 equal portions and turn each piece to brown on other side. Sprinkle with nutmeg. Serves 4.

Try caraway seeds sprinkled over french-fried potatoes.

Calories	147	Protein	2 g.
Fat	7 g.	Carbohydrate	19g.
Saturated Fat	1 g.	Sodium	8 mg.
Cholesterol	tr	Potassium	296 mg.

LYONNAISE POTATOES

Lyonnaise is a method of slicing cold boiled potatoes, frying with onions, and serving garnished with parsley.

1 medium onion sliced fine

2 tablespoons unsalted butter

4 cold, boiled potatoes

Pepper to taste

1/4 teaspoon rosemary

Parsley

Fry the onion in the butter and cook until light brown. Slice the potatoes thin, sprinkle them with pepper and rosemary. Place in the frying pan and cook with onion until a rich golden brown. Garnish with parsley. Serves 4.

Calories 229	Protein . . . . 3 g.
Fat . . . . 12 g.	Carbohydrate . . . . . 30 g.
Saturated Fat . . . . 7 g.	Sodium . . . . 9 mg.
Cholesterol . . . . . 31 mg.	Potassium . . . . . 487 mg.

BAKED SWEET POTATOES

Wash and dry medium-size sweet potatoes. Pierce with fork. Bake until tender in a hot oven (425 degrees). If you want the skin to be soft, rub a little unsalted butter or margarine on before baking.

Cut crisscross gashes in the skin of the baked potato, then pinch them so that some of the soft inside pops through the opening. Drop in one of the following:

1. **1 tablespoon low-sodium peanut butter or 8 chopped roasted peanuts; then add 1 tablespoon orange juice**
2. **1 tablespoon unsalted butter plus a dash of nutmeg and sherry**
3. **1 tablespoon honey and 1 tablespoon unsalted butter**

1 serving:

Calories 105	Protein . . . . 2 g.
Fat . . . . tr	Carbohydrate . . . . . 25 g.
Saturated Fat . . . . tr	Sodium . . . . 12 mg.
Cholesterol . . . . tr	Potassium . . . . . 324 mg.

MICROWAVE SWEET POTATO

A native Southerner (who rarely uses the microwave) says this is the best way to cook sweet potatoes.

2 potatoes
Paper towel

Place sweet potatoes on paper towel. Pierce with a fork. Microwave on high for about 15 minutes or until tender. Serve with yogurt and honey and a sprinkling of nutmeg. Serves 4.

Calories	105	Protein	2 g.
Fat	tr	Carbohydrate	25 g.
Saturated Fat	tr	Sodium	12 mg.
Cholesterol	tr	Potassium	324 mg.

GLAZED SWEET POTATOES

4 medium-size sweet potatoes
¼ teaspoon nutmeg
6 tablespoons honey
4 teaspoons unsalted butter
2 oranges

Pare sweet potatoes and cut in half. Drop into enough boiling water to just cover. Add nutmeg, honey, and butter. Cover and boil until potatoes are tender. If liquid has not cooked down enough by the time they are tender, remove cover and boil rapidly until a syrup is formed. Baste sweet potatoes occasionally with the syrup. Garnish with sliced oranges. Serves 4.

Calories 285	Protein. . . . . 3 g.
Fat . . . . 5 g.	Carbohydrate . . . . . 61 g.
Saturated Fat. . . . . . . 3 g.	Sodium. . . . . 17 mg.
Cholesterol. . . . . . 11 mg.	Potassium . . . . . 346 mg.

STUFFED SWEET POTATOES

4 large sweet potatoes

¼ cup honey

¼ cup raisins

2 to 3 tablespoons orange juice

1 teaspoon cinnamon

¼ teaspoon nutmeg

¼ teaspoon ginger

1 peeled orange, chopped

1 tablespoon melted unsalted butter

Bake sweet potatoes at 375 degrees for about an hour or until tender. Let cool slightly. Slice in half lengthwise and scoop out potato, leaving about ¹/₄ inch wall near skin. In a bowl mash sweet potatoes and add remaining ingredients. Mix until fluffy and pile into potato shells. Heat in 350-degree oven for about 15 minutes. Serves 6 to 8.

Calories 171	Protein. . . . . 2 g.
Fat . . . . 2 g.	Carbohydrate . . . . . 38 g.
Saturated Fat. . . . . . . 1 g.	Sodium. . . . . 10 mg.
Cholesterol. . . . . . . 5 mg.	Potassium . . . . . 371 mg.

STOVE-TOP SUMMER STEW

This recipe was originally Diana Kennedy's, but it came to us via Deborah Madison. It's a greatly simplified version of a wonderful combination of flavors.

3/4 cup nonfat plain yogurt mixed with 1 tablespoon cornstarch
1/4 teaspoon cloves
1/4 teaspoon ground pepper
1/2 teaspoon ground coriander
1/2 teaspoon cinnamon
1/2 cup chopped fresh cilantro leaves
5 mint leaves, chopped
1 jalapeño pepper, seeded and sliced
1 1/2 lbs. zucchini and/or other summer squash
1 cup frozen corn or kernels from 2 ears
1 tablespoon peanut oil
1 small onion, chopped
1/2 cup boiling low-sodium vegetable broth
1 large tomato, chopped
Freshly ground pepper
Chopped cilantro leaves for garnish

In a saucepan combine yogurt with the cloves, pepper, coriander, cinnamon, cilantro, mint, and 1/2 jalapeño. Heat through but do not boil. Remove from heat and let stand so that the flavors may mingle. Cut the squash into chunks. Scrape kernels from the corncob if you are using fresh ears. In a nonstick skillet heat oil and sauté onion until soft. Add the zucchini, corn, and other half of the jalapeño pepper. Continue to sauté for another minute or 2 and then add broth to allow the vegetables to simmer until they are just tender. Add the yogurt mixture and tomato and allow the mixture to heat through gradually. Do not boil. Sprinkle freshly ground pepper on top along with cilantro leaves. Serves 4 to 5.

Calories	133	Protein	5 g.
Fat	4 g.	Carbohydrate	23 g.
Saturated Fat	1 g.	Sodium	47 mg.
Cholesterol	2 mg.	Potassium	796 mg.

WINTER VEGETABLE BOUQUET

4 carrots

2 broccoli stems

2 parsnips

1 rutabaga

1 turnip

4 cups water

1 tablespoon unsalted butter

2 tablespoons honey

1 teaspoon nutmeg

1 teaspoon cinnamon

Parsley

Peel vegetables and cut into equal-width 2-inch pieces. Bring water to boil in saucepan, add vegetables, and simmer covered until tender. In nonstick skillet melt butter over low heat and add honey, nutmeg, and cinnamon. Toss gently with vegetables and arrange in colorful spokes. Sprinkle with fresh parsley. Serves 6.

Calories 123	Protein. . . . . 3 g.
Fat . . . . 3 g.	Carbohydrate . . . . . 24 g.
Saturated Fat. . . . . . . 1 g.	Sodium. . . . . 64 mg.
Cholesterol. . . . . . . 6 mg.	Potassium . . . . . 552 mg.

BASIC STIR-FRY

A stir-fry is a quick and healthful dish and can be made with a wide variety of vegetables. It may be cooked in a wok or a large frying pan or saucepan. A sweet-and-sour sauce is added at the end. Serve it with grilled chicken or pork or over rice.

Sauce

3 tablespoons cornstarch

½ cup water (or orange juice)

3 cloves garlic, minced

2 tablespoons fresh chopped ginger

2 tablespoons honey

2 tablespoons cider vinegar

2 tablespoons sherry

1 teaspoon sesame oil

¼ cup lemon juice

1 teaspoon low-sodium soy sauce

Mix water and cornstarch in bowl until cornstarch is softened. Add remaining ingredients. Mix thoroughly.

Vegetables

2 tablespoons peanut or olive oil

1 finely chopped onion

1 bunch scallions, cut in 2-inch lengths

1 bunch broccoli, cut in florets (stems can be cut
  in rounds)
½ lb. mushrooms, sliced
4 cups of chopped bok choy (or other cabbage)
1 red pepper, seeded, cored, and sliced in strips
1 zucchini, washed and cut in chunks

Heat oil in wok or large skillet or pan. Sauté onion until soft. Add scallions, broccoli, and mushrooms and stir-
fry for a minute. Add bok choy, pepper, and zucchini and
continue to stir-fry for another minute. Add prepared
sauce and stir-fry for another 2 minutes. Serves 4 to 6.

Calories 219		Protein . . . . 7 g.	
Fat . . . . 9 g.		Carbohydrate . . . . . 32 g.	
Saturated Fat . . . . . . 1 g.		Sodium . . . . 121 mg.	
Cholesterol . . . . 0 mg.		Potassium . . . . . 946 mg.	

TOFU STIR-FRY

1 tablespoon sesame oil
1 onion, sliced
3 cloves garlic, sliced
½ cup scallions, chopped
1 tablespoon chopped fresh ginger
1 teaspoon mustard seeds
10 oz. firm tofu, cut into ¼-inch cubes
1 teaspoon low-sodium soy sauce
1 cup broccoli, chopped
½ cup parsley, chopped
Freshly ground pepper
1 tablespoon sherry

In a nonstick skillet heat oil and cook onion until soft. Add garlic, scallions, ginger, and mustard seeds and cook at a low heat about 1 minute. At medium heat cook tofu until crisp. Add soy sauce and broccoli. After broccoli turns bright green, add parsley, pepper, and sherry. Toss gently and serve with rice or noodles. Serves 4.

Calories	13	Protein	7 g.
Fat	7 g.	Carbohydrate	7 g.
Saturated Fat	tr	Sodium	66 mg.
Cholesterol	0 mg.	Potassium	205 mg.

VEGETARIAN PIZZA

Pizza Dough

½ cup hot water

½ cup milk

1 tablespoon yeast

Pinch of sugar

1 tablespoon olive oil

1¼ cup white flour

¼ to ½ cup whole wheat flour

Mix water and milk. Add yeast and pinch of sugar. Stir. Let sit until bubbles form, about 10 minutes. Add olive oil and flour to mixture. Knead, adding more flour as necessary, until dough is smooth and elastic, about 10 minutes. Place in oiled bowl and let rise for about 30 minutes. Roll out and spread on large, oiled pizza or oblong pan. Preheat oven to 500 degrees. Spread filling (see below) over dough and bake for 20 minutes.

Pizza Filling

1 large onion, chopped

3 cloves garlic, sliced

1 tablespoon olive oil

1 cup mushrooms, sliced

1 28-oz. can Italian tomatoes, no salt added

1 teaspoon oregano

1 teaspoon basil

¼ teaspoon black pepper

In nonstick skillet sauté onion and garlic in oil. When onion is soft add mushrooms and cook until limp. Add remaining ingredients and simmer for 30 minutes or until thick. Let cool slightly before spreading on pizza dough.

ADDITIONAL PIZZA TOPPINGS

Sliced green, red, or yellow peppers

Zucchini wedges

Broccoli florets

Onion rings

Grated, skim milk mozzarella

Variation: Calzones are great for lunch and can easily be adapted from this recipe. Roll out pizza dough into 6-inch circles. Fill with topping suggestions. Bake in oven for about 10 to 15 minutes or until done. Nutritional analysis would be about the same as for 1 slice of pizza.

Pizza dough/filling:

Calories 162	Protein. . . . . 5 g.
Fat . . . . 4 g.	Carbohydrate . . . . . 27 g.
Saturated Fat. . . . . . . 1 g.	Sodium. . . . . 23 mg.
Cholesterol. . . . . . . 1 mg.	Potassium . . . . . 376 mg.

Pizza with mozzarella:

Calories 179	Protein. . . . . 7 g.
Fat . . . . 5 g.	Carbohydrate . . . . . 27 g.
Saturated Fat. . . . . . . 1 g.	Sodium. . . . . 56 mg.
Cholesterol. . . . . . . 5 mg.	Potassium . . . . . 382 mg.

BOK CHOY

Bok choy, a kind of Chinese cabbage, has a distinct flavor all its own and can be steamed for a few minutes and served simply with freshly ground pepper. The top, green leaves can be used in salads, as well as the tender, inner leaves. The thicker leaves can be saved for cooked dishes, stews, and soups. This recipe was inspired by Jane Grigson's *Vegetable Book.*

1 tablespoon peanut oil

1 finely chopped onion

3 cloves garlic, finely chopped

1 tablespoon grated ginger

1 lb. shredded bok choy

1 teaspoon sugar

2 tablespoons sherry

1 teaspoon low-sodium tamari

1 teaspoon sesame oil

1 teaspoon toasted sesame seeds

Heat the peanut oil and stir-fry the onion, garlic, and ginger. Add the bok choy and sprinkle with sugar, stirring constantly for 2 to 3 minutes. Add sherry and tamari and continue to cook for another 2 to 3 minutes, adding water by the spoonful if necessary. Before serving toss with a teaspoon of sesame oil and the sesame seeds. Serves 4 to 5.

Calories	71	Protein	2 g.
Fat	4 g.	Carbohydrate	6 g.
Saturated Fat	1 g.	Sodium	96 mg.
Cholesterol	0 mg.	Potassium	282 mg.

WILTED GREENS

Mix and match from greens such as spinach, chard, endive, bok choy, dandelion, mustard, or beet, or select 1 or 2. The sodium content in all but endive and bok choy is somewhat higher than other vegetables, but unless your doctor tells you otherwise, you can still enjoy greens from time to time.

1½ lbs. fresh greens

1 tablespoon sesame oil

5 cloves garlic, sliced

1 tablespoon rice vinegar

1 tablespoon toasted sesame seeds

Wash and drain greens, leaving some water on the leaves. Cut in large pieces. Heat oil in nonstick skillet and sauté garlic until tender. Toss greens in hot oil in small batches until they are wilted. Sprinkle vinegar and sesame seeds on top and mix thoroughly. Serves 4.

Calories	82	Protein	4 g.
Fat	5 g.	Carbohydrate	8 g.
Saturated Fat	1 g.	Sodium	87 mg.
Cholesterol	0 mg.	Potassium	771 mg.

BAKED CHERRY TOMATOES

1 pint cherry tomatoes

1/4 cup low-sodium herbed bread crumbs

1 medium onion, sliced in rings

1/2 cup chopped fresh parsley

1 tablespoon extra-virgin olive oil

2 cloves garlic, minced

1/2 teaspoon dried thyme

Ground pepper to taste

Spread tomatoes in an 8-inch baking dish. Combine remaining ingredients, stirring well, and spoon over tomatoes. Cover loosely with foil and bake at 425 degrees for 6 to 8 minutes. Serves 4.

Calories	79	Protein	2 g.
Fat	4 g.	Carbohydrate	10 g.
Saturated Fat	1 g.	Sodium	11 mg.
Cholesterol	tr	Potassium	266 mg.

MASHED POTATOES AND PARSNIPS WITH ROASTED GARLIC

This recipe was adapted from Molly O'Neill's column in the Sunday *New York Times Magazine*.

1 lb. parsnips, peeled and cut into chunks

6 large baking potatoes, peeled and quartered

1/2 cup lowfat milk

3 tablespoons unsalted butter

1 large whole roasted garlic

Ground pepper to taste

In a large saucepan place parsnips and potatoes. Cover with water and bring to a boil. Simmer for about 20 minutes or until they are tender. Drain and remove vegetables. Heat milk and butter in same saucepan. When they are heated through, add parsnips and potatoes and mash until smooth. Squeeze pulp of roasted garlic into mixture and stir in thoroughly. Add ground pepper and serve at once. Serves 8 to 10.

Calories	212	Protein	4 g.
Fat	5 g.	Carbohydrate	40 g.
Saturated Fat	3 g.	Sodium	21 mg.
Cholesterol	12 mg.	Potassium	686 mg.

RAITA

This Indian vegetable dish is especially cooling on a hot summer day and can be easily altered to fit whatever you have on hand or whatever fresh produce is in abundance.

1 eggplant, boiled for 5 minutes, drained, and chopped

1 cucumber, peeled, seeded, and chopped

1 green pepper, seeded and chopped

2 tomatoes, seeded and chopped

Cayenne pepper to taste

Freshly ground pepper

2 cups nonfat plain yogurt

Mix all ingredients and chill for at least an hour before serving. Serves 4.

Calories 117	Protein. . . . . 8 g.
Fat . . . . 1 g.	Carbohydrate . . . . . 21 g.
Saturated Fat . . . . tr	Sodium. . . . . 97 mg.
Cholesterol. . . . . . . 2 mg.	Potassium . . . . . 800 mg.

ROOT VEGETABLES WITH ROSEMARY

This is adapted from a recipe created by our local
health-food store, Bread and Circus.

1 small rutabaga, cubed

1 sweet potato, cubed

1 large parsnip, scrubbed and cubed

10 shallots, peeled and cut in half

3 tablespoons olive oil

4 cloves garlic, minced

3 tablespoons fresh rosemary leaves, chopped

³⁄₄ cup water

1 small turnip, cubed

2 cups butternut squash, peeled and cubed

Ground pepper, to taste

Preheat oven to 400 degrees. In a large baking
dish, place rutabaga, sweet potato, parsnip, and shallots.
Sprinkle half of the olive oil, garlic, and rosemary over
the vegetables. Add water. Then layer the turnip and
squash on top of the first set of vegetables. Sprinkle with the remaining olive oil, garlic, and rosemary.
Place in oven and bake for 20 minutes. Remove vegetables from oven, add ground pepper, and stir to

combine. Replace in oven and cook an additional 15 minutes.

Calories	114	Protein	2 g.
Fat	5 g.	Carbohydrate	17 g.
Saturated Fat	1 g.	Sodium	19 mg.
Cholesterol	0 mg.	Potassium	361 mg.

Desserts

A lovely platter of fresh, ripe fruit is really the healthiest way to end a meal. Naturally low in sodium, most fruits are high in Vitamin C and potassium as well. But in most cases you can make your favorite cake and pastry recipes healthier without compromising taste by replacing high-sodium ingredients with their low-sodium versions. Use canola oil or unsalted instead of salted butter in batters and crusts. Featherweight Baking Powder, available in most supermarkets, is low in sodium and also free of aluminum. Unrefined flours, nuts, and seeds will increase the potassium level of the recipe.

To get you started, here are our recipes for a number of basic, ever-popular desserts. Some old favorites are higher in fat. If your doctor permits, enjoy them occasionally, but you must compensate over time. Nothing sparks a baker's creativity, however, more than fruit picked at its peak. We also include—thanks to our family and friends—a collection of treasured recipes, each one a product of such seasonal inspiration.

Please note all nutritional information refers to 1 serving size, unless otherwise noted.

DOUBLE-CRUST PIE DOUGH

2 cups sifted flour
¼ cup water
⅔ cup vegetable shortening
¼ teaspoon mace
½ teaspoon lemon rind
Add sesame seeds if you like them

Sift flour into a bowl. Remove ⅓ cup of this flour and mix with water, forming a paste. Set aside.

Add vegetable shortening, mace, and lemon rind to flour, and cut mixture, using a pastry blender or 2 knives, until pieces are the size of peas. Add paste mixture to flour mix and mix thoroughly until dough comes together and can be shaped into a ball. Divide into 2 parts. Chill. Roll ⅛ inch thick. Bake at 450 degrees for 15 to 20 minutes. Makes crust for 9-inch, 2-crust pie.

Calories. 2,055	Protein. . . . . 24 g.	
Fat . . . . 140 g.	Carbohydrate . . . . 176 g.	
Saturated Fat. . . . . . 35 g.	Sodium . . . . 7 mg.	
Cholesterol. . . . . . . 0 mg.	Potassium . . . . . 250 mg.	

BASIC APPLE PIE

The local wisdom here is that Gravenstein apples are the best for pies. Early McIntoshes are always good, however, and later in the season Cortlands are fine.

Low-sodium pastry for a 2-crust, 9-inch pie
4 cups apples
1 cup sugar

½ teaspoon cinnamon

½ teaspoon nutmeg

½ teaspoon vanilla

Grated rind from ½ lemon

1 tablespoon lemon juice

1 tablespoon unsalted butter

Make the pastry. Line a 9-inch pie pan with the pastry, saving enough for a top crust. Chill both in refrigerator while you prepare the filling. Heat oven to 450 degrees. Peel, core, and slice apples very thin. Mix sliced apples with sugar, cinnamon, nutmeg, vanilla, lemon rind, and juice. Fill unbaked pie shell with the mixture. Dot with butter and cover with top crust. Bake 10 minutes, then reduce heat to 350 degrees and continue baking 30 to 35 minutes more. During last 5 minutes of baking, brush pastry top with cream and sprinkle with granulated sugar. Serves 6.

Note: Apple pie spice is sodium-free and can be used instead of the spices in this recipe.

Calories 531	Protein. . . . . 4 g.
Fat . . . . 26 g.	Carbohydrate . . . . . 75 g.
Saturated Fat. . . . . . . 6 g.	Sodium . . . . 2 mg.
Cholesterol. . . . . . . 0 mg.	Potassium . . . . . 143 mg.

PUMPKIN PIE

1 tablespoon gelatin

¼ cup cold water

1½ cups cooked or canned pumpkin

¾ cup white or brown sugar

1 teaspoon cinnamon
2 teaspoons grated orange peel
½ teaspoon nutmeg
2 tablespoons rum or orange juice
2 tablespoons unsalted butter
1 baked low-sodium pie shell
½ cup chopped pecans

Soak gelatin in water for 5 minutes. Combine remaining ingredients in a medium saucepan, and cook until slightly thickened. Pour in pie shell. Place a few pecans on top. Cool. Serves 6.

Calories	397	Protein	4 g.
Fat	22 g.	Carbohydrate	49 g.
Saturated Fat	4 g.	Sodium	13 mg.
Cholesterol	0 mg.	Potassium	322 mg.

CRANBERRY TART

This is a delicious, festive dessert.

1 cup flour
1 stick unsalted butter
2 teaspoons vanilla

Mix flour and butter until it is crumbly. Add vanilla and mix. Dump mixture into a 9-inch pie tin or a tart pan. This will not look promising, but it will look better after you press the mixture thoroughly against the sides of the pan.

Note: This crust is a wonderful base for many fresh fruits. Choose choice seasonal fruits, just apples or pears, or combinations, such as peaches, blueberries, and kiwi. Arrange the fruit on top of this dough recipe and sprinkle with sugar, cinnamon, and vanilla. Bake at 400 degrees for about 25 minutes or until crust is golden brown.

Cranberry Filling:

Scant 1 cup sugar

2 tablespoons cornstarch

¾ cup water

1 tablespoon grated orange rind

1 package rinsed and sorted cranberries

½ cup coarsely chopped walnuts

Preheat oven to 400 degrees. Combine sugar, cornstarch, water, orange rind, and cranberries in saucepan. Bring to boil and cook over medium heat until cranberries pop and mixture thickens. (If this mixture does not appear thick enough, add 1 more tablespoon of cornstarch, softened in 1 tablespoon of water.) Add chopped walnuts. Check for sweetness. Remove from heat and cool. Pour into pie crust and bake for about 20 minutes or until crust is brown. Top with a tablespoon of lite dessert topping. Serves 8.

Calories	333	Protein	3 g.
Fat	16 g.	Carbohydrate	46 g.
Saturated Fat	8 g.	Sodium	4 mg.
Cholesterol	31 mg.	Potassium	98 mg.

BROWNIES

2 squares unsweetened chocolate
¼ cup unsalted butter
1 cup sugar
1 egg
½ cup flour
½ cup walnut meats, cut up
1 teaspoon vanilla

Melt the chocolate over hot water in saucepan. Remove pan from heat. Add the butter and stir until melted. Add sugar, egg, flour, nut meats, and vanilla. Spread the mixture evenly in a 8-inch-square shallow pan lined with heavy wax paper. Bake 1 hour in a slow oven, 300 degrees. Turn out on board and pull off the paper. Cut the brownies into squares while still warm. Makes 16 brownies.

Calories	132	Protein	2 g.
Fat	7 g.	Carbohydrate	17 g.
Saturated Fat	3 g.	Sodium	3 mg.
Cholesterol	21 mg.	Potassium	57 mg.

MARJORIE'S APPLE BARS

3 medium apples, peeled and sliced
¼ cup unsalted butter, softened
½ cup sugar
1 egg
½ cup walnuts, chopped
1 cup flour
2 teaspoons low-sodium baking powder
1 teaspoon cinnamon

Stir apples in butter and sugar. Add beaten egg. Mix in dry ingredients. Bake in greased and floured 9-by-9-inch pan at 350 degrees for 40 minutes or until done. Makes 16 squares.

Calories	214	Protein	3 g.
Fat	10 g.	Carbohydrate	30 g.
Saturated Fat	4 g.	Sodium	8 mg.
Cholesterol	38 mg.	Potassium	210 mg.

CHOCOLATE CAKE

Pureed prunes make this a moist, low-fat chocolate cake. The recipe was adapted from the *Los Angeles Times.*

  2 cups flour
  1 cup cocoa
  1½ cups sugar
  1 tablespoon low-sodium baking powder
  4 jars prune baby food
  2 teaspoons vanilla
  2 eggs
  1 cup low-fat milk mixed with 1 teaspoon white
     vinegar
  1 cup boiling water
  1 tablespoon instant coffee (espresso) powder

Preheat oven to 350 degrees. Sift dry ingredients into a bowl. Combine prunes, vanilla, eggs, and milk and blend with dry ingredients. Add boiling water to coffee powder and mix with batter. Pour into 2 greased and floured 9-inch cake pans and bake in oven for 25 to 30 minutes or until cake is done. Frost with Seven-Minute Mocha Frosting. Serves 12.

Calories 246	Protein. . . . . 6 g.
Fat . . . . 2 g.	Carbohydrate . . . . . 52 g.
Saturated Fat. . . . . . 1 g.	Sodium. . . . . 30 mg.
Cholesterol. . . . . 36 mg.	Potassium . . . . . 268 mg.

Seven-Minute Mocha Frosting

1 tablespoon instant coffee powder (instant espresso powder is delicious)

¼ cup hot water

3 egg whites

½ cup brown sugar

½ cup sugar

1 teaspoon cream of tartar

1 teaspoon vanilla

In top of double boiler combine coffee powder and hot water. Let cool and then add egg whites, sugars, and cream of tartar. Beat constantly for 7 minutes until icing is thick and forms peaks. Add vanilla. Ices 1 2-layer cake.

Calories 70	Protein. . . . . 1 g.
Fat . . . . 0 g.	Carbohydrate . . . . . 17 g.
Saturated Fat. . . . . . 0 g.	Sodium. . . . . 18 mg.
Cholesterol. . . . . . 0 mg.	Potassium . . . . . . 58 mg.

CHERRIES JUBILEE

2½ cups canned, pitted black cherries

2 thin slices lemon

¼ cup sugar

½ teaspoon cinnamon

½ cup brandy

Heat, but do not boil, cherries. Drain juice and add cherries to lemon in blazer pan or chafing dish. Mix sugar and cinnamon and sprinkle over the top. Add brandy, set ablaze. When flame dies out serve at once over Lemon-Orange Cake or low-fat frozen vanilla yogurt. Serves 8.

Calories	94	Protein	1 g.
Fat	tr	Carbohydrate	20 g.
Saturated Fat	tr	Sodium	2 mg.
Cholesterol	0 mg.	Potassium	119 mg.

LUSCIOUS LEMON-ORANGE CAKE

3 beaten egg yolks

½ orange (juice and grated rind)

½ lemon (juice and grated rind)

1 cup sugar

1 tablespoon plus 1 teaspoon flour

1 cup milk

3 stiffly beaten egg whites

Add egg yolks to juice and rind of orange and lemon. Beat well. Mix sugar and flour and add to mixture. Slowly stir in milk. Fold in stiffly beaten egg whites last. Pour in baking dish. Set in pan of hot water and bake at 350 degrees for 45 minutes. There will be a tasty lemon-orange custard at the bottom, with a layer of golden sponge cake on top. Serves 10.

Calories	113	Protein	3 g.
Fat	2 g.	Carbohydrate	22 g.
Saturated Fat	1 g.	Sodium	32 mg.
Cholesterol	65 mg.	Potassium	74 mg.

BAKED APPLES

8 tablespoons honey
4 teaspoons grated orange peel
1 teaspoon nutmeg, mace, or cinnamon
4 apples, cored, but unpeeled

Boil honey, orange peel, and nutmeg, mace, or cinnamon. Add apples. Cook about 5 minutes, turning apples often in syrup. Place apples in baking dish, spoon sauce over apples. Bake 15 to 20 minutes at 350 degrees, basting 2 or 3 times with sauce. Cool slightly and serve with hard sauce. Serves 4.

Calories	215	Protein	tr
Fat	1 g.	Carbohydrate	56 g.
Saturated Fat	tr	Sodium	3 mg.
Cholesterol	0 mg.	Potassium	188 mg.

Hard Sauce

Serve this on pumpkin pie or baked apples.

4 tablespoons unsalted butter
2 cups confectioners' sugar
1 egg
½ teaspoon vanilla
1 tablespoon sherry or brandy

Cream butter, sugar, and egg. Add flavorings, beat until creamy. Chill. Serves 12.

Total recipe:

Calories	1,279	Protein	7 g.
Fat	51 g.	Carbohydrate	203 mg.

Saturated Fat...... 30 g.	Sodium......... 71 mg.
Cholesterol..... 338 mg.	Potassium ...... 88 mg.

RICE PUDDING

1 cup rice
3 cups water
2 lemons (juice)
1 cup white sugar
¼ teaspoon cumin seed
½ teaspoon cinnamon

Boil rice and water in double boiler. When almost dry, mix with lemon juice, sugar, cumin seed, and cinnamon. Pour in mold. Serve cold with Hard Sauce. Serves 6.

Calories 237	Protein............ 2 g.
Fat................. tr	Carbohydrate ..... 58 g.
Saturated Fat .... tr	Sodium .... 6 mg.
Cholesterol....... 0 mg.	Potassium ...... 57 mg.

DOLORES RYAN'S PEACH AND MAPLE SYRUP CAKE

This recipe, which combines summer and winter flavors, came from a New England maple-sugaring family. Instead of peaches you can use apples, plums, or pears.

¼ cup unsalted light butter
½ cup maple syrup
1 egg
1 teaspoon vanilla

1 cup flour

1 teaspoon baking powder

1 teaspoon mace

½ cup walnuts (optional)

2 ripe peaches, peeled and sliced

1 tablespoon sugar

Cream butter and syrup. Add egg, vanilla, and sifted dry ingredients. Pour into greased 9-by-9-inch pan. Lay walnuts (if you choose to use them) and sliced peaches on top of batter. Sprinkle with sugar. Bake at 350-degrees for 20 to 25 minutes. Serves 9.

Calories	208	Protein	3 g.
Fat	10 g.	Carbohydrate	28 g.
Saturated Fat	4 g.	Sodium	27 mg.
Cholesterol	38 mg.	Potassium	152 mg.

FRUIT MERINGUES

This beautiful dessert is light and festive. If you prefer, and can afford the extra fat, you may substitute a small amount of whipped cream for the dessert topping.

2 egg whites

¼ cup sugar

1 cup softened lite dessert topping

2 to 3 cups fresh fruit, such as strawberries,
  raspberries, peaches, grapes, kiwi

Preheat oven to 250 degrees. In a mixing bowl beat egg whites until they form stiff peaks. Gradually add sugar. Spread baking sheet with waxed paper or parchment and spoon mixture on paper, forming mounds. Bake them for about 2 hours, until the meringues are dry, not sticky. Let cool, then spoon softened topping on each meringue and arrange sliced fruit in colorful designs on top. Serve with a fresh marigold, violets, and mint. Makes 6 meringues.

Calories	105	Protein	2 g.
Fat	3 g.	Carbohydrate	19 g.
Saturated Fat	3 g.	Sodium	22 mg.
Cholesterol	0 mg.	Potassium	145 mg.

PEACH BLY

The fact that homegrown peaches, blueberries, and plums all seem to ripen at the same time in our neck of the woods makes this a natural and delicious variation on Peach Melba.

½ cup blueberries
2 medium plums
½ cup water
2 tablespoons sugar
¼ teaspoon allspice
2 large peaches
2 cups nonfat vanilla frozen yogurt
Mint leaves

Combine blueberries, plums, water, sugar, and allspice in a saucepan. Bring to a boil and simmer for 5 minutes. Puree mixture in blender or food processor. Reserve. Poach peaches in water to cover until they are just tender when poked with a knife. Remove and drain. Rinse with cold water. Peel, halve, and remove pits. Cool. When ready to serve place peach half in dish, fill with frozen yogurt, and cover with blueberry-plum sauce. Garnish with fresh mint. Serves 4.

Calories 172	Protein. . . . . 3 g.
Fat . . . . tr	Carbohydrate . . . . . 41 g.
Saturated Fat . . . . tr	Sodium. . . . . 47 mg.
Cholesterol. . . . . . 5 mg.	Potassium . . . . . 323 mg.

BAKED RHUBARB

---

2 lbs. cut rhubarb

1 cup sugar

Wash rhubarb in cold water. Do not peel. Use your kitchen scissors so as not to tear. Cut stalks in 2-inch pieces. Place the rhubarb and sugar in a baking dish. Cover and place in preheated moderate oven for 20 minutes until sugar is melted. Remove cover and finish baking for 30 minutes in moderate oven. Serves 8.

Calories 114	Protein. . . . . 1 g.
Fat . . . . tr	Carbohydrate . . . . . 29 g.
Saturated Fat. . . . . . . 0 g.	Sodium . . . . 5 mg.
Cholesterol. . . . . . 0 mg.	Potassium . . . . 326 mg.

RHUBARB-STRAWBERRY CRUMBLE

An excellent dessert for celebrating the beginning of summer fruit.

Topping

$^1/_2$ cup sweet butter
$^1/_2$ cup brown sugar
1 cup flour
1 teaspoon cinnamon
$^1/_2$ teaspoon nutmeg
1 cup oats

Fruit

3 cups rhubarb, diced
$^3/_4$ cup sugar
1 pint strawberries, hulled and sliced
1 teaspoon ginger
$^1/_2$ teaspoon cinnamon
4 tablespoons tapioca

To make the topping, cream together the butter and brown sugar in a medium-size bowl. Sift together the flour and spices and add to the creamed mixture, beating until well blended. Stir in the oats.

To prepare the fruit filling, place the rhubarb and $^1/_4$ cup of the sugar in a medium-size saucepan and cook over medium heat for about 5 to 7 minutes or until the juices run and the rhubarb begins to soften. Pour into a 2-quart baking dish and add the strawberries. Mix in the spices and tapioca, stirring well. Crumble the topping over the fruit. Bake for 40 to 45 minutes or until the crumble topping is lightly browned. Serves 6 to 8.

Calories 524	Protein . . . . 8 g.
Fat . . . . 18 g.	Carbohydrate . . . . . 88 g.
Saturated Fat . . . . . . 10 g.	Sodium . . . . 12 mg.
Cholesterol . . . . . . 42 mg.	Potassium . . . . . 467 mg.

FROZEN STRAWBERRY DELIGHT

16-oz. bag of unsweetened strawberries

2 tablespoons sugar

½ cup nonfat plain yogurt

1 to 2 tablespoons frozen orange juice concentrate

Puree berries in a blender or food processor. Add remaining ingredients. Freeze. Garnish with a sprig of mint. Serves 6.

Note: Serve fresh strawberries with honey drizzled on top.

Calories 87	Protein . . . . 2 g.
Fat . . . . tr	Carbohydrate . . . . . 21 g.
Saturated Fat . . . . tr	Sodium . . . . 24 mg.
Cholesterol . . . . 1 mg.	Potassium . . . . . 276 mg.

BANANAS FLAMBÉ

2 tablespoons unsalted butter

4 medium-size bananas, peeled and split

1 tablespoon sugar

2 tablespoons lemon juice

¼ cup brandy

Melt butter in a large nonstick skillet over low heat. Add bananas and sprinkle with sugar and lemon juice. Sauté slowly until brown on one side (about 10 minutes). Turn with a wide spatula and brown on the other side. Remove bananas to a warm serving platter. Add brandy to skillet, stir to pick up brown bits. Pour over bananas and light. Serves 4.

Note: Serve over a scoop of frozen nonfat yogurt, and sprinkle with chopped walnuts.

Calories	204	Protein	1 g.
Fat	6 g.	Carbohydrate	30 g.
Saturated Fat	4 g.	Sodium	2 mg.
Cholesterol	16 mg.	Potassium	462 mg.

POACHED PEARS

1 cup red (or white) wine

3 cups water

¼ cup sugar

½ teaspoon (or 2 sticks) cinnamon

½ teaspoon nutmeg

1 teaspoon vanilla

4 firm pears, peeled and cored, with stem intact

1 tablespoon cornstarch mixed with 2 tablespoons water

In a heavy, medium-size saucepan mix wine, water, sugar, cinnamon, nutmeg, and vanilla. Bring mixture to a simmer and poach pears for about 20 minutes or until tender. Remove pears (and cinnamon sticks, if used) and place on serving dish. Reduce liquid by half. Add cornstarch mixed with water and allow sauce to thicken. Scoop onto pears. Serve with a dollop of nonfat frozen yogurt. Serves 4.

Variation: After poaching, add seasonal fruit, such as raspberries or blueberries, sliced peaches, or grated apple to liquid as you're reducing it. Proceed with rest of recipe.

Calories 190	Protein. . . . . 1 g.
Fat . . . . 11 g.	Carbohydrate . . . . . 43 g.
Saturated Fat . . . . tr	Sodium . . . . 8 mg.
Cholesterol. . . . . . . 1 mg.	Potassium . . . . . 262 mg.

DATE-FILLED PASTRIES

½ cup unsalted butter

3 teaspoons confectioners' sugar

1 cup bread flour

1 teaspoon vanilla

¼ teaspoon mace

Cream butter and sugar. Add flour, vanilla, and mace. Put teaspoon of mixture into tiny cupcake tins. Press with fingertips into pan. Bake at 350 degrees for 45 minutes or until light brown.

Filling

1 8-oz. package of dates (about 34 dates)

1 cup sugar

½ cup water

Chop dates, combine ingredients, and cook until slightly thickened. Mixture thickens as it cools. Fill pastries when the mixture cools. A jam or jelly may be used for filling, too. Makes 12 pastries.

Pastry:

Calories 112	Protein. . . . . 1 g.
Fat . . . . 8 g.	Carbohydrate . . . . . . 9 g.
Saturated Fat. . . . . . . 5 g.	Sodium . . . . 1 mg.
Cholesterol. . . . . . 21 mg.	Potassium . . . . . . 13 mg.

Date filling:

Calories 163	Protein. . . . . 1 g.
Fat. . . . . tr	Carbohydrate . . . . . 44 g.
Saturated Fat. . . . . . . 0 g.	Sodium . . . . 2 mg.
Cholesterol. . . . . . . 0 mg.	Potassium . . . . . 243 mg.

PECAN PUFFS

½ cup unsalted butter

2 tablespoons granulated sugar

1 teaspoon vanilla

1 cup flour, sifted

1 cup pecan meats, ground

¼ teaspoon nutmeg

½ cup confectioners' sugar

Cream butter until soft and blend in granulated sugar until creamy. Add vanilla. Stir flour, pecans, and nutmeg into mixture. Roll dough into small balls and place on a well-greased cookie sheet. Bake in 300-degree oven for about 45 minutes. Roll puffs in confectioners' sugar while hot and again when cold. Makes 2 dozen puffs.

Calories 94	Protein. . . . . 1 g.
Fat . . . . 7 g.	Carbohydrate . . . . . . 8 g.
Saturated Fat. . . . . . . 4 g.	Sodium . . . . 1 mg.
Cholesterol. . . . . . 10 mg.	Potassium . . . . . . 24 mg.

CHRISTMAS COOKIES

These are a delight.

1 cup unsalted butter
1 cup sugar
1 egg yolk
2 cups sifted all-purpose flour
2½ teaspoons cinnamon
¼ teaspoon mace
1 egg white
½ cup ground nuts, unsalted

Cream butter and sugar thoroughly. Beat in egg yolk, add flour, cinnamon, and mace, and blend well. Roll pieces of the dough into 1-inch balls between buttered palms. Place balls about 2 inches apart on ungreased baking sheet. Press out paper-thin with a floured spatula. Paint with egg white and sprinkle with ground nuts. Bake at 350 degrees for 10 to 12 minutes. Makes 6 dozen cookies.

Calories	49	Protein	1 g.
Fat	3 g.	Carbohydrate	5 g.
Saturated Fat	2 g.	Sodium	1 mg.
Cholesterol	10 mg.	Potassium	8 mg.

A PRETTY IDEA FOR MELONS

Halve, seed, and peel cantaloupe or honeydew melon. Cut in 4 wedges. Place on platter. Dip white seedless grapes in fruit juice and then roll in white granulated sugar. Place grapes in small bunches on melon. Add mint for color. Try a sprinkle of cardamom with fresh melon. Serves 4.

Sandwiches

The ingredients in a sandwich can quickly eat up a person's daily sodium allowance; deli meats and cheeses are notoriously high in sodium, as are many of the processed condiments we spread on bread. Even the bread itself is often loaded with salt; always check the nutritional facts found on the bread label if you don't have a reliable bakery that offers a selection of low-sodium loaves, or you can bake low-sodium bread yourself. Have low-sodium pita bread or flour tortillas on hand to make a quick sandwich. To avoid using unhealthy, salty processed food, cook extra portions of meat, poultry, and fish so that you'll have leftovers on hand, ready to slice or chop for fillings. Sliced vegetables like onions, cucumbers, and ripe tomatoes add crunch and juicy flavor. Add lettuce for texture. Varieties of pepper—raw sweet pepper rings, crushed pepper flakes, or freshly ground peppercorns—can add zest and bite to an otherwise bland sandwich. Below are some suggestions, organized in lists, to help you make low-sodium sandwiches delicious; mix and match them, experiment, and enjoy. In our Sauces and Condiments section, you'll find other recipes for low-sodium spreads, chutneys, and butters.

Unless otherwise noted, all nutritional information refers to 1 serving size.

CHICKEN / TURKEY

Cranberry sauce

Chopped cilantro

Butter or mayonnaise—flavored with curry powder, chopped thyme, tarragon, or sage

Pineapple bits

Bean or alfalfa sprouts

BEEF

Horseradish

Salsa

Tabasco

Mustard—dried or low-sodium prepared

Ground allspice, nutmeg, or cloves

Sliced onion

FISH

Butter or mayonnaise—flavored with chopped fresh dill, tarragon, or ginger

Fresh-squeezed lemon juice

Low-fat sour cream spiced with turmeric, garlic powder, and onion powder

LAMB

Chutney

Low-sodium mayonnaise spiced with cumin, curry, and garlic

Mint jelly

Yogurt with chopped mint and raisins

Olive oil with crumbled dried rosemary and ground pepper

PORK

Applesauce or sliced apples

Cranberry sauce

Low-sodium mayonnaise spiced with dried crumbled sage and a touch of dried mustard

VEAL

Olive oil with crumbled oregano and marjoram

Chopped basil and sliced tomato

TOFU

Bean sprouts

Chopped garlic and ginger

Tahini

VEGETABLES

Try grilling sliced vegetables like summer squash, eggplant, zucchini, bell peppers, and onion. Brush the slices with olive oil, sprinkle with freshly ground pepper, and grill, or place under a broiler, until golden brown. Meanwhile, brush crusty low-sodium or pita bread with roasted or pureed garlic. Broil until lightly toasted. Make open-faced sandwiches by arranging a selection of the grilled vegetables on top. Grated carrot and ginger or bean sprouts make good additions.

TOASTED CHEESE WITH TOMATO SANDWICH

Spread 1 slice of low-sodium bread with unsalted butter. Add sliced low-sodium cheese, and top with sliced tomato. Sprinkle with dry mustard and basil. Broil until cheese is bubbly. Serves 1.

Calories 295	Protein. . . . . 12 g.
Fat . . . . 18 g.	Carbohydrate . . . . . 23 g.
Saturated Fat. . . . . . 8 g.	Sodium. . . . . 81 mg.
Cholesterol. . . . . 47 mg.	Potassium . . . . . 302 mg.

PEANUT BUTTER AND RAISIN SANDWICH

Low-sodium peanut butter is available in most grocery and health-food stores. But it's easy to make at home. Here's a simple recipe:

2 cups roasted, unsalted peanuts
¼ cup peanut oil

Blend peanuts in a blender for 1 minute. With the motor still running, gradually add oil, 1 tablespoon at a time. Makes 1¹/₂ cups.
Variation: Add 2 tablespoons honey, or experiment with unsalted cashews or pecans instead of peanuts.

1 tablespoon low-sodium peanut butter
1 tablespoon raisins
2 slices low-sodium bread

Mix peanut butter and raisins and spread on low-sodium bread.

Peanut butter:

Calories 90	Protein. . . . . 3 g.
Fat . . . . 8 g.	Carbohydrate . . . . . . 2 g.
Saturated Fat. . . . . . . 1 g.	Sodium . . . . 1 mg.
Cholesterol. . . . . . . 0 mg.	Potassium . . . . . . 82 mg.

Peanut butter and raisin sandwich:

Calories 356	Protein. . . . . 10 g.
Fat . . . . 15 g.	Carbohydrate . . . . . 48 g.
Saturated Fat. . . . . . . 4 g.	Sodium . . . . 8 mg.
Cholesterol. . . . . . . 4 mg.	Potassium . . . . . 234 mg.

EGG SALAD SANDWICH

Remember 1 egg has 68 mg. of sodium, and that is a lot. Most of the sodium is in the white—the yolk has only 13 mg. Combine chopped egg and ¹/₂ table-spoon of low-sodium mayonnaise (3 mg.), a dash or two of herb vinegar and black pepper, and ¹/₂ tablespoon of chopped chives or parsley. Spread between low-sodium bread.

Calories 366	Protein. . . . . 11 g.
Fat . . . . 18 g.	Carbohydrate . . . . . 39 g.
Saturated Fat. . . . . . . 4 g.	Sodium. . . . . 92 mg.
Cholesterol. . . . . 219 mg.	Potassium . . . . . 128 mg.

FIG SANDWICH

1 cup dried figs

¹/₂ cup hot water

1 teaspoon lemon juice

3 chopped walnuts

Finely chop figs. Cook to a paste in water. Add lemon juice. Cool. Spread on low-sodium bread and dust with ground nuts.

Without bread:

Calories 37	Protein. . . . . 1 g.
Fat . . . . 1 g.	Carbohydrate . . . . . . 8 g.
Saturated Fat . . . . tr	Sodium . . . . 2 mg.
Cholesterol. . . . . . . 0 mg.	Potassium . . . . . . 93 mg.

WATERCRESS SANDWICHES

2 tablespoons watercress

1 tablespoon low-sodium mayonnaise

1 teaspoon onion, grated (or 1 teaspoon chives, chopped)

Low-sodium bread

Chop watercress, mix with low-sodium mayonnaise, add grated onions or chives. Spread on low-sodium bread.

Calories 417	Protein. . . . . 7 g.
Fat . . . . 26 g.	Carbohydrate . . . . . 41 g.
Saturated Fat. . . . . . 4 g.	Sodium. . . . . 60 mg.
Cholesterol. . . . . . . 8 mg.	Potassium . . . . . 143 mg.

SHRIMP SANDWICH

6 canned low-sodium shrimp, chopped

1 tablespoon low-sodium mayonnaise

1 teaspoon lemon juice

1 teaspoon chopped parsley, fresh

Low-sodium bread
Lettuce leaves

Mix shrimp with low-sodium mayonnaise. Add lemon juice and parsley. Spread between low-sodium bread. Place lettuce between slices. Serves 1.

Without bread:

Calories 125	Protein. . . . . 4 g.
Fat . . . . 12 g.	Carbohydrate . . . . . . 1 g.
Saturated Fat. . . . . . 1 g.	Sodium. . . . . 99 mg.
Cholesterol. . . . . 42 mg.	Potassium . . . . . . 55 mg.

MUSHROOM SANDWICH (OR CANAPÉ SPREAD)

³/₄ lb. mushrooms (about 12 large ones)
1 tablespoon unsalted butter or margarine
1 tablespoon sherry
¹/₂ tablespoon cornstarch
¹/₄ teaspoon pepper
2 teaspoons chopped fresh parsley

Chop mushrooms fine. Sauté in butter or margarine. Remove 1 tablespoon butter, cool. Lightly blend sherry with cornstarch. Stir until smooth. Add to mushrooms. Add pepper and cook, stirring until thick and smooth. Mix in parsley. Chill.

Calories 514	Protein. . . . . 8 g.
Fat . . . . 48 g.	Carbohydrate . . . . . 22 g.
Saturated Fat. . . . . 29 g.	Sodium. . . . . 14 mg.
Cholesterol. . . . 125 mg.	Potassium . . . . 1,206 mg.

The Last Touch: Condiments

Using condiments is one of the delights of eating. Being able to sprinkle a little of this or a dollop of that on our food is fun. We're able to continue creating right at the table, to add more color and texture and flavor and individuality to what's before us.

Choose 2 or 3 condiment recipes from the pages that follow and make them without even having an immediate use. Try catsup to start, and perhaps chutney next. None of these recipes takes very long and each adds remarkable zest to many dishes.

The following list will give you a sense of the widely available and commonly used condiments, sauces, or simple garnishes that you may have thought to be off-limits on a low-sodium diet. But you really can enjoy them—some with care and some with abandon. Remember that it is often what you add last to a dish that gives it its distinctive flavor.

Food	Measure or quantity	Sodium (in milligrams)
Parmesan cheese	1 tablespoon	88
Lea & Perrins Worcestershire	1 teaspoon	59
Angostura bitters	1 teaspoon	tr
Dijon mustard	$1/2$ teaspoon	75
low-sodium mustard	1 teaspoon	1
cinnamon sugar	1 teaspoon	0
currants	$1/4$ cup	5
honey	1 tablespoon	1
horseradish pared	1 oz.	2
horseradish prepared	1 oz.	27
lemon juice	1 tablespoon	<1
peanut butter	1 tablespoon	10
taco sauce	1 tablespoon	66
currant jelly	1 tablespoon	7
grated onion	1 tablespoon	1
Mission olive	1 large	36
almonds	1 oz.	45
grated apple	1 tablespoon	tr
apricot jam	1 tablespoon	2
bacon bits	1 teaspoon	52
bean sprouts	$1/2$ cup	2
grated carrot	1 tablespoon	5
catsup, low-sodium	1 tablespoon	6
maple syrup	1 tablespoon	6
nonfat plain yogurt	1 tablespoon	10
chopped tomato	1 whole	4
tamari lite	$1/2$ teaspoon	120
Bragg Liquid Aminos (soy-tamari alternative)	$1/2$ teaspoon	100–115

Refer to this list often to remind you of the great variety of flavors you can easily use to enhance your food. Remember, though a tablespoon of taco sauce has 66 milligrams of sodium, a tablespoon of salt has 100 times that amount!

LOW-SODIUM MAYONNAISE

This homemade low-sodium mayonnaise has much less sodium than most standard commercial low-sodium preparations.

1 egg yolk
Dash of cayenne
$1/2$ teaspoon dry mustard
$1/2$ teaspoon sugar
$1^1/4$ tablespoons vinegar
$3/4$ tablespoons lemon juice
1 cup olive oil or other vegetable oil

Place egg yolk in a deep bowl or into a blender or food processor. Mix in cayenne, mustard, and sugar. Stir in egg yolk and then add vinegar, lemon juice, and a drop or two of oil. Beat with fork or blend until thoroughly mixed. Continue adding the oil, a few drops at a time, beating vigorously or blending after each addition until about $1/4$ of the oil has been used. A wire whisk is wonderful for making mayonnaise. Beat in remaining oil, 1 or 2 tablespoons at a time. Mayonnaise thickens as it stands, but if too thick, it will separate on standing. Store in a covered jar in refrigerator or cool place. Lasts a few days.

Total recipe:

Calories.......... 1,983	Protein............ 3 g.
Fat .... 221 g.	Carbohydrate ...... 4 g.
Saturated Fat..... 31 g.	Sodium .... 8 mg.
Cholesterol..... 213 mg.	Potassium ...... 39 mg.

Tablespoonful:

Calories 99	Protein .... tr
Fat .... 11 g.	Carbohydrate........ tr
Saturated Fat....... 2 g.	Sodium............. tr
Cholesterol...... 11 mg.	Potassium .... 2 mg.

EGGLESS MAYONNAISE

½ teaspoon confectioners' sugar

¼ teaspoon dry mustard

¼ teaspoon paprika

Few grains cayenne

1 tablespoon vinegar

1 tablespoon lemon juice

¼ cup chilled evaporated milk

1 cup chilled olive oil or vegetable oil

Beat first 7 ingredients until well blended. Add ⅓ cup oil and beat. Add remaining oil and beat again. Makes 1½ cups.

Total recipe:

Calories.......... 2,009	Protein............ 5 g.
Fat .... 221 g.	Carbohydrate ..... 10 g.
Saturated Fat...... 32 g.	Sodium......... 67 mg.
Cholesterol...... 18 mg.	Potassium ..... 232 mg.

Tablespoonful:

Calories	84	Protein	tr
Fat	9 g.	Carbohydrate	tr
Saturated Fat	1 g.	Sodium	3 mg.
Cholesterol	1 mg.	Potassium	10 mg.

MUSTARD

Experiment with various vinegars and spices. Here's a way to begin:

1 tablespoon dry mustard

1 teaspoon turmeric

Sprinkling of mustard seed

Dash of allspice

1 teaspoon flour

⅛ teaspoon sugar

1 tablespoon cider or balsamic vinegar or lemon juice

Mix ingredients well. Yields 2¹/₂ tablespoons. Store in refrigerator for 2 weeks.

Total recipe:

Calories	24	Protein	1 g.
Fat	1 g.	Carbohydrate	5 g.
Saturated Fat	tr	Sodium	3 mg.
Cholesterol	0 mg.	Potassium	41 mg.

CATSUP

This has the most fragrant aroma while simmering on the stove.

1 6-oz. can tomato paste, no salt added
1 28-oz. can peeled tomatoes, no salt added or
    2 lbs. ripe tomatoes, chopped
1 onion, chopped
1 green pepper, chopped
1 stalk celery, chopped
1 cup water
½ cup vinegar
½ cup sugar
1 teaspoon cinnamon
1 teaspoon allspice
1 teaspoon cloves
½ teaspoon garlic powder
½ teaspoon pepper

Puree tomato paste and tomatoes in blender or food processor until smooth. Pour into saucepan. Combine onion, pepper, celery, and water in blender or food processor and puree. Add vegetable mixture to saucepan along with remaining ingredients. Simmer for 1½ to 2 hours, stirring occasionally, until catsup is thick. Pour into glass jars with lids to store in refrigerator (1 to 2 weeks) or into plastic containers to freeze (up to 6 months). Makes 1 quart.

Tablespoonful:

Calories 12	Protein . . . . tr
Fat . . . . tr	Carbohydrate . . . . . . 3 g.
Saturated Fat . . . . tr	Sodium . . . . 4 mg.
Cholesterol. . . . . . . 0 mg.	Potassium . . . . . . 62 mg.

ROASTED EGGPLANT PUREE

2 small or 1 large (2 lbs.) eggplant
1 tablespoon extra-virgin olive oil
3 tablespoons lemon juice
½ cup nonfat plain yogurt
3 cloves garlic, pressed
Freshly ground pepper
1 tablespoon fresh dill or basil

Broil eggplant 4 inches from flame, turning continuously until it's completely charred on the outside. (This may be done on the grill, as well.) When eggplant is cool, peel away the skin and squeeze the bitter juices out. Slice in half and scrape away seeds. Chop and puree in blender or food processor with remaining ingredients. This may be served with raw vegetables, crackers, or as an accompaniment to lamb. Keeps refrigerated for 3 to 4 days.

Tablespoonful:

Calories 17	Protein. . . . . 1 g.
Fat . . . . 1 g.	Carbohydrate . . . . . . 3 g.
Saturated Fat . . . . tr	Sodium . . . . 5 mg.
Cholesterol . . . . tr	Potassium . . . . . . 93 mg.

ROASTED PEPPER DRESSING

This is a simple and elegant dressing for meats, vegetables, or salads.

2 red peppers
¼ cup extra-virgin olive oil
3 tablespoons balsamic vinegar

Preheat oven to 450 degrees. Cut peppers in half, core, and seed. Place skin side up on foil-lined baking pan. Roast for about 25 minutes or until skin is charred and blistery. Remove from oven and cover with towel. Let sit until cool enough to handle. Remove skin and chop. Combine peppers with oil and vinegar and puree in blender or food processor. Makes about 1¼ cups.

Total recipe:

Calories	468	Protein	3 g.
Fat	41 g.	Carbohydrate	26 g.
Saturated Fat	6 g.	Sodium	11 mg.
Cholesterol	0 mg.	Potassium	477 mg.

CRANBERRY-ORANGE RELISH

4 cups cranberries (1 lb.)
2 oranges, quartered (seeds removed)
2 cups sugar
¼ teaspoon allspice

Coarsely chop cranberries and oranges (rind, too) in a blender or food processor. Stir in sugar and allspice and chill. This is wonderful with all meats and can keep for weeks in the refrigerator. Makes 2 pints.

Per serving:

Calories 66	Protein . . . . tr
Fat . . . . tr	Carbohydrate . . . . . 17 g.
Saturated Fat . . . . tr	Sodium. . . . . 12 mg.
Cholesterol. . . . . . . 0 mg.	Potassium . . . . . . 23 mg.

SUMMER CRANBERRY RELISH

This version of cranberry sauce is welcome during the winter holidays, as well.

1-lb. package fresh cranberries

1 cup sugar

Juice of 1 orange

1 teaspoon grated orange peel

1 cup water

1 bunch fresh mint, chopped

Chop cranberries coarsely with a knife or in a food processor. Combine with remaining ingredients in a saucepan and bring to a boil, stirring occasionally. Reduce heat and simmer for 5 to 10 minutes or until mixture thickens. Chill before serving. Makes 20 servings, or 3 cups.

Total recipe:

Calories. 1,784	Protein. . . . . 6 g.
Fat . . . . 2 g.	Carbohydrate . . . . 490 g.
Saturated Fat . . . . tr	Sodium. . . . . 14 mg.
Cholesterol. . . . . . . 0 mg.	Potassium . . . . . 940 mg.

Tablespoonful:

Calories	27	Protein	tr
Fat	tr	Carbohydrate	7 g.
Saturated Fat	tr	Sodium	tr
Cholesterol	0 mg.	Potassium	14 mg.

ONION RELISH

3 medium onions, chopped finely

1 green pepper, seeded, cored, and chopped finely

1 tomato, peeled, seeded, and diced

1 cucumber, peeled, seeded, and diced

Tabasco sauce

1 tablespoon sugar

1 tablespoon lemon juice

⅓ cup wine vinegar

2 tablespoons olive oil

Combine all ingredients and chill at least 1 hour or until serving time. Keeps refrigerated 1 to 2 weeks. Makes 6 servings.

Per serving:

Calories	85	Protein	1 g.
Fat	5 g.	Carbohydrate	11 g.
Saturated Fat	1 g.	Sodium	5 mg.
Cholesterol	0 mg.	Potassium	236 mg.

SWEET PEPPER RELISH

6 red peppers (not the hot variety)
6 green peppers
6 small onions, peeled
1 cup mild cider vinegar
¾ cup sugar

Coarsely chop peppers and onions in blender or food processor. Remove and transfer to a medium-size bowl. Cover with boiling water and let stand 10 minutes. Drain. Combine remaining ingredients in a saucepan and boil for 5 minutes. Add vegetables and boil 10 minutes. Keeps refrigerated for at least a few weeks.

Total recipe:

Calories 940	Protein . . . . 13 g.
Fat . . . . 2 g.	Carbohydrate . . . . 253 g.
Saturated Fat . . . . tr	Sodium . . . . 34 mg.
Cholesterol . . . . 0 mg.	Potassium . . . . 2,471 mg.

Tablespoonful:

Calories 10	Protein . . . . tr
Fat . . . . tr	Carbohydrate . . . . . . 3 g.
Saturated Fat . . . . tr	Sodium . . . . tr
Cholesterol . . . . 0 mg.	Potassium . . . . . . 26 mg.

CRANBERRY CHUTNEY

This is a perfect accompaniment for roasted chicken, fowl, or pork, and can be used cold as a spread on sandwiches.

1 lemon
1/2 cup apricot preserves
1/2 cup cider vinegar
1/2 cup firmly packed dark brown sugar
1 teaspoon curry powder
1 teaspoon ground ginger
1 cinnamon stick
1/4 teaspoon whole cloves
1 1/2 cups water
2 medium-size green apples, peeled, cored, and chopped
1 12-oz. package fresh cranberries (about 3 cups)
1/2 cup raisins
1/2 cup walnuts

Blanch lemon in boiling water to cover for 2 minutes. Drain. Do not peel. Coarsely chop and seed lemon. Combine chopped lemon, apricot preserves, vinegar, brown sugar, curry powder, and ginger in a large nonaluminum saucepan. Tie cinnamon stick and whole cloves in cheesecloth; add to saucepan. Add water. Bring to a slow boil over medium-low heat, stirring until sugar dissolves. Add apples; simmer 10 minutes. Add cranberries and raisins; simmer, uncovered, for 25 to 30 minutes, or until thickened, stirring occasionally to prevent sticking. Remove chutney from heat and discard cheesecloth bag.

Stir in walnuts. Refrigerated, chutney will keep for several weeks. To store for a longer time, place in clean, hot canning jars, leaving ¹/₄ inch head space, cover with clean, hot lids, and process in boiling water bath, with jars covered by 1 to 2 inches of water, for 10 minutes. Serves up to 20 as an accompaniment to meats.

Per serving:

Calories 91	Protein . . . . 1 g.
Fat . . . . 2 g.	Carbohydrate . . . . . 19 g.
Saturated Fat . . . . tr	Sodium . . . . 4 mg.
Cholesterol. . . . . . . 0 mg.	Potassium . . . . . . 97 mg.

GREEN TOMATO AND APPLE CHUTNEY

This recipe is adapted from *A Kitchen Garden, Volume 2*, from Shephard's Garden Seeds.

  5 cups green tomatoes, coarsely chopped

  3 cups Granny Smith or pippin apples, peeled, cored, and coarsely chopped

  1 large red bell pepper, seeded and coarsely chopped

  ¹/₂ cup raisins

  1 tablespoon fresh ginger, finely chopped

  3 cloves garlic, finely chopped

  ¹/₂ teaspoon ground cumin

  ¹/₂ teaspoon mustard seed

  1 teaspoon ground coriander

  ¹/₈ teaspoon nutmeg

  ¹/₈ teaspoon cayenne pepper

¹/₂ cup brown sugar
¹/₂ cup white sugar
1 cup mild white or rice vinegar

In a large 4- to 5-quart saucepan, combine all ingredients. Bring to a boil and then simmer, stirring occasionally, for about 45 minutes or until mixture is thickened. Let cool, then store in glass jars in refrigerator or heat the jars and process in a hot-water bath for 10 minutes for ¹/₂ pints and 15 minutes for pints. Let chutney mellow for a few days before serving. Makes 5 cups.

Total recipe:

Calories. 1,588	Protein. . . . . 17 g.
Fat . . . . 5 g.	Carbohydrate . . . . 407 g.
Saturated Fat. . . . . . . 1 g.	Sodium. . . . . 182 mg.
Cholesterol. . . . . . . 0 mg.	Potassium . . . . 3,803 mg.

UNSALTED PICKLES

You can make your own pickles (without brine) by boiling up 4 sprigs of fresh dill blossoms with seeds, 1 teaspoon pickling spice, 1 tablespoon sugar, and 1 cup white vinegar and then pouring over enough sliced cucumbers to fill a quart jar. Cover, cool, and refrigerate. This keeps for several weeks. The amount of sodium in this recipe is negligible.

CURRANT JELLY SAUCE

½ teaspoon dry mustard
⅛ teaspoon ground cloves
⅛ teaspoon cinnamon
1 tablespoon vinegar
½ cup currant jelly

Combine all ingredients in a saucepan. Cook over low heat, stirring constantly until jelly is melted. Serve hot with meat or vegetables.

Total recipe:

Calories 405	Protein . . . . tr
Fat . . . . tr	Carbohydrate . . . . 105 g.
Saturated Fat . . . . tr	Sodium . . . . 25 mg.
Cholesterol . . . . 0 mg.	Potassium . . . . . 122 mg.

Tablespoonful:

Calories 51	Protein . . . . tr
Fat . . . . tr	Carbohydrate . . . 13 mg.
Saturated Fat . . . . tr	Sodium . . . . 3 mg.
Cholesterol . . . . 0 mg.	Potassium . . . . . . 15 mg.

MUSTARD SAUCE

1 tablespoon low-sodium mayonnaise
2 tablespoons low-fat sour cream
1 teaspoon low-sodium prepared mustard

Combine ingredients. Mix well. Serve with cold meats and vegetables.

Per serving:

Calories	129	Protein	1 g.
Fat	14 g.	Carbohydrate	1 g.
Saturated Fat	2 g.	Sodium	61 mg.
Cholesterol	8 mg.	Potassium	28 mg.

SOUR CREAM AND WINE SAUCE

¹/₂ cup low-fat sour cream

2 tablespoons sherry

¹/₂ teaspoon nutmeg

Blend. Serve with soups, puddings, chilled fruit, vegetables, or meat.

Total recipe:

Calories	292	Protein	4 g.
Fat	25 g.	Carbohydrate	8 mg.
Saturated Fat	15 g.	Sodium	63 mg.
Cholesterol	51	Potassium	191 mg.

Tablespoonful:

Calories	29	Protein	tr
Fat	2 g.	Carbohydrate	1 g.
Saturated Fat	2 g.	Sodium	6 mg.
Cholesterol	5 mg.	Potassium	19 mg.

HERB BUTTER FOR FISH

This may be used on any fish to be baked or broiled.

¹/₄ cup unsalted butter

1 teaspoon grated onion

½ teaspoon lemon juice

½ teaspoon rosemary, dried

½ teaspoon tarragon, dried

½ teaspoon chopped fresh parsley

Pepper to taste

Combine ingredients. Serves 4.

Per serving:

Calories 415	Protein. . . . . 1 g.
Fat . . . . 46 g.	Carbohydrate . . . . . . 3 g.
Saturated Fat. . . . . . 29 g.	Sodium . . . . 8 mg.
Cholesterol. . . . . 125 mg.	Potassium . . . . . . 58 mg.

HERB BUTTER FOR BASTING FISH OR CHICKEN

2 tablespoons unsalted butter

¼ teaspoon lemon juice

⅛ teaspoon dry mustard

1 tablespoon chopped parsley or chives

Beat butter until soft. Add rest of ingredients and mix as well. Serves 2.

Per serving:

Calories 219	Protein. . . . . 1 g.
Fat . . . . 25 g.	Carbohydrate . . . . . . 1 g.
Saturated Fat. . . . . . 15 g.	Sodium . . . . 5 mg.
Cholesterol. . . . . . 66 mg.	Potassium . . . . . . 32 mg.

BASTING SAUCE FOR BROILERS

2 tablespoons melted unsalted butter

2 tablespoons sherry

½ teaspoon paprika

¼ teaspoon rosemary, dried

Combine all ingredients and use to baste chicken while broiling.

Total recipe:

Calories	259	Protein	1 g.
Fat	25 g.	Carbohydrate	4 g.
Saturated Fat	15 g.	Sodium	5 mg.
Cholesterol	66 mg.	Potassium	55 mg.

CHICKEN MARINADE

½ cup olive or vegetable oil

3 tablespoons white vinegar

½ teaspoon pepper

2 teaspoons minced fresh parsley

½ teaspoon dried rosemary, crumbled

½ teaspoon dried tarragon

½ teaspoon dried basil

1 clove garlic

Combine all ingredients and mix well. Marinate for 2 hours at room temperature.

Total recipe:

Calories 975	Protein. . . . . 1 g.
Fat . . . . 108 g.	Carbohydrate . . . . . . 5 g.
Saturated Fat. . . . . . 15 g.	Sodium . . . . 5 mg.
Cholesterol. . . . . . . 0 mg.	Potassium . . . . . 107 mg.

LEMON BASTING SAUCE FOR TURKEY OR CHICKEN

Melt 2 tablespoons unsalted butter. Mix and stir into melted butter the following:

2 teaspoons paprika

1 teaspoon sugar

½ teaspoon black pepper

¼ teaspoon dry mustard

Few grains cayenne pepper

Blend in thoroughly:

½ cup lemon juice

½ cup hot water

2 teaspoons grated onion

Start the chicken cooking with the inside facing down, basting frequently with lemon sauce. Breasts will take 30 minutes or so depending on size. Use sauce for basting roast turkey or chicken.

Total recipe:

Calories. 1,288	Protein. . . . . 3 g.
Fat . . . . 139 g.	Carbohydrate . . . . . 22 g.
Saturated Fat. . . . . . 86 g.	Sodium. . . . . 26 mg.
Cholesterol. . . . . 374 mg.	Potassium . . . . . 315 mg.

CHERRY CHICKEN BASTE

1 8-oz. jar cherry preserves
1 tablespoon vinegar
4 cloves
¼ teaspoon allspice
¼ cup unsalted butter

Heat and use mixture to baste broiled or roast chicken.

Total recipe:

Calories. 1,037	Protein. . . . . 1 g.
Fat . . . . 46 g.	Carbohydrate . . . . 162 g.
Saturated Fat. . . . . . 29 g.	Sodium. . . . . 32 mg.
Cholesterol. . . . . 125 mg.	Potassium . . . . . 234 mg.

PEACH JUICE TURKEY BASTE

2 tablespoons unsalted butter
¼ cup sherry wine or apple juice
2 cups canned peach juice

Melt butter, add wine or apple juice and peach juice. Use peaches filled with cranberry sauce for garnish.

Total recipe:

Calories 754	Protein. . . . . 2 g.
Fat . . . . 46 g.	Carbohydrate . . . . . 75 g.
Saturated Fat. . . . . . 29 g.	Sodium. . . . . 43 mg.
Cholesterol. . . . . 125 mg.	Potassium . . . . . 253 mg.

CUCUMBER SAUCE

Serve this with cold salmon.

1 medium cucumber
1 tablespoon vinegar
⅛ teaspoon pepper
Few grains cayenne
1 teaspoon minced onion
1 tablespoon dill weed, finely chopped

Peel the cucumber, chop very fine. In a small bowl, mix cucumber with the remaining ingredients. Add ½ cup sour cream if you can afford the sodium count and the calories.

Total recipe:

Calories 33		Protein. . . . . 1 g.	
Fat . . . . tr		Carbohydrate . . . . . . 8 g.	
Saturated Fat . . . . tr		Sodium . . . . 6 mg.	
Cholesterol. . . . . . . 0 mg.		Potassium . . . . . 345 mg.	

OYSTER SAUCE

½ cup white wine vinegar
1 teaspoon black ground pepper
3 shallots, chopped fine
Few grains cayenne

Combine ingredients. Store covered in refrigerator 3 days and serve cold with oysters.

Total recipe:

Calories	62	Protein	2 g.
Fat	tr	Carbohydrate	18 g.
Saturated Fat	tr	Sodium	6 mg.
Cholesterol	0 mg.	Potassium	248 mg.

SAUCE PIQUANT

Good with cold meats and fowl.

1 cup red wine or dry Sauterne

1 cup olive oil

2 chopped onions

1 teaspoon rosemary

2 cloves garlic, chopped

¼ cup wine vinegar

⅛ teaspoon dried red pepper

Mix all ingredients thoroughly, stir until well blended. Put in jar to marinate for 24 hours. This sauce may be used on sandwiches or to baste meats and fowl while roasting or broiling.

Total recipe:

Calories	2,180	Protein	3 g.
Fat	216 g.	Carbohydrate	29 g.
Saturated Fat	29 g.	Sodium	23 mg.
Cholesterol	0 mg.	Potassium	655 mg.

Tablespoonful:

Calories	50	Protein	tr
Fat	5 g.	Carbohydrate	1 g.
Saturated Fat	1 g.	Sodium	1 mg.
Cholesterol	0 mg.	Potassium	15 mg.

STEAK MARINADE

Cooking over charcoal gives meat and poultry a wonderful flavor, and seasonings are not really as necessary as they are in other methods of cooking. Try this marinade for indoor cooking. Everyone will enjoy the flavor.

1 cup red wine
½ cup olive or vegetable oil
⅓ cup brown sugar
¼ teaspoon marjoram
¼ teaspoon rosemary
2 large onions, thinly sliced
1 clove garlic

Combine all ingredients and mix well. Allow steak to marinate at least 4 hours or, better yet, overnight.

Total recipe:

Calories	1,513	Protein	4 g.
Fat	109 g.	Carbohydrate	101 g.
Saturated Fat	15 g.	Sodium	43 mg.
Cholesterol	0 mg.	Potassium	1,001 mg.

Festive Seasonal Menus

JANUARY
*Roast Pork, Hopping John, Carrot Salad,
Poached Pears*

FEBRUARY
*Hearty Beef Soup, Apple and Curry Bread,
Chocolate Cake*

MARCH
*Chicken Fajitas, Black Bean Salad, Salsa, Frozen
Strawberry Delight*

APRIL
*Lamb Fibonacci, Mashed Potatoes with Parsnips,
Broccoli with Lemon, Fruit Meringues*

MAY
*Chinese Noodles with Peanut Sauce, Green Salad,
Melon and Grapes*

JUNE

*Broiled Fresh Salmon Steaks, Lemon New Potato
Salad, Pea Pods with Mushrooms, Rhubarb and
Strawberry Crumble*

JULY

*Jody McKenzie's Chicken Salad, Wild Rice Salad
and Corn, Baked Cherry Tomatoes, Peach Bly*

AUGUST

*Quonquont Farm Raspberry Soup, Bluefish with
Ginger, Carol's Corn Salad, Stuffed Zucchini,
Peach and Maple Syrup Cake*

SEPTEMBER

Vegetarian Pizza, Green Salad, Fresh Fruit

OCTOBER

*Traditional Meat Loaf, Stuffed Sweet Potatoes,
Poached Artichokes, Apple Pie*

NOVEMBER

*Venison Stew, Swift River Squash, Risotto,
Luscious Lemon Cake*

DECEMBER

*Roast Chicken with 40 Cloves of Garlic, Lemon-
Parsley Rice, Ratatouille, Cherries Jubilee*

·Acknowledgments·

Many, many people have contributed to this cookbook over the years. Certainly a few are aware of how deeply they have helped us; others might be quite surprised that, by the merest gesture or offhand phrase, they urged us along. We thank you all.

At every turn, people shared their recipes, books, and ideas with us. We would like to thank in particular Larry and Carol Sheehan, whose kitchen and library and friendship are a constant inspiration. We are grateful to Ann Patchett, Jody McKenzie, Susie Greenberg, Marilyn Patti, Carla Ness, Chris Bagg, Greg Rowehl, M. E. Malone, Deanna Cook, Ruth Craft, Lisa Newman, Donna Cusimano, Dolores Ryan, Kathy Precourt, Maude Davis, Sarah Schoedel, Marilyn Kerivan, Tracy and Fran Kidder, Jan Dizzard, Deborah Wiesgall, Chris Jerome, Anne Mannarino, Brinna Sands, Jenny French, Melissa Bagg, Maisie Todd, Phyllis Kirkpatrick, Beth Long, Olivia B. Blumer, Penny Conaway, Barbara Purington, Edie Tucker, Dianne Grinnell, Michael Janeway, Kevin Blanchard, Carol LaBonte, Emily Todd, Priscilla Totten, Dee Notson, and Grace Ledbetter. We note here, as well, the help of Andrew Tucker, whose memory we cherish.

For technical help, we thank Kit Nylen, Doug Wilkens, and Nell Todd, and Laural Adams, of the Smith

College Science Library. We are forever indebted to Tom Looker, who selflessly led us through three generations of computer technology and whom we now call Saint Cyber. We also thank Sue Silvester and the Mohawk Print Shop for help in the early stages.

Several doctors spoke with us and/or shared medical information. We are grateful to Dr. Timothy Guiney, Dr. William Castelli, Dr. Wayne Callaway, Dr. George Webb, Dr. Norman Kaplan, Dr. Michael Glasscock, Dr. Kit French, and Dr. Alexander Leaf. We thank, also, Larry Lindner of the *Tufts Newsletter* and Mary D'Elia, pharmacologist, for giving their advice.

For nutritional information, we thank Dodie Anderson, Healthwitch, Elizabeth Heiser of *Eating Well* magazine, Michael McCusker, Terry Karr, and Sidney Flum.

For providing us with expert nutritional guidance and analyses, we thank Eileen Atallah of the University of Massachusetts and Dr. Mary Wasserman of Rutgers University. We are particularly grateful for Mary's careful reading of the nutritional material and her thoughtful advice. Eileen's eleventh-hour help will always touch us.

For editorial help, we thank Robert C. Notson, our uncle, who shepherded the first edition to publication and who, in his nineties, offered his abiding wisdom once again; Maria Mack, who initiated the project; Becky Cabaza, who enthusiastically encouraged our beginning steps; Fran McCullough, whose high expectations widened our horizons; Ryan Stellabotte and Katie Hall, whose careful reading guided the book to completion. We thank Katie, in particular, for her determination, and Ryan for his meticulous attention to the manuscript.

David Black, our agent at the start, investigated the history of this book with the skill and patience of an archivist. And his colleague, Susan Raihofer, encouraged us with grace, warmth, and magnanimous spirit.

Our deepest gratitude goes to our beloved family members—to Maisie for artful cooking, to Nell for bold action and typing, and to Emily for years of dedicated, scrupulous, and noble collaboration on all aspects of this project. They are a tribute to their grandmother. Liam Harte heroically, chivalrously, assembled the manuscript. We are thankful for Mary Bagg's sharp, organized editorial eye and vast knowledge of cooking and for Richard Todd's gentle wit and kind heart.

But it took all of us, those listed above and we, the children of Elma and Ted Bagg, joining together to continue the work one woman began—with genius and playfulness and great good sense—over three decades ago, out of caring for her husband.

·References·

American Heart Association Booklets: Your 500 Milligrams Sodium Diet; Your 1,000 Milligrams Sodium Diet; Your Mild Sodium Restricted Diet.

American Heart Association. Cooking Without Your Salt Shaker. Cleveland: American Heart Association Northeast Ohio Affiliate.

American Spice Trade Association Booklets: A History of Spices; How to Use Spices; Spices.

Ballentine, Rudolph, M.D. *Diet & Nutrition: A Holistic Approach.* Honesdale, PA: Himalayan International Institute, 1978.

Boxer, Arabella, et al. *The Encyclopedia of Herbs, Spices, and Flavorings.* New York: Crescent Books, 1984.

Bradley, Alice V., M.S. *Tables of Food Values.* Peoria, IL: Charles A. Bennett Co., 1931.

Brenner, Eleanor P. *Gourmet Cooking Without Salt.* Garden City, NY: Doubleday & Company, 1981.

Bounds, Sarah. *No-Salt Cookery.* Northamptonshire, U.K.: Thorsons Publishers Limited, 1984.

Brody Jane. *Jane Brody's Nutrition Book.* New York: Bantam Books, 1981.

Claiborne, Craig, with Pierre Franey. *Craig Claiborne's Gourmet Diet.* New York: Wings Books, 1980.

Eagle, Haber, & Austen DeSanctis. *The Practice of Cardiology. The Medical and Surgical Cardiac Units at the Massachusetts General Hospital I, Second Edition.* Boston: Little, Brown.

Gebhardt, Susan E., and Ruth H. Matthews. *Nutritive Value of Foods.* Home and Garden Bulletin Number 72. U.S. Department of Agriculture: Human Nutrition Information Service, Revised June 1991.

Gerson, Max, M.D. *A Cancer Therapy.* Bonita, CA: The Gerson Institute, 1990.

Gittleman, Ann Louise, M.S., C.N.S. *Get the Salt Out.* New York: Crown, 1996.

Gittleman, Ann Louise, M.S., with J. Maxwell Desgrey. *Beyond Pritikin.* New York, Bantam Books, 1988.

Kilham, Christopher S. *The Bread & Circus Whole Food Bible.* Reading, MA: Addison-Wesley, 1991.

Klempner, Walter, M.D. *Radical Dietary Treatment of Hypertensive and Arteriosclerotic Vascular Disease, Heart and Kidney Disease and Vascular Retinopathy.* Durham, NC: Duke University School of Medicine.

Leaf, Alexander, M.D. *Youth in Old Age.* New York: McGraw-Hill, 1975.

Lloyd, Nancy. *Salt-Free Recipes: Eating Well on a Low Sodium Diet.* Northamptonshire, U.K.: Thorsons Publishers Limited, 1984.

Martin, Rux, et al. *The Eating Well Cookbook*. Charlotte, VT: Camden House, 1991.

Matthews, Ruth H., and Young J. Garrison. *Food Yields Summarized by Different Stages of Preparation*. Agriculture Handbook Number 102. U.S. Department of Agriculture: Agriculture Research Service, Revised September 1975.

McCance, R. A., & E. M. Widdowson. *The Chemical Composition of Foods*. Brooklyn, NY: Chemical Publishing Company, 1947.

Mindell, Earl, R.R.Ph., Ph.D. *Earl Mindell's Food As Medicine*. New York: Simon and Schuster, 1994.

Moore, Richard D., M.D., Ph.D., and George, D. Webb, M.D., Ph.D., *The K Factor*. New York: Macmillan, 1986.

National Research Council, "Sodium-Restricted Diets," National Academy of Science, Publication #32, July 1954.

Natow, Annette B., Ph.D., R.D., and Jo-Ann Heslin, M.A., R.D. *The Sodium Counter*. New York: Simon and Schuster, 1993.

Netzer, Corinne T. *The Complete Book of Food Counts*. New York: Dell Publishing, 1997.

Ornish, Dean, M.D. *Stress, Diet & Your Heart*. New York: Signet, 1984.

Peterson, Skinner. *Elements of Food Biochemistry*. New York: Prentice-Hall, 1943.

Polin, Bonnie Sanders, Ph.D., and Frances Towner Giedt. *The Joslin Diabetes Gourmet Cookbook*. New York: Bantam Books, 1993.

Reader's Digest. *Great Recipes for Good Food*. Pleasantville, NY: Reader's Digest Association, 1988.

Riccio, Dolores. *Superfoods: 300 Recipes for Foods that Heal Body and Mind.* New York: Warner Books, 1992.

Rogers, Jean. *The Healing Foods Cookbook.* Emmaus, PA: Rodale Books, 1991.

Sands, Brinna. *King Arthur Flour 200th Anniversary Cookbook.* Norwich, VT: Sands, Taylor, & Wood Co., 1991.

Sherman, Henry C., Ph.D., Sc.D. *Chemistry of Food and Nutrition.* New York: Macmillan, 1946.

Shulman, Martha Rose. *Mediterranean Light.* New York: Bantam Books, 1989.

Shulman, Martha Rose. *The Vegetarian Feast.* New York: Bantam Books, 1989.

Starke, Rodman, D., M.D., Mary Winston, Ed.D., R.D. *American Heart Association Low Salt Cookbook.* New York: Random House, 1990.

Trattler, Ross. *Better Health Through Natural Healing.* London: Thorsons, 1987.

United States Department of Agriculture. *Dietary Guidelines for Americans.* Washington: U.S. Government Printing Office, 1990.

United States Department of Agriculture. *Composition of Foods . . . Raw, Processed, Prepared.* Agriculture Handbook 8: AH8-1 to AH8-21.

United States Department of Agriculture. *Manual of Food Codes and Conversions of Measures to Gram-Weight for Use with Individual Food Intake Data from 1977–78 Nationwide Food Consumption Survey.* Science & Education Administration. Human

Nutrition Center: Consumer and Food Economics Institute, November 1979.

Williams, Sue Rodwell, M.R.Ed., M.P.H. *Nutrition and Diet Therapy.* Saint Louis: The C. V. Mosby Company, 1969.

The computer program used for the analyses:
Nutritionist III
version 7.0
N-Squared Computing
3040 Commercial Street SE
Suite 240
Salem, OR 97302

· Index ·